WOODSTOCK

WOODSTOCK
THEN AND *NOW*: A 50TH ANNIVERSARY CELEBRATION

EDITED BY
ALEX LUDWIG AND
SIMONE PILON

© 2022 Clemson University
All rights reserved

Paperback edition
ISBN: 978-1-63804-047-7

First hardcover edition published in 2021.
ISBN: 978-1-63804-005-7

Published by Clemson University Press.
Please visit our website: www.clemson.edu/press.

Interior designed by Andrea Reider.
Cover designed by Lindsay Scott.
Front cover image courtesy of Elliott Landy.
Back cover image courtesy of Henry Diltz.

CONTENTS

Acknowledgments	vii
List of Illustrations	ix
Introduction	xiii
Berklee College of Music's Celebration of Woodstock	xvi
About This Book	xviii
1: Behind the Scenes at Woodstock	1
2: Woodstock Fifty Years Later	59
3: Woodstock's Stardust	107
4: Playing With Jimi Hendrix	147
Profiles of Woodstock Luminaries Featured in the Book	165
Henry Diltz	165
Rona Elliot	167
Bill Hanley	170
Elliott Landy	173
Michael Lang	173
Chip Monck	176
Gerardo Velez	177
Index	181

ACKNOWLEDGMENTS

We would be remiss if we did not thank the many people who made the 50th anniversary celebration of Woodstock at Berklee College of Music and this book possible. This was a team effort, and many members of the Berklee community helped make it happen. A big thank you to Mike Mason, Kali Noonan, Darla Hanley, Kate Kelleher, Allen Bush, Tracey Gibbs, and members of the Conference and Events, David Friend Recital Hall, Public Safety, and Video Services teams. We would like to recognize the efforts of the Liberal Arts work-study students who took a first pass at the transcriptions—Christine Bernard, Samuel Chong, Charles Fuertsch, and Aarya Ganesan—and Kali Noonan, who supervised that work.

In addition, we would like to recognize the faculty and staff members who led ensembles, organized exhibits, gave talks, or moderated sessions during Woodstock Week. These include Tom Baskett, Sofía Becerra, Deborah Bennett, Mason Daring, Kenwood Dennard, Wayne Marshall, Maureen McMullan, Rekha Menon, Gretchen Moore, Bob Mulvey, Patricia Peknik, Zoë Rath, Mark Simos, and Aja Burrell Wood. We would also like to acknowledge the members of the conference committee who helped select the academic presentations: Alicia Bower, Patrick Burke (of Washington University in St. Louis), Patricia Peknik, and Ron Reid.

While the contributions of the Berklee College of Music community were invaluable, this event would not have been possible without the participation of our Woodstock luminaries: Henry Diltz, Rona Elliot, Bill Hanley, Elliott Landy, Michael Lang, Chip Monck, and Gerardo Velez. Because it was the fiftieth anniversary of Woodstock, 2019 was a particularly busy year for all of these people. Michael Lang was in the middle of organizing the Woodstock 50 festival, which was set to begin just a few months after the Berklee celebration; Henry Diltz talked about the increased interest in his photos because of the anniversary; and Rona Elliot was preparing to teach a course, "Woodstock at 50," at New York University in the summer of 2019, with Karen Curry, former network executive and adjunct professor at NYU. Everyone's willingness to take time from their other projects, travel to Boston, and share their experiences and insights with us was most appreciated.

However, the contributions of our luminaries did not stop after the April 2019 event, since each of the participants contributed to the content of this book. In particular, we would like to thank Henry Diltz and his partner Gary Strobl, Elliott Landy, and the estate of Dan Garson for contributing their photos to this publication. Michael Lang provided information for the sidebar on Woodstock 50, and Tom Jablonka contributed background information about the creation of the Woodstock site drawings. Rona Elliot not only wrote the profiles included at the end of the book, but also worked with the other roundtable participants and members of the Woodstock community to confirm some of the names and information. Rona has a wealth of Woodstock knowledge.

Finally, a big thank you to Alison Mero and the Clemson University Press staff for believing in this project.

Michael Lang passed away shortly after the hardcover release of this book. His humanity, focus on community, love of music, and respect for people and the planet forged Woodstock into one of the most iconic events in music history and its impact is still felt more than fifty years later. The editors of this book had the privilege to spend time with Michael in April 2019 when he came to Berklee to celebrate the fiftieth anniversary of Woodstock. He lived up to his reputation as an incredibly passionate, down-to-earth, and laid-back person. Michael was supportive of the event we held and contributed immensely to the book that you are reading now. We would like to dedicate this work to his memory.

LIST OF ILLUSTRATIONS

1. Black and white photograph of Chip Monck, Rona Elliot, Michael Lang, Henry Diltz, Elliott Landy, and Bill Hanley at Berklee's Woodstock anniversary celebration in April 2019. Photograph by Dave Green. xvii

2. Black and white scan of the map created by the architectural team of the Woodstock site. xxii

3. Black and white scan of the map of the stage, with Filippini's Pond notated by the wavy lines. xxiii

4. Black and white scan of the map of the foot trails in the shopping area known as the Bindy Bazaar xxiv

5. Black and white photograph of festival attendees swimming in a pond. The reflection in a side mirror of a car parked nearby shows the long lines of people making their way to the festival. Photograph by Henry Diltz. 14

6. Black and white photograph of Chip Monck and Michael Lang in Max Yasgur's field, prior to the start of the festival. Photograph by Henry Diltz. 21

7. Black and white photograph of members of the Hog Farm in a large circle in a field, holding hands. They are marking a landing spot for helicopters. Photograph by Henry Diltz. 24

8. Black and white photograph of a helicopter landing, with the crowd and tents visible in the background. Photograph by Henry Diltz. 34

9. Black and white photograph of Tim Hardin on August 15, 1969, seated at a table, holding the guitar with its strap and handwriting his setlist, using his left hand and a felt-tipped marker. Photograph by Henry Diltz. 35

10. Black and white photograph of two of the three turntables on an empty Woodstock stage on August 18, 1969. The field is visible in the background, with just a few people and large quantities of garbage. Photograph by Henry Diltz. 39

11. Black and white photograph of the field at the end of the festival. A few people remain, collecting their belongings, lying on the ground, or cleaning up the large quantities of garbage that are visible in the photograph. Photograph by Henry Diltz. 41

12. Black and white photograph of Max Yasgur making a peace sign with his left hand and addressing the crowd. Martin Scorsese is in the lower left corner of the photograph, in "the pit," a term Henry Diltz uses in chapter 2, to describe the area below and in front of the stage. He is also making a peace sign. Photograph by Elliott Landy. 43

13. Black and white photograph of Janis Joplin performing. Photograph by Henry Diltz. 49

14. Black and white close up of Richie Havens singing and playing the guitar. Photograph by Henry Diltz. 50

15. Black and white photograph of a woman crowd surfing at Woodstock '94. Photograph by Henry Diltz. 62

16. Black and white photograph of Mel Lawrence in an office trailer at Woostock. Photograph by Henry Diltz. 67

17. Black and white close-up photograph of the stage being built at the base of the sloping field, with scaffolding in place. Photograph by Henry Diltz. 69

18. Black and white photograph of Swami Satchidananda on stage, flanked by associates. The photograph is taken from the stage, showing the back of Swami Satchidananda and the vastness of the crowd. Photograph by Elliott Landy. 77

19. Black and white photograph of Jimi Hendrix playing guitar. Photograph by Henry Diltz. 87

20. Black and white photograph of the back of John Sebastian, who is onstage facing the audience and holding a guitar. Photograph by Henry Diltz. 93

LIST OF ILLUSTRATIONS   xi

21. Black and white photograph of members of Jefferson Airplane - Sally Mann, Paul Kantner, and Grace Slick, with a cigarette in her mouth - seated on the side of the stage along with Bill Graham, who is kneeling. Photograph by Henry Diltz.   96

22. Black and white photograph of Chip Monck working with cables under the stage. Photograph by Henry Diltz.   112

23. Black and white photograph of the crowd and some of the scaffolding, with rain clouds and muddy ground. Photograph by Dan Garson.   116

24. Black and white photograph of the stage at the base of the sloping field, showing the landscape of the area. Photograph by Henry Diltz.   123

25. Black and white photograph of the Eagles standing beside a cactus in Joshua Tree National Park. Photograph by Henry Diltz.   132

26. Black and white photograph of Ravi Shankar playing the sitar. Photograph by Henry Diltz.   141

27. Black and white photograph of festival attendees climbing and sitting on the scaffolding. Photograph by Dan Garson.   151

28. Black and white photograph of a road lined on both sides with cars, and with crowds walking down the middle, to and from the festival site. Photograph by Henry Diltz.   155

29. Black and white photograph of Gerardo Velez standing behind a conga, on stage with Billy Cox, Larry Lee, Juma Sultan, and Jimi Hendrix. Photograph by Henry Diltz.   158

30. Black and white wide-angle shot of the field and stage, with farms in the background. Photograph by Henry Diltz.   162

INTRODUCTION

In the summer of 1969, a dairy farm in upstate New York hosted an event that would be marked as a pivotal moment in the history of pop music. Two years after the so-called "Summer of Love" and one year after the tumultuous events of 1968, the Woodstock Music & Art Fair, which was billed as an "Aquarian Exposition: 3 Days of Peace and Music," took place during the weekend of August 15–17, putting an exclamation point on an undeniably transformational decade. Watching the coverage of the festival from a New York City hotel, Joni Mitchell wrote the song "Woodstock," which captures the opposition that defined the turbulent and divisive era in which she was living. She wrote, "We are stardust . . . / Caught in the devil's bargain / And we've got to get ourselves back to the garden."

Her evocative lyrics highlight the multivalent impulses at the heart of Woodstock. The musical lineup included not only Janis Joplin, the Grateful Dead, and Jimi Hendrix, but also Ravi Shankar, Carlos Santana, and Sha Na Na, an anachronistic doo-wop group. The behavior of the audience at Woodstock was exceedingly peaceful, whereas several other festivals in the 1960s were marred by violence, particularly Denver Pop, in June 1969, and Altamont, in December 1969. Woodstock functioned as an idyll amidst much of the social and political turmoil of the 1960s because cofounder Michael Lang imbued the festival with the fundamental characteristics of the counterculture: three days of peace and music, as it was billed on the poster. Woodstock dedicated space not only for music but also for progressive organizers to proselytize in a tent known as Movement City, and for audiences to view art in a pavilion displaying work by Native Americans.

But the question remains: why does Woodstock have such staying power in popular culture? Woodstock was neither the first festival to feature pop music nor the largest of its generation; the Monterey Pop Festival in

1967 is generally regarded as the first major festival in the United States, and the Watkins Glen Summer Jam in 1973 hosted over six hundred thousand people, more than the highest estimated attendance at Woodstock.

Woodstock's place in American culture rests in part on its reputation as a hotbed of chaos, owing mostly to behind-the-scenes complications. Initially, festival cofounder Michael Lang and his partner Artie Kornfeld sought funding to build a recording studio in the bucolic town of Woodstock, in the Hudson River valley of New York. Lang and Kornfeld approached John Roberts, heir to the Polident fortune, and his partner Joel Rosenman for financial support, with the quartet forming Woodstock Ventures. But Roberts and Rosenman, who had just built a recording studio in New York City, were more interested in funding a music festival. When an adequate location in the town of Woodstock could not be found, the foursome turned their attention to the town of Wallkill, in Orange County, New York. In Wallkill, the organizers found an appropriate site, but citizens of the town banded together to thwart the festival. Authorities in Wallkill denied the application for permits with only three weeks left until Woodstock's advertised opening day.

Growing more desperate by the hour, the organizers searched throughout the region for a natural amphitheater, even using a helicopter to look from the air. They soon discovered a dairy farm owned by Max Yasgur in Sullivan County, but were left with just three weeks to adapt the plans and build the infrastructure for a major festival. The festival organizers planned for fifty thousand attendees, but on the first day the gates were quickly overrun, forcing the organizers to make the festival free and open to the public. In the end, various estimates put the attendance somewhere between four hundred and five hundred thousand people. The unexpected number of attendees put a strain on the festival's facilities, and organizers struggled to provide basic necessities, like food, water, and portable toilets. Despite the overcrowding, the festival doctor, William Abruzzi, reported that no injuries were incurred from violence during the festival.

A number of bands used Woodstock to launch their careers. The backing group for Bob Dylan, known collectively as The Band, had released their first album, *Music from Big Pink* (1968), the previous summer. The Band's live performance at Woodstock, and later that year with Bob Dylan at the Isle of Wight Festival in the UK, cemented their legacy as an alternative to the extravagant studio productions of the Beatles in the mid-1960s.

Crosby, Stills, Nash & Young's performance at Woodstock marked only their second as a quartet. They were in the midst of recording their first album, *Déjà Vu* (1970), which remains their most popular to date, selling more than eight million copies. It features singles like "Our House," and their cover of Joni Mitchell's song, "Woodstock."

After his iconic performance at Woodstock, Joe Cocker embarked on an American tour with bandleader Leon Russell.[1] Cocker's cover of the Beatles' song "With a Little Help From My Friends" tapped into the optimism of hippie culture, and the song became the unofficial anthem for Woodstock.

Perhaps more than any other, Carlos Santana capitalized on the exposure from his Woodstock performance. Prior to the festival, Santana was relatively unknown on the national stage; he only had a recording contract and a manager, Bill Graham. At Graham's insistence, Santana's band was added to Woodstock, and their debut album was released two weeks after the festival, peaking at number four on the *Billboard 200*.

The size and scope of Woodstock is one of its most important legacies. By gathering thirty-one acts for one event, the organizers of Woodstock proved to Wall Street that popular music could still be a money-making venture. Woodstock was also a turning point in the business of running a major music festival. Whereas Michael Lang was not necessarily driven by the desire to make money, promoters that followed in his footsteps were less idealistic. To reduce the financial risk of hosting such large events, they turned instead to single-day festivals held in sports arenas and convention centers, which provided protection from inclement weather, improved sanitation facilities, and fixed seat locations. Though more common, these rock music tours of the 1970s and 1980s featured decidedly less diverse musical acts.

For Woodstock's twenty-fifth anniversary in 1994, Woodstock Ventures held a festival in Saugerties, New York. Woodstock '94, as it was known, had corporate sponsorship and advance sale of the media rights, but its gates were overrun on the first day, turning it into a free festival just as the original had been. Five years later, Woodstock '99, organized in part by Michael Lang and held at a former Air Force base in Rome, New York, featured an all-star lineup of mostly alternative rock and pop music bands, attracting more than two hundred thousand people. But it, too, devolved into chaos,

---

[1] Born John Robert Cocker (1944-2014), "Joe" Cocker was an English singer whose performance style paired convulsive tremors with an evocative voice. His career was plagued by addictions to alcohol and drugs, yet some of his song covers were tremendously successful: "With a Little Help from My Friends" became the theme song for the late 1980s family comedy *The Wonder Years*, and "You Are So Beautiful," peaked at number 5 in the US. Michael Lang, one of the producers of Woodstock, began managing Cocker in 1976.

ending with widespread rioting and arson. Despite these negative associations, the memory of Woodstock lives on.

BERKLEE COLLEGE OF MUSIC'S CELEBRATION OF WOODSTOCK

In April 2019, the Liberal Arts Department at Berklee College of Music in Boston held Woodstock Week, a weeklong celebration of the fiftieth anniversary of the 1969 Woodstock Festival. Berklee is an institution founded on the study of popular music, and its Liberal Arts Department focuses on the connection between music and society through the study of fine arts, the humanities, and the natural and social sciences. This made Berklee a logical home for a celebration of Woodstock.

The celebration at Berklee started with events primarily for the campus community, including screenings of the 1969 film *Easy Rider* and the 1970 documentary *Woodstock: 3 Days of Peace and Music*, directed by Michael Wadleigh, and for which a young Martin Scorsese served as one of the assistant directors; an exhibit titled "Peace, Love, and Music at Berklee: Archival Highlights from the Woodstock Era;" and a performance by Berklee's Jimi Hendrix Ensemble. The week closed with a symposium during which scholars from the United States and Europe shared their research on Woodstock. Topics included Woodstock reincarnations in Central Europe, gender parity at music festivals, and presentations on Jimi Hendrix. In between academic sessions, student ensembles performed, including the Sly and the Family Stone Ensemble and a second performance by the Jimi Hendrix Ensemble.

The high point of Berklee's celebration was a series of roundtable discussions and interviews with the people who we called our "Woodstock luminaries." These were Michael Lang (Woodstock cofounder); Chip Monck (emcee, stage and lighting designer); Bill Hanley (audio engineer); Henry Diltz and Elliott Landy (photographers); Rona Elliot (public relations); and Gerardo Velez (percussionist for Jimi Hendrix). Meeting all together for the first time since 1969, these luminaries shared Woodstock stories, talking about the impact of the festival on their careers and on society as a whole.

These luminaries came from all corners of the United States and from as far away as Australia. Michael Lang and Elliott Landy drove to Boston from Woodstock, New York. Henry Diltz and Rona Elliot are both based in Los Angeles. Gerado Velez lives in Miami, and Bill Hanley in Medford, Massachusetts. Chip Monck traveled from Melbourne, Australia, where he has lived since 1988. Attendees at the event included members of the

INTRODUCTION xvii

1. Black and white photograph of (from left to right) Chip Monck, Rona Elliot, Michael Lang, Henry Diltz, Elliott Landy, and Bill Hanley at Berklee's Woodstock anniversary celebration in April 2019. Photograph by Dave Green.

Berklee community, as well as members of the public who joined from the Boston area and other parts of the United States, while others came from international locales, including Denmark and Poland.

Despite not having been together for fifty years, this group shared a deep and palpable sense of camaraderie and respect. There was much laughter as the participants told their stories and chided each other in a friendly way. Michael Lang appeared as laid back as others have described him to be. Henry Diltz snapped pictures throughout the entire event. And Chip Monck and Bill Hanley displayed an incredible aptitude for technical details, whether troubleshooting feedback from the microphones or relaying stories about the technology they deployed at Woodstock.

In the larger roundtables, featured in chapters 1 and 2, photos by Henry Diltz and Elliott Landy were shown as the panelists spoke. The audience watched as a group of old friends reminisced, getting caught up in the images and stories, and in their continued commitment to peace, love, and music. While some of this dynamic does not translate to the written page, we did our best to convey the warmth that was felt in that room. Most importantly, we wanted to capture this historic event, the first reunion of this group of people in fifty years, for posterity. As we prepared this book, one of the participants shared with us that the event brought them closer together and cemented their friendship and commitment to each other.

ABOUT THIS BOOK

Each chapter of this book consists of a transcript of a specific session at Berklee's Woodstock celebration. The first chapter, "Behind the Scenes at Woodstock," features a roundtable discussion held on Saturday, April 6, 2019, with Henry Diltz, Rona Elliot, Bill Hanley, Elliott Landy, Michael Lang, and Chip Monck. This session, which was called "Woodstock Then," was led by Berklee faculty member and Woodstock attendee Bob Mulvey, and centered on a series of Woodstock photos taken by Henry Diltz and Elliott Landy. This pictorial journey through the history of Woodstock, from the organizers checking out the site and building the stage, to cleaning the field at the end of the festival, framed the conversation and allowed the roundtable participants to reminisce. Some of the pictures referenced in this conversation are included in the book; others are described as they are brought up.

In the second chapter, "Woodstock Fifty Years Later," Alex Ludwig, assistant professor of liberal arts at Berklee, moderated another roundtable, called "Woodstock Now," with Henry Diltz, Rona Elliot, Michael Lang, and Chip Monck. This roundtable also was held on April 6. We were pleasantly surprised when Gerardo Velez arrived earlier than expected and joined this second roundtable. In this discussion, the participants talked about the impact of the festival on the music industry as well as on society as a whole. The session featured a sneak peek at a yet-to-be-released documentary on Woodstock by PBS's *American Experience*. The clip focused on Wavy Gravy and the Hog Farm, which opened a discussion about their roles at the festival. In addition, a surprise video message from Ringo Starr was played for Henry Diltz, and is transcribed in chapter 2.

The third chapter, "Woodstock's Stardust," is transcribed from an interview with Henry Diltz, Rona Elliot, and Chip Monck held on Thursday, April 4, 2019, for Berklee students enrolled in the Professional Development Seminar. In this conversation, Henry, Rona, and Chip consider the impact of Woodstock on their careers and reckon with both the challenges and the opportunities for young musicians today.

The fourth and final chapter, "Playing with Jimi Hendrix," is an edited transcription of an interview with Gerardo Velez, one of Hendrix's percussionists at Woodstock, in which Velez shares his experiences both as one of

Hendrix's percussionists and as his roommate. This interview was held on Sunday, April 7, 2019.

The book concludes with profiles of each of the luminaries, written by Rona Elliot in collaboration with the subjects. Rona's background and experience as a music journalist helped to elicit personal and vivid stories grounded in biographical information. Once Rona entered the planning process for the conference and especially for this book, she became a tireless source of information and connection to the larger community of Woodstock participants.

The transcripts of the conversations published in these chapters are as close to the original as possible. They have, however, been edited for clarity and readability. Abbreviations such as "gonna" and "wanna" have been rewritten in more formal English as "going to" and "want to." Repeated filler phrases such as "you know" have been deleted, and missing words have been added in square brackets. In some cases, sentences have been rearranged or rewritten for clarity. Parts of the discussions that did not clearly connect with the topic of the chapter or question posed by the moderator have been deleted.

We loosely borrowed formatting from playwriting traditions in order to highlight the characters in each chapter, and to help convey the unspoken elements of each session. While there was much more laughter than is conveyed in the following pages, we tried to share some moments when there was laughter, as well as to indicate when someone interjected or gestured. These appear italicized and set apart in brackets.

A variety of other editorial decisions were made in order to provide unity throughout the work. Several participants mention years or decades, and these have been written in full, for example, "the 1960s." The initial festival, held in 1969, is referred to as "Woodstock," "the festival," or "Woodstock '69." The subsequent festivals are "Woodstock '94" (the twenty-fifth anniversary of the original festival, held in 1994), "Woodstock '99" (held in 1999), and "Woodstock 50," which was scheduled to be held in 2019 but was cancelled shortly before it was supposed to start. Spelling of names of bands (the/The; &/and) were based, when possible, on the standards of the Rock & Roll Hall of Fame; however, we have used the spelling "rock and roll" throughout.

The event was live-streamed and the recordings archived. The transcripts that make up this book are based on those recordings. Unfortunately, at times the panelists forgot to use their microphones, making some words or passages unintelligible in the recordings. A common refrain during the first roundtable was Bill Hanley (and the others, at times) reminding Chip Monck to use his microphone. As a result, snippets of conversations were lost. We did our best to reconstruct these passages, but occasionally it was not possible. We should add that Bill Hanley and Chip Monck showed their continued commitment to their craft by suggesting lighting and sound improvements throughout the event. Again, those were not included in the book as they do not pertain to the topic at hand.

In order to help the reader understand what the panelists are saying and to place the events in their cultural, musical, and historical contexts, clarifying and additional information has been placed in footnotes. In addition, topics and events of particular significance are presented in greater detail in sidebars throughout the book. These transcripts are based on recollections from fifty years ago. We tried to corroborate and fact check as much as possible, and when we did find a discrepancy, we noted it in the text.

While we made editorial decisions to try to make the book more consistent and readable, the reader should keep in mind that these are conversations and, in the case of the first chapter, conversations among a large number of people. The sessions were lively as the participants reconnected with each other for the first time in fifty years and enjoyed reminiscing about the festival. The resulting narrative isn't always linear, as the participants regularly interrupted each other (or "interjected," as we say in the book), took the conversation in varied directions, and repeated themselves. While we did eliminate some repetitions, we also wanted to capture the essence and energy of these conversations. We tried to standardize some elements of the text, as stated above, but we also wanted to maintain each participant's voice so that the reader could get a feel for the different personalities and perspectives. We hope that the different work styles and approaches of the participants come through in the text, as this is something that they themselves raise.

This book, like the Woodstock festival itself, is a project of collaboration and commitment to a common goal. For this reason, we would like to dedicate it to all the people who made the festival possible: those who worked behind the scenes and those who performed; those who joined us in person for the fiftieth anniversary celebration and those who were with us in spirit; those who are alive today and who continue to share their experiences; and those who have passed. Peace and love to all.

Alex Ludwig and Simone Pilon

WOODSTOCK SITE PLANS

*Provided by Neal V. Hitch, PhD,
courtesy of The Museum at Bethel Woods*

Drawn with exquisite detail and dotted with delightful characters, the Woodstock site plans offer a fascinating look at Woodstock's landscape. The plans were drawn by Tom Jablonka and dated August 11, 1969, just four days before the festival's opening day. The plans reveal the immense size and scope of Woodstock beyond its stage for music.

It is easy to see how the organizers laid out the site. The campgrounds occupy the largest open parcels of land (see the western or left-hand side of the map), and the main gate funnels the attendees eastward through the Bindy Bazaar and on toward the stage. Flanking the main gate to the north is Movement City, a space allocated for progressive speakers including members from the Students for a Democratic Society (SDS) and various other political groups, and to the south is one of many free Food for Love kitchens set up by the Hog Farm.

The Bindy Bazaar separated the campgrounds from the stage area. The bazaar was located in a hilly, wooded area with various trails linking together about twenty-five vendors in pop-up booths, in which one could buy pottery, fabric, and other items. The northeast corner of the bazaar held the Indian Pavilion, which featured works by Native American artists.

Moving east from the Bindy Bazaar, one finds a large open field, sloping downward toward the stage, which was located near the intersection of West Shore and Hurd Roads. Behind the stage and across the street, the organizers erected a pavilion for the performers and their dressing tents, a crew mess hall, and a series of other trailers. Looking closely at the stage, one sees extraordinary details like the four light towers and the bridge built over the road for the performers to move safely from their pavilions to the stage

The main plan also reveals two farms adjacent to Max Yasgur's. The Gempler Farm, located to the south of the Bindy Bazaar, was not officially part of the festival, and the Filippini Farm, located to the north of the Performers' Pavilion, was rented at the last minute. In

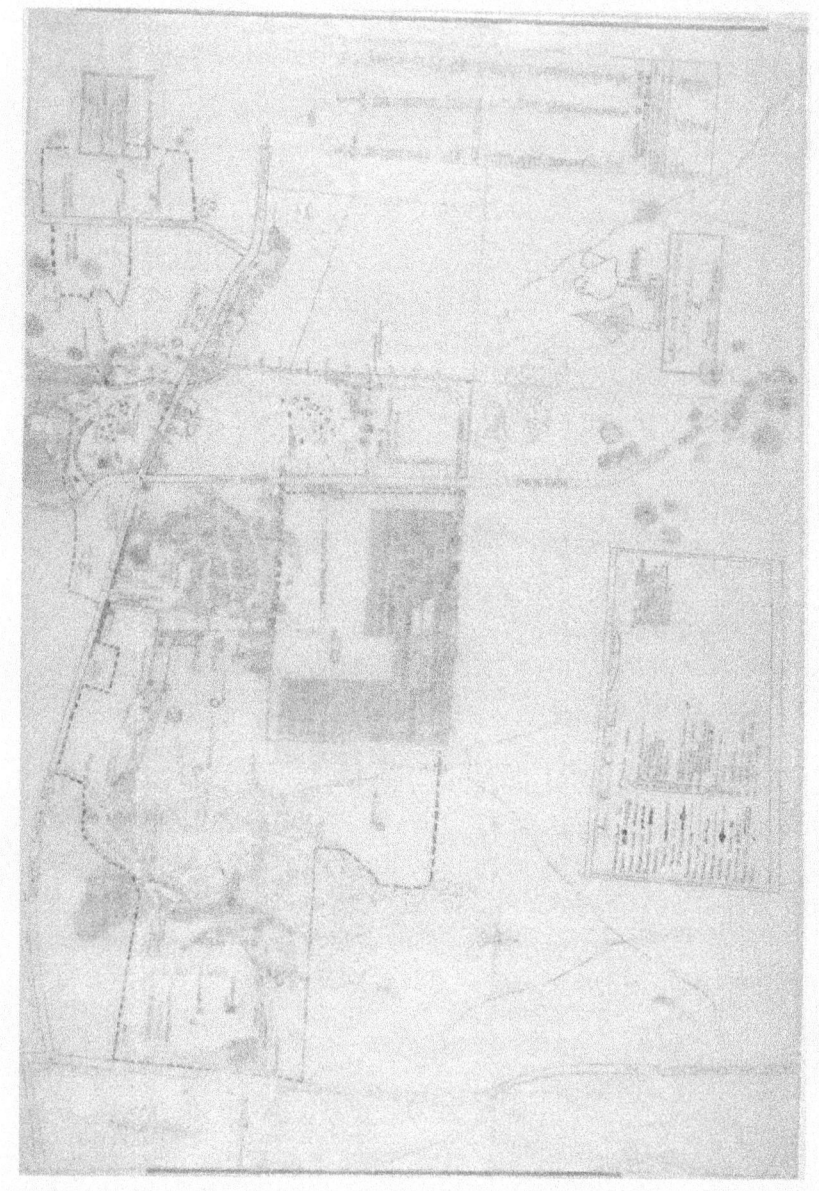

2. Black and white scan of the map created by the architectural team of the Woodstock site.

fact, Filippini's Pond was a major source of drinking water for the festival, before being overrun (famously) by nude bathers.

The plans are replete with unusual features and hand-drawn characters. Look for Penny Lane in the southwestern quadrant, or the Puppet Theater near Crystal Pond, or the ladybug and turtle alongside more abstract characters in the Bindy Bazaar.

In a telephone interview with the editors of this book, Tom Jablonka stated that he was brought into the Woodstock family when its technical director, Chris Langhart, entered Jablonka's furniture store in New York City. Langhart was looking for wooden stakes to

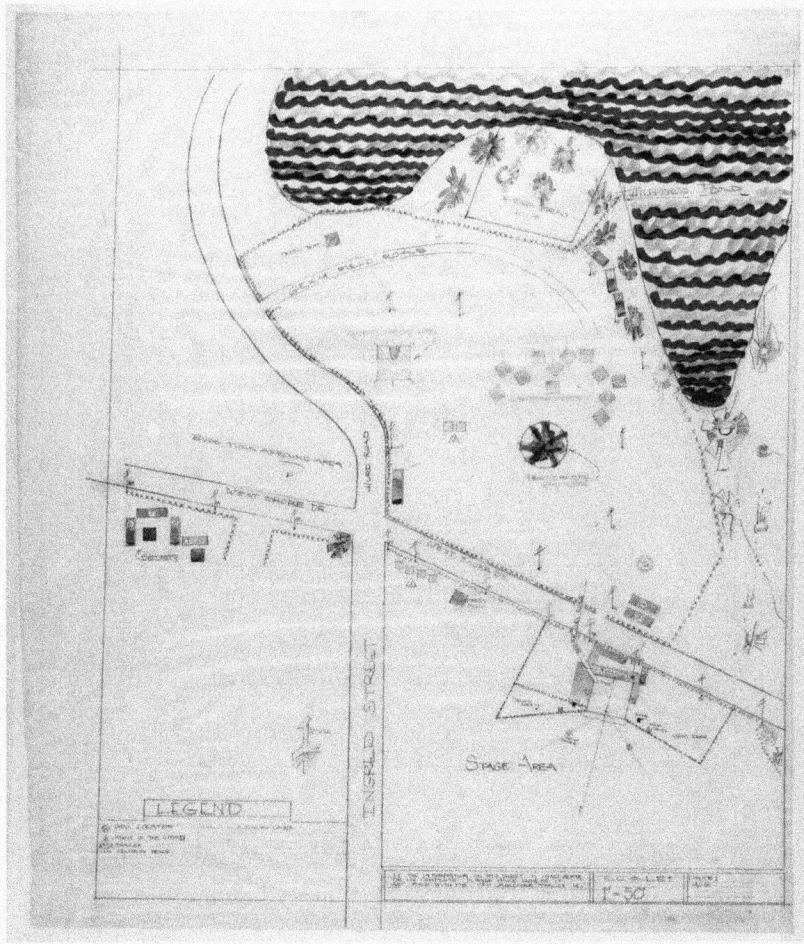

3. Black and white scan of the map of the stage, with Filippini's Pond notated by the wavy lines.

help make a landscape survey, and asked Jablonka, who had taken drafting classes in high school, if he wanted to help. Jablonka was on site for about a month, and noted that he started his map by tracing over existing surveys. Next, he was tasked with identifying the location of every telephone pole, each of which is meticulously marked on the plans. For the most part, his drawings were aspirational, and did not necessarily detail exact locations of existent structures. Interestingly, Jablonka also informed us that the fanciful doodles and character sketches scattered throughout the plans were hand-drawn by his office assistant, Denise Lawrence.

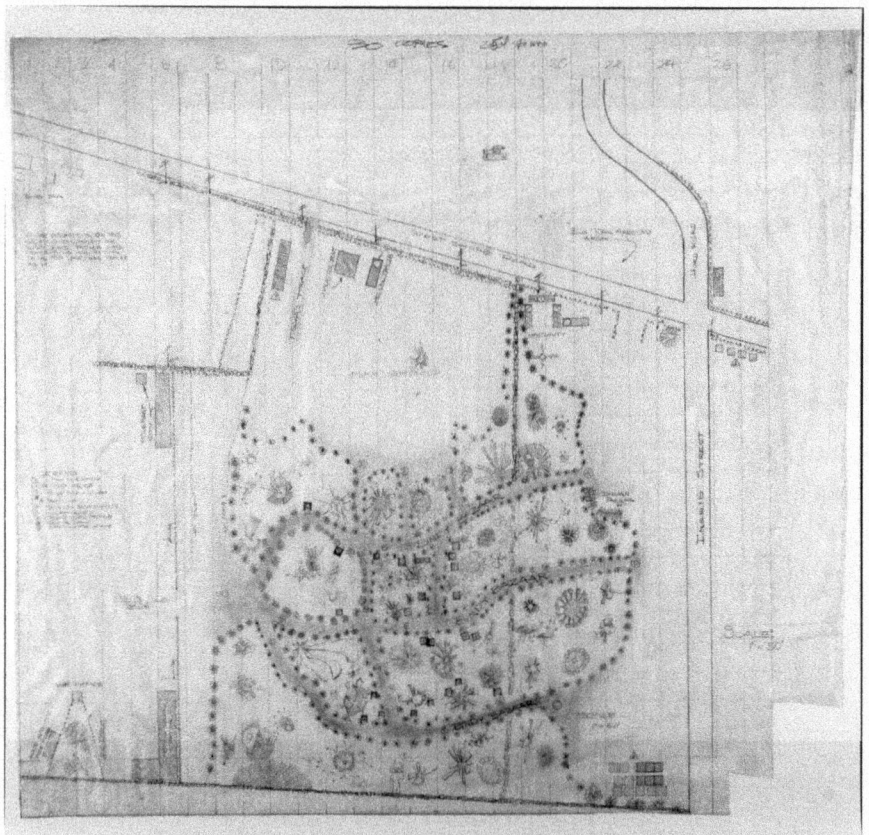

4. Black and white scan of the map of the foot trails in the shopping area known as the Bindy Bazaar.

Provided by Neal V. Hitch, PhD, courtesy of The Museum at Bethel Woods.

CHAPTER 1

BEHIND THE SCENES AT WOODSTOCK

Saturday, April 6, 2019, 12:45–2:45 p.m. EDT
David Friend Recital Hall at Berklee College of Music
Boston, Massachusetts

Participants:
Henry Diltz, photographer
Rona Elliot, public relations
Bill Hanley, sound engineer
Elliott Landy, photographer
Michael Lang, cofounder
Chip Monck, lighting designer and emcee

Moderated by Bob Mulvey, associate professor of professional music, Berklee College of Music

Moderator: Welcome to this roundtable, what we're calling "Behind the Scenes at Woodstock." We are going to try to cover both visually and through commentary the time before the festival, the festival, and after the festival as well.[1] [We have] an amazing panel of Woodstock luminaries here.

---

[1] Throughout the roundtable, pictures taken at Woodstock by Henry Diltz and Elliott Landy were projected behind the participants. They would frequently comment on those pictures, and we have tried to include those photos or else describe them for the reader.

It looks like the hall is full; it doesn't look like it is overfull. I had a joke about too many people showing up but I think we are okay. What we are going to do is take a pictorial journey through those three phases of the festival. [*pointing to Henry Diltz who is snapping pictures of the group with a small digital camera*] He's not going to stop taking pictures.

I think that I'm right, that this is the first time that this group of people has been together in fifty years. All together, collected? Collectively together for the first time, and they haven't changed a bit.

So I'm Bob Mulvey, an associate professor in the professional music department here at Berklee. And that's not as important as the fact that in 1969, in the summer of 1969, I was seventeen years old. I was working a summer job and waiting to go to college in September. I saw an ad for a concert that was happening in New York, in the Catskills. I was in New England, so I wasn't too far away; it seemed doable. Everybody who I was listening to, collecting the music of, and trying to play the music of, was performing; it was an incredible roster. So I went and bought a ticket. I reminded Michael [Lang] that I bought a ticket so I don't owe him. [*to Michael Lang*] I don't owe you any money.

Rona Elliot: [*interjecting*] You're the only one!

Moderator: I still have that eighteen-dollar ticket.

Michael Lang: It helped.

Moderator: Glad I could help. I couldn't resist the lineup of artists. Obviously, none of us checked the weather forecast for New York before we left. Not that I think it would have made a lot of difference, anyway. I'm pretty sure we still would have gone.

So let me introduce our panel of luminaries, and I'm going to give very brief introductions because we want to get to some of these visuals. Their resumes are phenomenal, and would take much too long to completely cover.

Henry Diltz is a music photographer, well-known for over two hundred album covers and thousands of publicity photos from the 1960s and 1970s, and later than that too. His photographs have been published in *Rolling Stone* magazine and *Life* magazine, among others. He was contacted by the Woodstock producers to chronicle the festival. Am I right?

Henry Diltz: [*pointing to Chip Monck*] By Chip.

Moderator: Welcome to Henry. Rona Elliot is an acclaimed music journalist who worked in radio and became music correspondent for the *Today Show* in 1985. In 2010, she became a board member of the Rock & Roll Hall of Fame, where her papers are included in its archive of rock history memorabilia. She was hired by the Woodstock producers to do public relations—Community relations? Local relations?—for the festival in 1969.

To my immediate left is Chip Monck, a celebrated lighting designer who was drafted as the stage announcer at Woodstock. So if you've listened to the recording or seen the film, you've heard Chip. After building, staging, and lighting the festival he became the announcer. He came to the festival with a history of lighting, at the Village Gate in New York and the Monterey Pop Festival. He also worked on the Rolling Stones tour in 1972, and the Summer Olympics in Los Angeles in 1984. Welcome to Chip.

In the middle is Michael Lang. We're really glad that Michael could make it. He's one of the cofounders of the Woodstock Festival. He had produced the Miami Pop Festival the year before, in 1968. And he has produced subsequent Woodstock festivals, including Woodstock 50 this summer, which we'll get a chance to talk about, hopefully, too. It's in Watkins Glen, am I right?

Michael Lang: Yes.

Moderator: And he's managed the careers of Joe Cocker, Rickie Lee Jones, and Willy DeVille. He's also worked in film production. His organization has worked with artists as diverse as Steely Dan, Missy Elliott, Bruce Springstein, and the Red Hot Chili Peppers.

Over next to Henry is Elliott Landy. Elliott is known as a photojournalist of the socio-political changes that were happening in the 1960s, and for his classic rock photography for his work with Bob Dylan, The Band, Van Morrison, and Jimi Hendrix, as well as many others. His work has been exhibited in galleries and museums worldwide, and published in *Rolling Stone*, the *New York Times*, and *Life* magazine. He, too, was allowed by the festival producers to photograph the festival. [*pointing to Henry and Elliott*] So we have two visual chroniclers of the festival.

And on the end is Bill Hanley. He is regarded as the "Father of Festival Sound." Bill was hired by the Woodstock producers to build the sound system for the festival because of his sound experience at the Newport Folk and Jazz Festivals, the Philadelphia Folk Festivals, and most of the major festivals in the 1960s and 1970s. He also did sound for the Beatles and at Madison Square Garden. Welcome to Bill.

Since we're discussing the behind-the-scenes of Woodstock with this great collection of people that we have here, I just wanted to give a quick historical context, and talk about the year of 1968, the year before Woodstock. It was a seminal year in youth culture in the United States and around the world.

In January was the Tet Offensive of the Vietnam War, which probably meant more draftees into the army to go to a very unpopular war. A lot of young people were affected by that.

In April was the assassination of Martin Luther King Jr. in Memphis, and obviously that impacted the entire civil rights movement, but it was also very important to the young people who had been working in the civil rights movement at the time.

In May of that year, students took to the streets of Paris. I don't know if people remember the riots in Paris of 1968, but they were joining with unionists, fighting against what they deemed an authoritarian regime in France at the time, under Charles de Gaulle.

In June of 1968, a month later, Robert Kennedy was killed in Los Angeles after winning the California primary, which probably would have projected him to the Democratic nomination. That affected young people, as he was an antiwar candidate, and had a lot of strong youth support for his campaign.

In August of that year was the Democratic [National] Convention in Chicago, for people who remember that. It was a very tense place; the police and young antiwar demonstrators clashed in the park. It was projected at the convention and on TV, and had a lot to do with the changing of the tide and the feelings on the Vietnam War.

In November, Richard Nixon was elected president because of some of the turmoil in the Democratic Party, and Nixon and his vice president Spiro Agnew were inaugurated in January of 1969, and both within five years were out on corruption and cover-up charges.

There were a couple of bright spots of 1968. One was the lovely photograph of the Earth from Apollo 8—if people remember *Earthrise*? The blue globe, kind of a marble in the sky. That was at the very end of the year, and it symbolized the fragility of where we all are, and also the beauty of the space program, which in the summer of 1969 was marked by the moon landing.

And some of the music that came out in 1968: *Astral Weeks* by Van Morrison; *Tommy* from the Who; *The White Album* from the Beatles; *Cheap Thrills* from Big Brother and the Holding Company, featuring Janis Joplin; *Beggars Banquet* by the Rolling Stones; and the second [eponymous] Blood, Sweat & Tears album, which actually has Fred Lipsius on it; and Fred has been a faculty member here at Berklee for I don't know how many years in the Woodwinds Department.[2]

I think those events in 1968 may have contributed to the large number of people at the festival who decided that they needed to gather, renew, and realize how many other young people still believed in the same things.

I have to start with Michael and just ask him, what were you thinking? But really, how did you conceive of the whole festival? What were you planning it to be? What was the image you had for it?

Michael Lang: It was pretty much what happened, only on steroids. It was, as you say, following a terrible year in 1968; the Summer of Love [in 1967] was kind of over, this dream of peace and compassion was disappearing, and a lot of the political groups were turning violent. So Woodstock was conceived as a last-ditch "let's get together" on our own, and see if we can make it work. And that was the impetus for Woodstock.

So when we planned it, when we were working out the details of it, there was this idea that music related to the counterculture should be free, because it belonged to the counterculture. And there was no rationale for the fact that bands had to get paid, and sound systems and stages had to be put up. It turned out that at most of the events that summer in 1968 there were mini-riots with tear-gassing. People would want to crash the gates, and the cops would be prepared for that in their gear. It was like a set-up, a conflict. Our concept was "no conflict." Police were there to help people.

We arranged initially for people who could pay, to pay a very reasonable price: seven dollars a day, eighteen dollars for three days, including camping and parking, which turned out to be the New York State Thruway. Then we arranged for free campgrounds, free stages, and free food, for those who came and couldn't afford to pay. We wanted everybody to be able to be a part of it, who wanted to be a part of it. We felt people would pay a fair price

---

[2] Fred Lipsius (b. 1943), is the original saxophonist for the band Blood, Sweat & Tears. He is a graduate of Berklee College of Music, class of 1961, and taught there from 1984 to 2019.

for a great event, and be happy to do it, and those that couldn't would be welcome as well.

We brought the Hog Farm in;³ it was Stan Goldstein's brilliant idea to bring the Hog Farm in to be a part of it.⁴ They were a commune from New Mexico, who were used to outdoor camping and to big outdoor events. We were bringing people from the inner cities who had no idea how to survive for a day out in the country. So they would welcome these people and help them set up a campsite and then encourage them to help the next people, and that started this community, which grew up through that weekend to half a million people who were basically brothers and sisters by the time the weekend was over. Had to be. And everyone shared everything; everyone survived together.

There were problems with water and with bathrooms because we couldn't get our trucks in to clean them for a day or so. And because we had this incredible group of people working with us they were able to figure out ways around all of those things, and we got through the weekend pretty well.

Rona Elliot: Michael also had an idea, in the spirit of that, to hire policemen—[*speaking to Michael Lang*] I assume it was your idea—to hire policemen from the tristate area. He interviewed them to make sure they wouldn't harass or arrest kids who were smoking dope, so I think that that added to it.

Michael Lang: In looking for a head of security, I interviewed a lot of people, and again Stan Goldstein came up with Wes Pomeroy,⁵ who was

---

³ Founded by Hugh Romney (later known as Wavy Gravy), the Hog Farm was brought to Woodstock ostensibly to help with crowd control, but took on other additional tasks, helping with construction, food distribution, and medical aid.

⁴ Stanley Goldstein (1939–2014) was the official chief of staff and campsite coordinator at Woodstock, where he was by all accounts a jack of all trades. In a private communication, Michael Lang described him as "a constant source of invaluable information and personnel."

⁵ Wes Pomeroy (1920–1998), the chief of security at Woodstock, was known for his compassionate treatment of festival attendees. In addition to Woodstock, Pomeroy made his name working at large events, like the Republican National Conventions in 1964 and 1968, and the Led Zeppelin tours in the 1970s. He also held positions in both the Johnson and Carter administrations, including as the assistant director of the Drug Enforcement Agency.

THE CHICAGO DEMOCRATIC NATIONAL CONVENTION IN 1968

Held in Chicago during the week of August 26, 1968, the Democratic National Convention was marred by turbulence inside and violence outside. The backdrop for these divisions was the Vietnam War, especially considering that the current Democratic president, Lyndon B. Johnson, had broken promises not to increase the United States' overseas involvement.

When Johnson decided not to seek reelection, Robert F. Kennedy rose in popularity, but his assassination on June 5, 1968, left the Democratic Party split among the sitting vice president and eventual nominee, Hubert Humphrey, and antiwar senators Eugene McCarthy and George McGovern, who ran as stand-ins for Kennedy.

The political divisions were accentuated outside the convention when the mayor of Chicago, Richard J. Daley, denied permits for various antiwar demonstrations, antagonizing groups like the Students for a Democratic Society (SDS) and Youth International Party (the so-called "Yippies"), led by Abbie Hoffman and Jerry Rubin.

Daley was increasingly hostile to the protestors; he restricted demonstrations from taking place near the convention itself and called up the Illinois National Guard. On the evening of August 28, a riot erupted with police spraying tear gas and beating protestors. Fleeing Grant Park, the protestors marched toward the convention center where they were assaulted again by police. This time, however, television cameras captured the scene, with footage broadcast on the nightly news of protestors chanting "The whole world is watching."

After the convention, the federal government brought charges against several organizers of the protests. One group of eight coconspirators charged included activist and Black Panther cofounder Bobby Seale, but his trial was eventually severed from that of the other defendants, who became known as the Chicago Seven. This group included Hoffman and Rubin, along with David Dellinger, Tom Hayden, Rennie Davis, John Froines, and Lee Weine. Overseen by Judge Julius Hoffman, the contentious trial saw Bobby Seale bound and gagged for multiple days, and Abbie Hoffman and Jerry Rubin openly mock the judge. The trial itself became a cause célèbre for the antiwar movement, and eventually all the charges were overturned.

part of a three-man crime commission under Nixon, and was the only sane voice at the Democratic National Convention [in Chicago], with Mayor Daley trying to kill everybody. A lot of the security guys would come up with these ideas: "We're going to have two rows of fencing with barbed wire on top, and then we'll have attack dogs in the middle." And we knew that wasn't the answer. Wes understood that you can't really do that, you can't control what we were looking at—two hundred thousand people—let alone half a million, and that you had to give them a space that encourages them to be part of what you're talking about, which is three days of peace and music.

In thinking about the security, it was Wes that came up with the idea of using the New York City cops, because they were used to dealing with people on the Lower East Side and the counterculture, and knew the limits and how not to create a problem out of a situation. So we had this list of questions for the interview of these cops, and one question was, "If someone blows pot in your face, what would you do?" "Beat them over the head and arrest them" was the wrong answer; "Inhale" was the right answer. About three days before the festival, the police commissioner pulled these cops from being able to come up officially, which devastated Wes, as he felt like he was just completely blindsided. It created a huge political mess, in any case. But the cops came up anyway, and they used names like Mickey Mouse and Donald Duck, and we paid them in cash. And most of them showed up. And they did what they were supposed to do; they were wearing red "peace" jackets and they were there to help. And they did.

Moderator: Can we talk briefly about the financing and how that was going to be done?

Michael Lang: Artie Kornfeld and I became friends in that year, and we put this idea together, Artie and I.[6] And then we went out to look for funding. We were looking at doing this festival, and also at doing a remote recording studio in Woodstock. We were introduced to John Roberts and Joel

---

[6] Artie Kornfeld (b. 1942) is an American concert promoter and record executive. He began working at Capitol Records in his early twenties, serving as the vice president of rock and roll music, the first time such a position was created in the industry. In 1969, he left Capitol to begin working on Woodstock, with Michael Lang as a cofounder.

Rosenman by Artie's attorney, and we went to visit them.[7] I guess I looked like somebody from Mars to them; they were kind of straight, yuppie kind of guys, but really nice. We decided to do it together. John Roberts had an inheritance from his family and he put up the money.[8] We had figured a half a million dollars was going to do it; of course, that went south as soon as we had to move from Wallkill, [New York].[9] And John really stood up and paid all the bills. We were $1.3 million in the hole after the festival.

Moderator: [*interjecting*] In 1969—

Michael Lang: That's a lot of money.[10]

Moderator: Rona, how did you get involved? And what were you asked to do?

Rona Elliot: I was in Algeria in early May of 1969 and I was a veteran of two pop festivals already. One was the other Miami Pop Festival in 1968 that Henry and I worked on, as opposed to Michael's Miami Pop in 1968. I always have to say there were two Miami Pop Festivals. The other pop festival that I had worked on was the Newport Pop Festival.[11]

The guy who would go on to be the director of operations at Woodstock

---

[7] Joel Rosenman (b. 1942) and John Roberts (1945–2001) were the financiers responsible for bankrolling the Woodstock Festival. Their first collaboration, building Mediasound, a recording studio in Manhattan, brought them to the attention of Michael Lang and Artie Kornfeld, who approached Roberts and Rosenman with a proposal to build a recording studio in Woodstock, New York. Roberts and Rosenman countered with an idea for a music festival. The four created Woodstock Ventures using funds from Roberts's recent family inheritance.

[8] On his twenty-first birthday, John Roberts received an inheritance of $250,000 (roughly the equivalent of $2 million in 2019) from his grandfather, the founder of the Block Drug company, best known for the Polident and Poli-Grip denture products.

[9] After failing to find a suitable venue for the festival in the actual city of Woodstock, New York, the organizers kept the name but moved on to the Mills Industrial Park in Wallkill, New York. After the festival organizers spent months of planning and negotiating with the town, the Wallkill Zoning Board of Appeals (ZBA) denied the application for a permit, thwarting the Woodstock organizers with less than one month to go before the festival.

[10] The 2019 equivalent of $1.3 million is just over $9 million.

[11] Not to be mistaken for the Newport Folk or Jazz Festivals in Rhode Island, the Newport Pop Festival was held in Costa Mesa, California, on August 3 and 4, 1968. The festival featured Jefferson Airplane, Country Joe McDonald, Tiny Tim, and Sonny and Cher, among others.

THE TWO MIAMI POP FESTIVALS

In 1968, a horse racing track just north of Miami hosted two separate pop-music festivals, both of which are known today as Miami Pop. Promoted by Michael Lang and Richard O'Barry, the first Miami Pop Festival took place on May 18 and 19, 1968, in front of an estimated crowd of twenty-five thousand people. Lang's involvement guaranteed the perception of Miami Pop as a dress rehearsal for Woodstock, and the analogy is apt. Both festivals featured the Jimi Hendrix Experience as headliners, and included unique ways of presenting the artists: in Miami, Michael Lang decided to stage the bands on flatbed trucks so they could be rolled off and on for a quick turnover between acts; at Woodstock the following year, the stage consisted of three giant turntables that emulated the flatbed trucks.

Key personnel at Woodstock also worked at Miami Pop, including Stan Goldstein, then working at Criteria Records in Miami, who ran sound at the festival; and Eddie Kramer, who later helped to record audio of Woodstock, photographed Miami Pop. Just as happened at Woodstock, the original promoters of Miami Pop, Lang and O'Barry, were essentially bankrupted by the festival after a rainout on the second day hampered their ability to take in ticket sales, forcing them to forgo payment for services rendered, including to those who recorded sound and footage of the festival.

The second Miami Pop Festival, held over three days at the end of December 1968, also shared many parallels with Woodstock. The second Miami Pop was produced by Tom Rounds and Mel Lawrence, the team that had produced the Fantasy Fair and Magic Mountain Music Festival in 1967, largely thought of as the first rock festival in the United States. Lawrence would later go on to be the director of operations at Woodstock. Six of the performers at this Miami Pop would later play at Woodstock, including Richie Havens, the Grateful Dead, and the Paul Butterfield Blues Band. The second Miami Pop festival was notable for its crowd size, with an estimated one hundred thousand people attending, making it the largest such festival on the East Coast up to that point, and for the fact that it ran two simultaneous main stages, also a first in rock-festival history.

[Mel Lawrence] sent me a telegram, which I wish I had kept, saying, "Come home, festival in upstate New York." I was planning on staying in Algeria because there was the Pan-African Cultural Festival scheduled that had Eldridge Cleaver and Timothy Leary.[12] That sounded pretty interesting, but then I thought, "The Catskills... That sounds so Catskill-like," having grown up in New York and having gone to camp in bungalow colonies in the Catskills. So I got there with Mel Lawrence in May of 1969, and Mel said, "Just talk to Michael [Lang] about what you want to do."[13]

A large PR company, Wartoke, had already been hired in New York, and I was pretty good at dealing with people individually, so I kind of made up this job that I would go into the local community, talk to the radio, and the TV, and the press people, and the Kiwanis Club, and organize a square dance, and Michael went for it, which was great, obviously. I have pictures of the square dance. So that's what I did that summer. When we started, there were thirteen of us in that motel.[14] We watched the moon landing together in July, and on the last day, there were four hundred

---

[12] The Pan-African Cultural Festival drew thousands of artists, poets, and musicians to the city of Algiers during the last ten days of July 1969. The festival was held to promote a postimperial Africa, and it attracted delegates from more than thirty countries across the continent. It featured performances by the likes of Archie Shepp and Nina Simone. Eldridge Cleaver (1935–1998) was an activist affiliated with the Black Panther Party. After being charged with murder, he fled the country to Cuba and then Algeria, the site of the Pan-African Cultural Festival. Timothy Leary (1920–1996) was a psychologist best known for the phrase "turn on, tune in, drop out," which he deployed when promoting the use of psychedelic drugs.

[13] Mel Lawrence (1935–2016) was an American documentarian and concert promoter. He was the director of operations at Woodstock after also having worked on most of the earlier important rock festivals in the 1960s, including the Magic Mountain Music Festival and Monterey Pop Festival, both in 1967, and the second Miami Pop Festival in 1968. A decade after Woodstock, Lawrence began producing documentaries, including *Koyaanisqatsi: Life Out of Balance* (1982), presented by Francis Ford Coppola, and *Paha Sapa: The Struggle for the Black Hills* (1993), a documentary for HBO that was nominated for an Emmy Award.

[14] Located in Bethel, New York, the El Monaco Motel was home base for the organizers of Woodstock. Elliot Tiber (1935–2016) owned the motel, which was subsequently used during the festival for housing and as a ticket office. Other spaces in Bethel that Woodstock workers used included the old New York Telephone Building in nearby Kauneonga Lake, and the Diamond Horseshoe Hotel. Although Tiber's property was deemed unusable for the festival itself, he happened to possess a permit allowing for a theatrical performance on his property, which he transferred to the Woodstock organizers.

of us. So that's what I did. But my most memorable thing was trying to convince the Kiwanis Club that we would be good for their community. I think they looked at me like I was from outer space. But looking back, when you watch the movie and consider how people thought of the event later, there were people who recognized their own children out there and who fed them.

Michael Lang: [*interjecting*] I just want to say that it's no reflection on Rona that they kicked us out three months later.[15]

Moderator: Let's go to the photographers here and then we'll get to Chip and Bill. So Henry, how did you get involved?

Henry Diltz: Well, I got involved because of a phone call from Chip, my friend Chip Monck. I was a folk singer in the early 1960s, and in some of our concerts, Chip was the lighting guy and the staging guy. So I'd met him in the early 1960s, and then we worked on Monterey Pop. I was there shooting photos, as well as at the Miami Pop Festival. So I knew Chip pretty well.

Anyway, he called me one day. I was in my kitchen in Laurel Canyon,[16] and he said, "Henry, we're going to have a huge music festival; you ought to be here." I said, "Chip, I've heard about it. I would love to, but I don't know those people; how am I going to get a photo pass?" He said, "I'll speak to the producer." And the next day, Michael Lang, whom I'd never met, called me, and he said, "Chip says we need you; I'm sending you an airline ticket and five hundred dollars," and that was it. So I flew to New York and I was there two weeks before the festival.

I stayed in a little boarding house with a lot of the people who were working on the grounds, the artwork, and all that. My job every day was to just go out and photograph everybody. The hippie carpenters sawing and

---

[15] On July 15, 1969, the Zoning Board of Appeals in Wallkill, New York, denied the Woodstock organizers' application for a permit for the festival, which was scheduled to begin exactly one month later.

[16] Laurel Canyon, located in the Hollywood Hills neighborhood of Los Angeles, was home to a burgeoning collection of singer-songwriters in the 1960s and 1970s. The music associated with Laurel Canyon features a wide range of styles and artists, including Joni Mitchell, Neil Young, Carole King, the Mamas and the Papas, the Eagles, and David Crosby, among many others.

THE MONTEREY POP FESTIVAL

Taking place during the weekend of June 16–18, 1967, Monterey Pop is largely thought of as having launched the so-called Summer of Love. The producers, including Lou Adler and Beatles publicist Derek Taylor, sought to promote the burgeoning rock scene with a festival that in retrospect set the template for future large-scale rock festivals, including Woodstock two years later.

The mix of musical styles was truly radical: West Coast mainstays such as Jefferson Airplane and the Grateful Dead played alongside new bands from the UK, such as the Who and the Jimi Hendrix Experience, neither of which had toured extensively in the United States. Otis Redding, backed by Booker T & the MGs, found an entirely new audience, as did Ravi Shankar, the Indian sitar virtuoso. The celebrated rock documentarian D. A. Pennebaker filmed the festival, producing footage that cemented the festival's status. The single most indelible image in the film is of Jimi Hendrix on his knees, coaxing a rising flame from his guitar, captured by Chip Monck's evocative lighting design.

---

hammering and building this huge deck, and the girls would come over with lunch. It was like summer camp; it was wonderful. It was upstate New York in the sunshine, and I was shooting all this stuff happening. I was documenting the Hog Farm; we would go swimming nude in the lake in the afternoon with everybody. And I was just photographing, documenting, which is what I love to do.

Then one day I saw six or eight people sitting up on the grass, up on the hillside, and I thought, "What are those people doing there? Oh yeah, I forgot there's going to be this huge concert." Then the next day there were hundreds of thousands of people there. You know, I was on the stage most of the time, and we didn't quite know how huge the whole thing was until somebody on Saturday afternoon brought a copy of the *New York Times* with an aerial picture. I remember everyone crowding around saying "Oh my God!" It showed the whole countryside and the closed freeways and everything. We couldn't see beyond the crest of the hill, and all the other stuff that was going on. And then I just kind of stayed on the stage for three days shooting everything that happened.

5. Black and white photograph of festival attendees swimming in a pond. The reflection in a side mirror of a car parked nearby shows the long lines of people making their way to the festival. Photograph by Henry Diltz.

Moderator: So Chip, let me go to you. How did you get involved in this idea?

Chip Monck: I had a weekly visit to the William Morris Agency, a talent agency, and one of the younger folks was an agent there, and I would contact him each week to see who was doing what, why, and where. And he said, "There's a curly-headed kid [Michael Lang] that is hiring everything in Christendom." Hector Morales was the agent, and he said, "Go get him." So I figured, okay, let's do this.

So I asked Mr. Lang, "Do you mind if I light it?" and Michael was kind enough to say, "By all means, please go right ahead." That was about the essence of the design criteria, and we just went to work. It was quite that simple; it was very relaxed, there were no papers. I think we just nodded and left it at that. It was quite sufficient. That's the way it is best to do deals with Michael; everyone else will tailor them after the fact, and Michael just leaves it exactly as it was, which was a reward that we all were very grateful for.

Just one thing about Michael that's really the essence of what we're here for, is that there is no reason that you can't do whatever you so wish. All you have to do is sharpen the bow, sharpen the arrow, tweak the bow; find the facilities with which to create; and tell others how to do it. And I'm sure you can, but don't forget that that's the essence of what we're here about.

Moderator: Thank you, Chip. Bill: how did you get contacted, and how did it start for you?

Bill Hanley: Stan Goldstein called me about Miami Pop, after I did that one for him. And I kept waiting and waiting and waiting [to hear about Woodstock], but I didn't get a word from him. Finally I showed up at his office on Sixth Avenue, wasn't it? Second floor. And then he told me the budget that he had for me. And he was going to get one hundred thousand people and that was it. So then I showed up at Bethel. He had fought with Judy over the price until she couldn't squeeze any more money out of him.[17] So we took that and ran with it.

We went back and built special speakers. But first of all, we showed up at the owner's property, Mr. Yasgur, and went down and on to this house. I can't remember if we went back to Boston or whether we went straight to his house from Bethel. And I can't remember who was in the car with me, but we went out the front door, down the street, take a left, and take another left, and then take a right. And then I saw this incredible field! And I looked that over and I said, "Gee, that would be a great amphitheatre."

Chip Monck: [*interjecting*] Bill arranged a rather sensible solution to the fact that we were on a fairly steep incline, or a raked, almost a raked theatre, with his scaffolding arrangement.

Bill Hanley: Well, we found out there were holes in the hill at the back of the house, and that's why the speakers were up so high. They were special speakers; we wanted to get line of sight, and it's best for audio, too. And that's how the design came about for the second tier of speakers.

Chip Monck: That was neat; Bill certainly did cover it.

Michael Lang: Here's a little anecdote about how Bill was hired and created this sound system, because nobody ever built a sound system for that many people before. He was probably one of the most experienced, or one

---

[17] Judy Bernstein, Bill Hanley's assistant.

of the two most experienced people with large PA [public-address] systems in existence. The other was Stanley Owsley [sic].[18] And Stanley Owsley was the Grateful Dead's sound man and built all of their outdoor speaker systems. The other thing that Owsley did was he was a major producer of LSD in America. So we thought it would be smarter to go with Bill.

Bill Hanley: Never happened.

Moderator: Wise choice.

Bill Hanley: I'm a teetotaler, totally, and don't even drink tea or coffee.

Moderator: Let's go to Elliott [Landy]. How did you get involved?

Elliott Landy: In 1967, I started photographing peace demonstrations and working with underground newspapers in New York City, and I did that through 1968 to try and help stop the Vietnam War, and to help communicate that war was bad. In those years, rock and roll music was part of the underground culture, was part of the "stop-the-war" culture, part of the "let's find a different way to live" culture. That led me to photographing The Band and then Bob Dylan. Because of that, I moved up to Woodstock. In those years, Woodstock was considered the music mecca because Dylan lived there, and The Band was just coming out. That was the place to be. [*to Michael Lang*] Which I imagine is what brought you to Woodstock?

Michael Lang: Not really; I was living in Coconut Grove, Florida. After the Miami Pop Festival, I wanted to move back to New York because we had lost all our money and I thought it was time for a change. But I loved the experience of living in a small, creative community, which is what Coconut Grove is. Woodstock was kind of a similar town; it was an artist community and two hours from New York City, so I thought it was a great place to go.

Elliott Landy: So I got to know Mike. His girlfriend was a friend of my sister's, and we used to hang out in the town square. And then one day, Mike called me and said, "I want to come up and see you." So he drove up to

---

[18] Augustus Owsley Stanley III (1935–2011), known professionally as "Bear," worked as the sound engineer for the Grateful Dead while also claiming responsibility for making millions of doses of LSD in the mid-1960s.

my house on his motorcycle, and he said, "I'm producing a festival, do you want to photograph it?" And I asked, "Who's playing?" and he named some of the famous groups. I don't remember which ones, but I was impressed. I said, "Sure, I'll do it." He said, "Okay, I'll see you later." We didn't even shake hands. It was that kind of time, and that's very indicative of what the 1960s were like. You said something and you meant it; and it was cool, and you did it. So that's how I came to photograph the festival.

Moderator: Let me go back to the prefestival. So how much time after the permit fell through in Wallkill? And then how much time after you had already started selling tickets?

Michael Lang: We lost our . . . I don't know what you call it. The town of Wallkill passed something called "Local Law Number One." This should give you an idea of how these things worked in those days. This law basically prevented us from being able to do the festival there. They created conditions that were impossible to meet. They were wrong, and we could have gone to court and we would have won six months later.

Rona Elliot: They were harassing the staff. If we drove around, they would stop us; they were just harassing us. They didn't want us.

CULTURAL HISTORY OF WOODSTOCK, NEW YORK

Located in Ulster County, the town of Woodstock, New York, has a long history as a cultural mecca, beginning with the painters of the Hudson River School in the late 1800s. In the 1960s, Albert Grossman encouraged Bob Dylan and The Band, both artists that he managed at the time, to visit Woodstock, where they were embraced by the vibrant folk-music scene. Café Espresso, on Tinker Street, hosted many of the major folk singers of the period, including Joan Baez and Peter Yarrow, and other musicians followed, as the Woodstock Sound-Outs, a series of small rock festivals, gained momentum with performances from Richie Havens and Phil Ochs, among others. Michael Lang was so impressed by the bohemian nature of the town that he hoped it would be the site of the original Woodstock Festival, and even kept the name when the town passed on hosting.

Michael Lang: It was called the "Concerned Citizens Committee" that was formed to really get us out of there. We got to Wallkill, and my partners, John and Joel, went and met with the town council, and they looked kind of yuppie-ish, and they described this idea of minstrels wandering through the property in the afternoon with a little jazz, a little folk, a little of this, and a little of that. Then we started moving in with our crew and they didn't look like John and Joel, so things started to change.

The 1960s were a time when our generation was feared by our parents' generation. There was this huge generation gap. We didn't think alike. They grew up in the Eisenhower years, when America had God on its side and never did anything wrong. And then we were in the 1960s and that was no longer true. We were coming out of the civil rights movement, or we were in the middle of the civil rights movement. John F. Kennedy was president and he was empowering the youth. Somehow we figured out that we could really make a difference. So we got very energized and very engaged in a lot of the social lessons of the day, which were women's rights, civil rights, the environmental movement, which began in the 1960s, and the idea of healthier food to put into your body.[19] A lot of those kinds of concepts were developed and generated in the 1960s. A lot of them have come home to roost it seems these days as well. I forgot where I was going. . . .

Rona Elliot: [*interjecting*] They hated us and we had to move.

Michael Lang: On the fifteenth of July, one month before the festival, we had to leave Wallkill. The miracle of Woodstock is that we had been looking for a stage for months and took Wallkill just as a panic move because we were running out of time. When we lost Wallkill on the fifteenth of July, the miracle was that on the sixteenth of July, we got a call from this guy called Elliot Tiber who said that he had a permit for a festival and a site for a festival, and wouldn't we come up and take a look. Of course, we said "Eureka!" and we drove up to the El Monaco Motel, which was in White Lake, New York, and it looked like the motel from hell. There were doors on a couple of the rooms and there were black things crawling out of the pool.

---

[19] For example, one popular book at the time argued for a meat-free diet, for both dietary and environmental reasons. Written in 1971, Frances Moore Lappé's *Diet for a Small Planet* is a vegetarian cookbook with plans for hundreds of meat-free recipes. Frances Moore Lappé, *Diet for a Small Planet (New York: Ballantine Books, 1971).*

Mel Lawrence, who was kind of our site manager and operations chief, my assistant Ticia Bernuth and, I think Stan Goldstein [and I] met at the motel, and Elliot walked us down the hill to the festival field. Mel was walking out in front, and suddenly he disappeared, and then Stan disappeared after him, and we were in the middle of a swamp. I had to drag Mel off of Elliot Tiber's throat, and we went back up the hill.

But we had passed amazingly beautiful farms on the way to [the] El Monaco, so we asked Elliot to get a hold of a local realtor for us, and we went riding through the hills, and went down Hurd Road, came up over the top of the hill, and there was the magic bowl of our dreams. So I asked, "Who owns this?" "Max Yasgur." So we arrived at Max's house, picked him up, and went back to the field. Max and I walked out to the field, and he did a quick calculation. It was a wet summer, so he needed to buy a lot of hay. He was in the milk business, so he needed money. He was a smart guy. I will never forget, like it happened yesterday. He was out there and licked the tip of his pencil and started making notes: "It's going to cost me so much to reseed per acre," and "It's going to cost me so much to lose the crops," and "It's going to cost me so much for this," and blah, blah, blah. Seventy thousand dollars later, we made a deal. So we had literally a month to prepare for Woodstock.

Moderator: We're looking at one of Henry's photos, I think, and this looks to me like it's at some stage of construction. Chip, were you there? I'm guessing you are one of those people standing on that platform.

Chip Monck: No. That was a workbench. In other words, with the construction of the roof, which is five joists—they were each five feet high and tons of lumber, immense dimensions [of] timber—there had to be somewhere to build it. Couldn't build on an incline, couldn't build it on grass, so the stage had to be the very first thing that went up. That was the carpentry shop for all intents and purposes. Then the scaffolding went up, and I moved my towers and that was about it. The muscle for that was Leo Makota and two guys, who put up all that scaffolding.[20] They were quite amazing.

So much got done in so little time, but just not quite enough. The one [of two stage designs] that was aesthetically most pleasing, but a little bit

---

[20] Leo Makota worked on the stage crew at Woodstock, building the scaffolding that held up the lighting. After Woodstock, he worked for a short time as the road manager for Crosby, Stills, Nash & Young.

dangerous, had these two-hundred-and-ten-feet-tall telephone poles at a slight angle with a strange mushroom cap on the top. It had holes all the way around, and most of the cables went back down this way to be tethered to the earth, basically as counterweights. And it supposedly balanced. It was tethered together, mushroom to mushroom, and then into the earth on either side, until such time as the weight got on it.

One of Henry's pictures is very interesting: it's a fifty-five-gallon drum with a tether on it, or a bridle, and a person sitting in the drum, and sometimes there would be two and they're going up there with wrenches and doing what they have to do. But it certainly isn't the rigging facility that would've been perhaps a little more efficient. We were just doing it. "This has to be done; how do we do it?" or "This looks like the safest possible way," or "This is realistic, and okay, how do we get up there?" "Well, we only have one crane, and they're not ready to lift the roof pieces yet, the five trusses, so let's use that to get the guys up there and put all the cables on the mushrooms, and we'll just go step by step." There could have been another way to do it, but there was no planning time available. The idea was, "Here's your site and here's the problem. Here's what everybody's decided on. It's about time we got it built."

And lighting we'll speak of later, and it was a very interesting challenge to me in my excessive OCD modes of production. I now present every client with maybe five absolutely different analogies or concepts so that we have someplace to go when we are a little tight on time or materials don't come and things like that. [*picture on screen changes*] Did you see the previous one? With Michael praying? I missed it. Michael's looking for divine assistance in that one.

Rona Elliot: [*interjecting*] And they came through.

Chip Monck: [*echoing Rona*] Indeed they did.

We were in a very, very strange position. I mean every time something failed, of which the list is not particularly long, but every single one of them was essential; there was reason to everything. Just very quickly: the turntable sections—and I won't go into how they were built and how they worked—but we had five different half-circle wagons, and they stuck together with a propeller in the middle of a great staff into the ground. Our turnover would have been very quick; we could've done probably ten-minute turnovers because the upstage act, or the one that was behind the one

6. Black and white photograph of Chip Monck and Michael Lang in Max Yasgur's field, prior to the start of the festival. Photograph by Henry Diltz.

that was performing, is being set up while the downstage act is performing. And then we'd just swing it around like that, and whoopee! we're ready for maybe a turnaround in ten minutes.

But the problem is that if we were so efficient as we wished to be, there's X amounts of acts in sixteen hours for all intents and purposes. What are they going to do for the other eight hours? Everything worked in our favor, peculiarly enough, and everything that broke in the rain, everybody got wet. You couldn't tell the difference between the performers or the stage people and the audience; everyone looked exactly the same. They were drenched, and the one safe place in the roof where there was a tarpaulin, a portion of our roofing system, there was a big puddle of water. And normally you'd bring all the equipment that you wanted and you would put it in the safe place underneath this tarp, and you'd push a two-by-four up against the water, the belly, and all the water would spill out on the sides. Well this young fella had this grand idea so he tied his pen knife to a bamboo pole and stuck a hole in the middle of the fucker. [*laughing*] Anyways, I guess it's somebody else's turn now. I've just sort of summarized my feelings about it.

Rona Elliot: [*interjecting*] And this is fifty years later!

Moderator: These are great stories!

Rona Elliot: [*looking at a projected picture of herself from the festival*] Picture by Henry Diltz.

Moderator: That's Rona.

Moderator: So Bill, what about the sound? These towers: what was the plan?

Bill Hanley: That was the plan. [*laughs*] The towers! Just the way it would sit there.

Chip Monck: And actually, Bill told them what to do and they put it up.

Bill Hanley: I'll tell you why the roof didn't get finished, though. Do you know? Because someone, when they were moving from Wallkill, someone broke twenty feet off of one of the telephone poles, and that's what happened to the roof. And instead of splicing in the pole in the middle where it broke, they decided to cut the other one off and so the cables were now at too wide of an angle, and they overloaded the cables. Steve [Cohen] dragged me over there and asked me what to do about it.[21] And that's what happened. That's why it didn't get finished.

Michael Lang: [*to Chip*] And that's what happened to your lights!

Bill Hanley: Oh the lights! That's right, the lights went down with the whole roof!

Chip Monck: Six hundred and fifty thousand watts of lights, and six hundred and fifty instruments, living underneath the deck waiting to be hung, plus floor masking and all sorts of stuff, all of the tools with which we worked. And so it sat there, and there were twelve follow spots: two, four, four, and two; forty-five degrees left and right of the centerline; and then fifteen degrees down center from horizontal, so that you don't

---

[21] Steve Cohen (b. 1940) was the production stage manager at Woodstock, and designed its physical platform and stage.

get a nose shadow on this side of your face. We have to do these things that way.

Bill Hanley: [*jokingly*] Chip, someone else has something to say.

Chip Monck: By all means; you told me to speak.

Moderator: When did it dawn on you that there were already people there and that there weren't ticket takers at the gate? Was it a couple of days before any music was starting? When did you realize there were already people there?

Rona Elliot: You looked out over the road and they were there. They were on the field; they were everywhere!

Michael Lang: The problem was we never got the ticket booths in place.

Rona Elliot: [*interjecting*] Or the fences.

Michael Lang: Well, the fences went up, and then they came down. And they went up and then they came down. But there was nobody to take tickets. People were looking for a place to buy tickets, but they weren't there. So we declared what was obvious to everyone else, which was that it was now a free festival.

Rona Elliot: There were people on the staff who never got there because the roads were impassable, and there were just people everywhere. It was like the lemmings heading to the sea, and they just kept coming. There was no end in sight, and that was on Thursday. By Friday, they were just *really* there.

Michael Lang: People were coming up with ideas like "Send women out in diaphanous dresses with baskets to try and get people to contribute."

Rona Elliot: Whose idea was that?

Michael Lang: That was Artie's idea, but we kind of nixed all that, and just accepted what was going on and paid attention to what we had to do.

Rona Elliot: I would say, and this will be said by other people probably far more articulately than me, but whenever there was an emergency, everybody on the staff rose to the occasion and worked together. If one thing was failing, you just went and did the next thing, whether it was digging the trenches to empty the toilets or to help with the food.

Henry Diltz: [*looking at a photo*] I just want to say that we're still a little bit before all the people arrived. This is the Hog Farm, the commune from New Mexico that was setting up the campsites. This is all still a few days before the people arrived.

Michael Lang: And they weren't praying, they were creating a circle for the helicopter to land.

7. Black and white photograph of members of the Hog Farm in a large circle in a field, holding hands. They are marking a landing spot for helicopters. Photograph by Henry Diltz.

Henry Diltz: Here's the Hog Farm ladies preparing all the coleslaw and brown rice that fed the masses after the first day when they ran out of food. And here's the Hog Farm and their bus from New Mexico. Every afternoon they would get in the bus and go down to the lake and swim in the lake; all the kids, and the babies. This is the Hog Farm bus, going down to the lake to go swimming. There they all are in the water.

Rona Elliot: [*interjecting*] They're all bankers now.

Henry Diltz: I always love this sequence, it's so beautiful. These are the people arriving. You see how the cars were parked on both sides of the street, with people in the middle. My boarding house was about a mile down that road, but after the first day I couldn't get home, and I just slept in my station wagon parked behind the stage.

Moderator: So the festival is set to begin on Friday afternoon. Friday at four. And how ready are you to put out music at that point?

Michael Lang: We had a problem getting equipment in, as you can imagine. So the way we had scheduled Friday was kind of out the window. And so it was kind of like, who can perform? Who's ready to perform? It took me an hour to convince Richie Havens to open the festival, and at five o'clock Richie went on stage, started to sing, and the PA worked.[22] That was my favorite moment at Woodstock.

Bill Hanley: Thank you.

Rona Elliot: [*laughing*] It's the little things!

Bill Hanley: They made it all the way through, too! No major hassles.

Moderator: So that's a sign. . . .

Henry Diltz: That was the first act Friday afternoon.

Rona Elliot: [*to Bill Hanley*] Did you think that the PA would work?

Bill Hanley: Did I think? It was designed to work. Yes, absolutely. That's what I designed it to do. There was a problem: it was another console made

---

[22] Richie Havens (1941–2013) was an American singer-songwriter known for his incorporation of rhythm and blues, soul, and folk styles. His debut album, *Mixed Bag* (1967), features the antiwar ballad "Handsome Johnny," made famous in the *Woodstock* film documentary.

similar to the one at the Fillmore East. It went into parasitic oscillations[23] and I had to kick-start it.

Moderator: [*to Bill Hanley*] Richie Havens started the show. Were you doing the sound? Were you at the sound board for that?

Bill Hanley: Some of it, yeah. As soon as I walked the house, I went back to try to make the console, the other console I built, work right, and it never worked right. It had parasitic oscillation problems.

Michael Lang: So then there was a truck that was brought to the site to house the recording equipment because we were recording and filming the festival.

Bill Hanley: That was my responsibility.

Michael Lang: And Bill arranged for this truck, with two eight-track recording machines and some great engineers, and he locked them in a truck for three days. Every once in a while, he'd open the door and throw in a piece of meat and close the door again. And they did a beautiful job!

Bill Hanley: Lee Osbourne did a wonderful job with that, too, in the mixdown, and doing the master recording.[24]

Moderator: Was the intention always to record everything?

Michael Lang: Yes, absolutely.

Moderator: And record everything from the start?

Michael Lang: I had filmed Miami Pop, and I knew that that was really an important aspect of things. We tried to get a deal with a studio to pay for the filming, but Monterey Pop had come out, and that [is a] brilliant film, but it didn't do well at the box office, so we couldn't get anybody to go for it.

---

[23] Often caused by feedback, parasitic oscillations create distortions of an audio signal and can even melt down a connected speaker.
[24] Lee Osborne and Eddie Kramer were independent engineers responsible for recording the festival because the audio rights had already been sold to Atlantic Records.

Artie Kornfeld had a friend named Freddy Weintraub.[25] Artie had been head of A&R [Artists and Repertoire] at Capitol Records, so he had a lot of contacts in the music business. Freddy was a manager and owned a club called The Bitter End in New York City, and he had been hired by Warner Brothers that year to be their in-house "hippie." Artie contacted him and made a deal for the festival to be filmed the day before it started.

Bill Hanley: And they bought all the film!

Moderator: [*looking at Henry Diltz's photo of John Sebastian in tie-dye in front of the crowd*] And this gentleman on stage wasn't originally scheduled to play, correct?

Henry Diltz: Right.

Moderator: But he was there?

Henry Diltz: John Sebastian lived in the town of Woodstock, and he just came over that afternoon to see his friends. He wasn't on the bill and he had taken some LSD.

Rona Elliot: He had taken a lot of LSD.

Henry Diltz: Yeah! So he was on the stage and the next helicopter hadn't arrived yet with the next act, so somebody stuck a guitar in his hand, I understand.

Michael Lang: [*interjecting*] That somebody was Chip, and not only did he stick a guitar in his hand, but he held his hand for the first two songs! [*laughs*]

Chip Monck: Well, he was just too caring, really. It looks pretty strange because he's got his hand behind when he's not playing the guitar and he's hanging onto my hand! But we were basically inseparable! [*laughs*]

---

[25] Fred Weintraub (1928–2017) ran The Bitter End, a coffee house in Greenwich Village, before being hired by Warner Brothers. His connections in the industry helped bring together Michael Lang and Michael Wadleigh, the director of the *Woodstock* film. After Woodstock, Weintraub started his own company, producing more than forty films, including Bruce Lee's *Enter the Dragon* (1973).

Rona Elliot: I did an interview with him and he insists it was the worst performance of his life. No one else agrees.

Henry Diltz: No, I didn't think that! I thought it was amazing. The part I remember is him singing a song about the children and he spoke to that crowd like it was his best friend.

Rona Elliot: Yes!

Chip Monck: Acid! It was all the acid! All he wanted to do was to see or do what he was doing and that was it. It was a very simple thing, you know? One channel.

Moderator: Relatively intimidating crowd, though!

Chip Monck: Yeah! You don't crush the fly on the mirror, that's fine. But you talk, and you do what you want to do. He gave a brilliant performance! He was just perfect.

Rona Elliot: How many songs did he sing?

Michael Lang: I think six.

Henry Diltz: How much is in the movie? I don't remember.

Michael Lang: One of his.

Henry Diltz: One song. The one about the children?

Michael Lang: Yeah!

Henry Diltz: That was great, yeah.

Moderator: Elliott, where were you during all of this? Were you in the crowd, or were you backstage?

Elliott Landy: I was actually on stage most of the time because Michael had told all the stage crew to let me up whenever I wanted to go. That was both good and bad: it was good because I was on the stage; it was bad because I wasn't out among the people as much as I would be if I were doing it these days. And the festival was really about the people. It was a transformative moment for almost everyone who was there. That's where I was.

Moderator: Joan Baez was the last performer? And so the night closes; what happens during that night into the next day? Are you guys restaging? Then finishing things?

Michael Lang: Well, people party and then they sleep. We didn't sleep.

Rona Eliot: Somebody brought a Ferris wheel adjacent to the property and it was on fire! Do you remember that? I was not stoned: there was a fire on a Ferris wheel. I thought, "God, people would really take advantage of the opportunity," you know?

Michael Lang: You know, I think you probably were stoned, because I don't remember any of that! [*laughs*] And I haven't seen it in any of the pictures.

Rona Elliot: No? Oh well!

Chip Monck: There was no permit for Ferris wheels!

Bill Hanley: I don't remember hearing about it.

Moderator: So Joan Baez closes the night and then the next day . . . ?

Michael Lang: So we're resetting as much as we can; we're trying to figure out how to get food in and how to get toilets cleaned. We had an early plan that we were going to do slit trenches and put toilets over them, and when they were full, move to the next slit trench and backfill it. So Mel [Lawrence] went to that solution halfway through, and the water system was efficient.

Think about this: creating a city for what we thought was a quarter million people, and it turned out to be five hundred or six hundred thousand. But creating a city: you need medical, you need water, you need food, you need all these things to keep people alive and well through the period, and Max [Yasgur] wouldn't let us bury any of the pipes. Chris Langhart, who was our resident genius about doing anything, had figured out where the

LIST OF PERFORMANCES AT WOODSTOCK

Friday (8/15) – Saturday (8/16)	Saturday (8/16) – Sunday (8/17)	Sunday (8/17) – Monday 8/18
Richie Havens (began at 5:07 p.m.)	Quill (began at 12:30 p.m.)	Joe Cocker and the Grease Band (began at 2:00 p.m.)
Satchidananda Saraswati	Country Joe McDonald	Country Joe and the Fish
Sweetwater	Santana	Ten Years Later
Bert Sommer	John Sebastian	The Band
Tim Hardin	Keef Hartley Band	Johnny Winter
Ravi Shankar	Canned Heat	Blood, Sweat & Tears
Melanie	Mountain	Crosby, Stills, Nash & Young
Arlo Guthrie	Grateful Dead	Paul Butterfield Blues Band
Joan Baez (finished around 2:00 a.m.)	Creedence Clearwater Revival	Sha Na Na
	Janis Joplin	Jimi Hendrix (finished just after 11:00 a.m. on Monday morning)
	Sly and the Family Stone	
	The Who	
	Jefferson Airplane (finished around 9:40 a.m.)	

pipes would break and how to get to them quickly to repair them.[26] And so all of those things were kind of developed overnight, out of necessity. And again, it was just the amazing talent of this crew that we had working on Woodstock that made it work.

Moderator: Sounds like a lot of ingenuity on the fly.

Michael Lang: Absolutely.

---

[26] Chris Langhart (b. 1940) was the technical director at Woodstock. He was one of the earliest workers to arrive on the site, and among other things he built a heliport and an elevated walkway that connected the stage to the artists' pavilion, which he also built.

Moderator: Resilience, kind of pulling it together. So, Saturday. I don't know if it was Santana or Quill . . . ?[27]

Michael Lang: It was probably Quill, because they were a local band from Boston and Rona had drafted them into doing community service in exchange for playing at Woodstock. They would play at the local prisons and Moose Clubs, so they opened. And then Carlos [Santana] went on next, but he wasn't really scheduled to go on, and so he dropped acid thinking that he had plenty of time. And we informed him that he didn't have plenty of time, and if he wanted to play, he had to get on stage and play. So he grabbed his guitar, which started squirming in his hands. It tried to attack him and he prayed pretty much through that whole set that he would stay in tune and stay alive. And you know, the rest is history. They amazed everybody and became huge stars after that.

Rona Elliot: Michael Shrieve, the drummer, was seventeen years old, and Carlos was Bill [Graham]'s act, so it was very important for Bill Graham that he be in this show.[28]

Moderator: Yeah, a lot of people didn't know Santana yet. They were—

Michael Lang: Nobody knew them; they hadn't recorded.[29] They were just a local San Francisco band. Bill Graham sent me a tape of them, and I had

---

[27] Founded by Jon (b. 1947) and Dan Cole (b. 1948), Quill was a psychedelic/progressive rock band from New England. In the late 1960s, Quill opened for a number of major acts, including the Who, the Kinks, Sly and the Family Stone, and Janis Joplin. Similarly, they were the opening act on day two of the festival. They also spent the week leading up to the festival playing at nearby state prisons and halfway houses as a gesture of goodwill to the community.

[28] Bill Graham (1931–1991) was a German-American rock concert promoter, famous for fostering rock in the 1960s and 1970s. His venues in San Francisco (the Winterland Ballroom and Fillmore West) and in Manhattan (Fillmore East) were the launching pad for everyone from the Grateful Dead to Otis Redding. Graham managed many of these artists, including Jefferson Airplane, and discovered Carlos Santana, whose performance at Woodstock came about at Graham's pugnacious insistence.

[29] Santana's eponymous debut album, which was recorded prior to their performance at Woodstock, wasn't released until August 30, 1969, two weeks after their performance at Woodstock. Michael Shrieve (b. 1949) is an American percussionist, best known for playing with Santana at Woodstock. He was actually twenty years old at that time. His extended drum solo during "Soul Sacrifice" is still regarded as a musical high point of the festival.

grown up on Latin music and loved it. And this synthesis of Latin and rock just knocked me out, so it was a great pick. Fifteen hundred dollars, the best buy of the festival.

Moderator: Wow, yeah. So are people still working on this as these acts are going and people still—

Michael Lang: [*interjecting*] Sure.

Moderator: —having to still, on the fly, pull things together?

Rona Elliot: We had a press tent. I was in the press tent with people from New York, and it was quickly taken over by the medical people who were taking care of the people who had OD'd [overdosed], so you just had to move around quickly.

Michael Lang: They weren't ODs; they had bad trips.

Rona Elliot: They had bad trips; they were suffering but they didn't die.

Michael Lang: They took bad LSD, and the Hog Farm was responsible for and experienced in dealing with that and getting them to sort of calm down, and then welcomed the next person who was having a bad trip and talked them down. It was a very efficient way of dealing with that. And then, soon after Chip's announcement, the famous announcement about the brown acid.

Rona Elliot: [*turning to Chip*] Do you want to say it? Oh, come on!

Chip Monck: I can't remember it!

Rona Elliot: You can't remember? Michael will tell you.

Chip Monck: I just remember that at the end of it, "It's not specifically too good, but it's your trip, so be my guest." "The brown acid that is circulating around us is not specifically too good." What do you say when your knees are knocking together and you don't know how to phrase it? It's a very awkward announcement, you know? You get halfway into it and, "Oh, shit!" Somebody just flopped over over there and you could be . . . It's too difficult.

Moderator: How did you get recruited to be the onstage announcer?

Chip Monck: I was just at the right place at the right time.

Moderator: Right place at the right time?

Chip Monck: Yeah. Michael just suggested that I continue. Go further downstage and start talking.

Moderator: Good choice!

Michael Lang: Actually, I came up to him at eight o'clock in the morning, and I said, "Chip, your lights are not happening. So you're the PA, you're the announcer."

Chip Monck: And the people are a little too close to the stage, so I turned that into, "Ladies and gentlemen: please pick up all the baggage that you have. This is going to be a little arduous for you, but you've made little divots in the earth and everything is very comfortable, but now I am going to ask you to do something because it's necessary for your pleasure. You're a little too close to the stage, and as the pressure comes from behind you, you will be pressed up against the plywood and you'll be looking at plywood for three days, and that is not exactly why you intended to come."

Rona Elliot: And listen to that voice: Michael made the right call!

Chip Monck: Basically what it was is, "Now I am going to help you by counting down these ten backward steps that you're going to take. You're not going to be confronting anybody like this; you're going to do it backwards. And they can't even move, right? So one, two"—[*aside*] holy shit!—"three, four," and they got to ten, and we put up the two little stakes and the clothesline again, the line of demarcation, our barrier, and everything was just fine.

Moderator: [*pointing to a photo of Chip kneeling, with a mic in one hand and many slips of paper in the other*] This is a great photo, Henry. This is wonderful!

Henry Diltz: That's Chip reading all the announcements. People would hand little bits of paper up on the stage.

Chip Monck: The interesting thing is when everybody ran out of paper. I have three rocks at home: one went through a bass drum, one hit me, and one was just lobbed. It was large enough not to be a piercing concern. And it's got written on it "Help James," and you had to find out that "James, you're supposed to go to this place. Now if anybody knows James and has his diabetes pills," that's obvious. Interesting code for anything he wants. "Please go and find so and so at. . . ." There were no numbered stations; there were no positions to tell. "You two go over there and have a nice time. Oh, you're looking for . . . ? Oh, I got it, right, okay." This time, we may be able to do it in a more efficient fashion since everyone has a cell phone.[30]

Moderator: So, Saturday happens. It was raining midday Saturday, if I remember correctly.

Michael Lang: It rained on and off.

Moderator: [*referring to a photograph of an aerial shot of the field, in the rain, with the crowd below*] Yeah, this is an unbelievable shot. The size of the crowd.

8. Black and white photograph of a helicopter landing, with the crowd and tents visible in the background. Photograph by Henry Diltz.

---

[30] When Chip Monck says "this time," he is referring to the Woodstock 50 Festival, which was still in the planning stages at the time of the Berklee celebration.

Henry Diltz: That's the acid casualty place where the Hog Farm was, in that tent. Very lovely, you know? I went in there. People were having a little problem with their trip, and somebody would talk them down, reassure them. It was all really, really great.

Michael Lang: It was mostly telling them, "This will end and you'll be fine."

Henry Diltz: There's a casualty right there. [*laughs, referring to a series of pictures of Tim Hardin and Richie Havens*]

Moderator: Tim Hardin and Richie Havens. That's a great shot.

Henry Diltz: [*referring to a picture of Tim Hardin seated with a guitar and a piece of paper and pen*] He's making his set list.

Moderator: If I remember correctly, the acts were delayed because of rain and things got pushed back and back and back. By evening time on Saturday, what's happening?

9. Black and white photograph of Tim Hardin on August 15, 1969, seated at a table and holding a guitar with its strap while handwriting his setlist, using his left hand and a felt-tipped marker. Photograph by Henry Diltz.

MEL LAWRENCE, IN AN INTERVIEW CONDUCTED BY RONA ELLIOT ON NOVEMBER 14, 2008

Mel Lawrence: I think that storm had a great deal to do with the turning point at Woodstock. Because of the rain, because of the mud, because of the miserable feeling of being wet, I think it became a great equalizer. It became a moment that we're all in this together. Being able to recognize your brother, it was hard before that; then all of a sudden, we are brothers and sisters all in this together. We're cold and muddy and wet, but we got to keep it going because we love the music and the music is something we all agree on. That was a turning point, and after that there was no doubt in my mind that everything was going to be okay.

Michael Lang: Acts are going on until sundown, sunbreak, until the sunrise. And I think the last act was the Who. Yeah, it was the Who.

Moderator: So there's a great story about Abbie Hoffman.[31] Can you relay that story to us with the Who?

Michael Lang: [*to the audience*] Do you people know who Abbie Hoffman is?

Audience: Yeah!

Michael Lang: Good. Abbie arrived with a printing press to sort of publish a paper to help these kids deal with the weather and deal with whatever. His father had been in the medical supply business, so Abbie was taking over the medical tents and organizing supplies and really working through the night. He arrived at the stage at around three in the morning, just before the Who were going on, and he grabbed me and he said, "Did you see this guy running around with a gun?" And I said, "What are you talking about?" And he said, "Yeah, there's a guy running around with a gun." So we went

---

[31] Abbie Hoffman (1936–1989) was an American political activist and cofounder of the Yippies (Youth International Party). Hoffman was known for his involvement in various antiwar movements in the 1960s and 1970s. For more, see the sidebar above on the Chicago Democratic National Convention in 1968.

downstairs and we went off the stage. We were looking around for this guy with a gun, and at some point the gun turned into a knife, and I realized that Abbie had imbibed.

I said, "The Who are about to go on; let's go watch them." So we got up and we went up to the stage. We were sitting on the side of the stage watching the Who, and Abbie said, "I have to say something about John Sinclair."

John Sinclair was a guy who had been arrested; he was an activist, and had been arrested for two joints of marijuana and sentenced to fifteen years in jail. And Abbie was dying to make a statement about him. I said, "Well, you can't when the bands are on. When they're over, I will let you say something."

We had a policy of no politics from the stage, but this was kind of different; I was happy to do it.[32] But he just kept trying to pop up, and I'd pull him down. At one point, Pete [Townshend] turned away from the audience to adjust his amplifier, and Abbie slipped out of my grip. He went to the microphone and started talking about John Sinclair. Pete turned around and saw this crazed guy at his microphone. Pete took his guitar, and swatted Abbie across the head, and Abbie went down on one knee, got back up, and jumped off the front of the stage and off into the audience and wasn't heard from again.

Moderator: It's a great story. So Bill, where are you during all of this? Are you and your crew perched on . . . ?

Bill Hanley: Every once in a while I'd check the sound system, but otherwise I was working on the mixer.

Moderator: [*looking at Henry's photo of the Who, with the sun rising*] This is obviously the Who. This is when in the morning?

Michael Lang: The sun is rising.[33]

Henry Diltz: Dawn is breaking over there on the side, you can see.

Chip Monck: Peter [Townshend] did everything that was possible to have

---

[32] For more on the politics at Woodstock's Movement City tent, see Patrick Burke, *Tear Down the Walls: White Radicalism and Black Power in 1960s Rock* (Chicago: University of Chicago Press, 2021).

[33] By most accounts, the Who played from five to six on the morning of Sunday, August 17.

[the Who] play at dawn. Poor John [Roberts] had to go wake the banker at such and such a time because when Mr. Townshend stepped out of the transport, he went knee-deep in mud. He was particularly annoyed about that, so then he decided he needed to be paid long before he went on stage. And he was looking at his watch, waiting for the sun to come up because that was a time he wanted to perform. It was wonderful to watch; it was very theatrical.

Rona Elliot: But Michael had to handle a lot of unexpected situations like that, and he did it with grace. You can imagine what it must have seemed like to have to hand over a bag of cash or a check.

Bill Hanley: What a headache!

Michael Lang: Yeah, they kind of cornered me by my trailer and said, "Which is the job of the road manager? We're not playing unless we get paid." And I said, "Well, you'll get paid on Monday. We'll give you a check. There's no cash on site because there was no box office." They just said, "We're not going to play." I said, "Well, okay great, just give me a couple minutes; I'll go make the announcement." "What announcement?" "The announcement that the Who is not going to play because there's no cash on site." And they played.

Moderator: [*looking at a picture of the turntable stage*] So this was the turntable idea, right? Am I correct on that, Chip? This is the idea?

Michael Lang: So this was an idea that I came up with: these three pieces of a pie. This turntable was an idea I came up with, and it worked fine until the Grateful Dead because it was—

Chip Monck: [*interjecting*] Everybody came up on stage and stood on it!

Michael Lang: [*continuing*] It was the [Grateful] Dead's equipment that was so heavy that it buckled the wheels at first, and then everybody came on, and that was the end of it.

Bill Hanley: The screws pulled right through the plywood, and that was the end of it. We were on the floor, floor to floor.

Rona Elliot: These are the urban myths that get developed. It smelled! This

10. Black and white photograph of two of the three turntables on an empty Woodstock stage on August 18, 1969. The field is visible in the background, with just a few people and large quantities of garbage. Photograph by Henry Diltz.

was a cow pasture with a lot of cow poop and fertilizer. [*pointing to a photo from after the festival, with all the debris on the ground*] Do you remember scratch and sniff? It smelled like manure. That really was, for me at least, what it was like.

Henry Diltz: Very heavy odor afterwards.

Moderator: I'm just going to let some of these photos sink in. [*referring to a series of photographs from the end of the festival being projected*].

Michael Lang: Mel [Lawrence]'s dog.

Rona Elliot: My dog.

Michael Lang: Oh, your dog.

Henry Diltz: Yeah, you know from the stage, looking out at all those soggy sleeping bags and blankets, it reminded me of one of those old Mathew Brady Civil War photos of dead horses in the field.[34] Especially after Jimi Hendrix played "The Star-Spangled Banner," it all seemed like a war zone, with all of the sound effects.

Chip Monck: The best part of it is there wasn't a winner, and there wasn't a loser; that's how Mr. Lang promotes and produces.

Moderator: So I want to make sure we have some time for questions from the audience. Before we do that, I want to ask everybody for one visual or audio moment that you remember, or that really stuck out in your mind. I will tell you mine. I was able to get pretty close to see Joe Cocker play. I had heard his music, but I didn't really know exactly how good he was, and he came out right before there was a rainstorm, and it was just a fantastic sound. He sounded great, and his band played great, and it was a beautiful afternoon before the rains came or that cloud came. That was my moment.

Bill Hanley: Chip, what would you say about your wildest moments of being in charge up there? Being on the stage, and making announcements, and keeping things together?

Chip Monck: It was just one continuous flow. It didn't peak, necessarily. I was very excited about the ten steps backwards, that was excessive. I chose the timbre of most of what I was doing to be very quiet, as calm as possible.

Bill Hanley: You did a great job.

Chip Monck: Thank you so much, Mr. Hanley. And so did you. We'll now spend fifteen minutes just congratulating each other! [*laughs*] We do that often at this age.

Michael Lang: So my favorite moment, musically, was Sly and the Family Stone. They were just mind-boggling; they turned the whole place into a church. There was this whole call-and-response with the audience, and it

---

[34] Mathew Brady (1822–1896) was an American photographer known for his vivid images of battlegrounds in the American Civil War.

11. Black and white photograph of the field at the end of the festival. A few people remain, collecting their belongings, lying on the ground, or cleaning up the large quantities of garbage that are visible in the photograph. Photograph by Henry Diltz.

went on and on. It was just magical. There were a lot of magical moments, musically, but that to me, that stood out as something special.

Rona Elliot: They were also one of the most integrated bands at the time, that included women in the band. They were really singular at the time, and it was incredible to have them there.

Chip Monck: So singular!

Rona Elliot: And you didn't see them again much after and he [Sly's] not very seeable in general now. He kind of is removed from reality, but it was amazing.

Elliott Landy: Right now, my favorite moments are the ones I got really good pictures of. I think the festival was an ongoing experience of incredible moments; it's hard to pick one out. I wish that my wife [*pointing to Linda Landy in the audience*] would come up here and tell us her story. But being at the festival was transformative for her, and there were four hundred and fifty thousand other people who had the same experience. And if you know almost anyone who was at the Woodstock Festival, they talk about it as a very special moment in their lives.

This picture of Max Yasgur is one of the moments. [*referring to a picture of Max Yasgur on stage, facing the crowd*] He's telling young people that this is what this generation is about: it's about peace and love. In those years there was a lot of bad press, there still is, about young people smoking pot and wanting to change the world and stop the war and so on. Max was the owner of the site; he rented it to Michael. [Max] got up there, and he's an older person, and in those years, it was like young people against older people as far as this kind of consciousness. The two generations seemed to be in different worlds. So he was an older person saying, "You're really showing the world what your generation is about." Down there in the lower corner is Martin Scorsese, answering him with the peace sign.[35]

Rona Elliot: He was probably fifty-five when we were twenty. How old was Max?

Michael Lang: Forty-five.

Rona Elliot: He was forty-five. He was *not* old. It just seemed like he was old.

Elliott Landy: And there's another moment I want to talk about, if you keep going, I'll—

Michael Lang: [*looking at a photo of Ravi Shankar, followed by one of the crowd in the rain*] That was Ravi Shankar playing in the rain, and that's a lot of people getting wet.

Rona Elliot: I'm just going to throw this anecdote: Martin Scorsese, who was

---

[35] Martin Scorsese (b. 1942) is an American filmmaker famous for embracing rock music from the 1960s in his film scores. One of Scorsese's earliest credits is as an assistant editor of the *Woodstock* documentary, for which he also served as a camera operator. He has directed and produced numerous important films about music and musicians, including *The Last Waltz* (1978) and *George Harrison: Living in a Material World* (2011).

12. Black and white photograph of Max Yasgur making a peace sign with his left hand and addressing the crowd. Martin Scorsese is in the lower left corner of the photograph, in "the pit," a term Henry Diltz uses in chapter 2, to describe the area below and in front of the stage. He is also making a peace sign. Photograph by Elliott Landy.

on the film crew, came that night with a set of cufflinks to wear when he was going to go out to dinner.

Elliott Landy: So this picture. When it started raining, I went under the stage to keep my cameras dry. I had a panoramic camera on my chest, and by accident I pressed the button and took this picture of the bottom of the stage area, and at the edge you can see the crowd and the rain. The other day, I realized how different things are now. The 1960s wasn't an era of selfies. To be under the stage at Woodstock and not take a pic of yourself there, that's the difference between these generations. We were so self-conscious. This is a "me" generation, and in those years I don't think it was about that.

Michael Lang: We were in the moment.

Elliott Landy: [*agreeing with Michael*] Yeah and there is a sign there that says "we are one," and that was the feeling of the 1960s. That's what it was about, to find our joint humanity—

Rona Elliot: [*interjecting*] "Joint" being the operative word.

Elliott Landy: [*continuing*] —and that's what the festival was about. [*responding to Rona's joke*] That's really good; absolutely, I like that. Because marijuana is really a very positive consciousness-expanding experience, if done in moderation.

Henry Diltz: Amen! [*laughs*] I like what you said about selfies; I forgot to take a selfie of myself the whole time.

Elliott Landy: Maybe you have a picture of me and I have one of you?

Henry Diltz: One of my moments was at one point I got off the stage. I thought I better get way at the back of the field and get a long shot down to the stage. It was in the evening, and I got way at the back, and I was just doing that, and I heard Chip on stage say, "Ladies and gentlemen, Crosby, Stills & Nash."[36] Oh my God! They were my friends! I'd just done their album cover a little while before they played there. I had to be there to photograph them. I had to run down through those hundreds of thousands of people to get there. I made it about halfway through the set.

Elliott Landy: [*looking at an image of himself*] This is a picture taken by Amalie Rothschild.[37] And I just want to point out those army bags that I used to carry my film and cameras because they didn't make comfortable camera bags in those days. I am wearing four different cameras and a panoramic camera, all cast-iron stuff, and two different light meters.

---

[36] The band performed at Woodstock under the name Crosby, Stills, Nash & Young. However, as Neil Young (b. 1945) spent most of his time backstage, Chip Monck introduced them only as "Crosby, Stills & Nash."

[37] Amalie Randolph Rothschild (b. 1945) is an American filmmaker and photographer, known for her photographs of important rock events from the late 1960s and for her award-winning documentaries.

Rona Elliot: I would say for me, my favorite memory is the opening bars of "The Star-Spangled Banner" [performed by Jimi Hendrix]. There were a million things that happened at Woodstock, but nothing compared to that. It just transported you; it was as if it was a shock. There were so many things that had happened, and we were all so involved in all these things, and then when those notes happened, it brought you back to some other place and to the music. I know everyone loves that performance.

Moderator: Let's open this up for some questions and answers.

Audience: Hello, thank you. When I saw *Woodstock* as a thirteen-year-old, it was my favorite film, and it remains my favorite film. Thank you all. So my question is, whatever happened to the baby who was born there, if you happen to know? And Johnny Winter and the [Grateful] Dead are not in the movie; was that just contractual? And as a quick aside, I heard Lou Adler speak in LA about Monterey Pop, and he said the only person that got paid, I believe he said, was [Jimi] Hendrix.[38] He said no one else got paid at Monterey Pop, which was weird for me to hear. Thank you.

Michael Lang: Everybody got paid at Woodstock—

Rona Elliot: [*interjecting*] And there was no baby.

Michael Lang: —and we don't know if there was a baby or not. Somebody had informed Chip along the way that there was a baby born. It turns out that there was a baby born at a hospital in Monticello.[39] And the woman had arrived pregnant and had her baby, and there's no record of where he is.

Rona Elliot: So for the Woodstock 40 book, we did a lot of research. We

---

[38] Lou Adler (born Lester Louis Adler, 1933) is an American record producer and talent manager. As a producer, Adler's earliest hits were with the Mamas and the Papas, including the songs "California Dreamin'" and "Monday, Monday," and with Carole King, whose album *Tapestry* (1971) earned Adler two Grammy Awards. Adler was one of the producers of the Monterey Pop Festival and also the executive producer of the film *The Rocky Horror Picture Show* (1975).

[39] Monticello and Bethel are both in Sullivan County, New York. Monticello is about 10 miles southeast of Bethel.

looked and looked—urban myth![40]

Audience: And the [Grateful] Dead and Johnny Winter?

Michael Lang: The Dead have always said that was the worst set they've ever played. Part of it was because just before they went on, Stanley Owlsey [*sic*], whom I mentioned a bit earlier, decided to rewire their stage, and so they were getting shocked by their instruments, and that was amplified by the LSD they'd taken. In their mind, it was a terrible set. I've seen it, and I didn't think it was that bad, but they didn't want to be in the movie. The movie was four and half hours long, and they had to cut it down. Warner Brothers was almost at gunpoint, trying to get them to do it in two hours, which was impossible, but they cut it down to three and a half hours and just took the best performances.

Chip Monck: Why wasn't Mountain included in the film?

Michael Lang: Again, I think it was just too much; Butterfield was the same. Bert Sommer, who was an artist that Artie was recording, was a great, brilliant singer-songwriter.[41] He was the last person to get cut from the film, and it would've made a complete difference in his life had he been in it. It's a shame.

Audience: Hi, thank you very much for being here.[42] This is an extremely rare and special occasion. I just want to acknowledge that. I'd like to make two acknowledgments rather than ask a question. Bill Hanley and Chip Monck both pretty much began their careers at Newport [Folk Festival] in 1959, and what a special occasion to have them both on stage. Mainly because of both of you, in lighting design and in sound reinforcement, are

---

[40] Michael Lang, Henry Diltz, and Dan Garson, *Woodstock Experience* (Guildford: Genesis Publications, Ltd., 2009).

[41] Bert Sommer (1949–1990) was an American folk singer-songwriter. His first album, *The Road to Travel* (1968), was produced by Artie Kornfeld, and he was the third performer on the opening day of Woodstock. Prior to the festival, Sommer was part of the Broadway cast of *Hair: The American Tribal Love-Rock Musical* (1967; opened on Broadway in April 1968), eventually playing the part of Neil "Woof" Donovan.

[42] This question was posed by John Kane, Bill Hanley's biographer. John Kane, *The Last Seat in the House: The Story of Hanley Sound* (Jackson: University Press of Mississippi, 2020).

pioneers; you helped shape the contemporary concert, rock and roll, and jazz industry. So thank you so much. I mean what a special honor that is. These guys are trailblazers; it's very important to note.

Secondly, I know a lot of money was lost on the *Woodstock* movie for some, but if we didn't have the *Woodstock* movie, how would we reference these times or this event? But in particular, Chip, right as Sha Na Na comes on before Hendrix, there was a gentleman from [Bill] Hanley's crew that was on the mixing platform. In the movie, you say, "Harold, turn up the mic," and Harold is here, he's in the back, Harold Cohen.[43] [*applause*]

Audience: I grew up in the New York area and was at the Fillmore East all the time getting the eleven o'clock show, because when the Grateful Dead played you got out at dawn. But that was when music was inexpensive, and you could go for six dollars and you could get into the Fillmore East. I was on the New York Thruway, so never got to Woodstock. Last night you spoke about how there was no real communication and no cell phones. The question is for Rona: How did the message get out to half a million people to be there?[44] The urgency, you've got to be there.

Rona Elliot: I'll say what I know, but I am going to defer to Michael. I know there was radio, and there was print advertising in local papers. I think the part I can talk to is the word of mouth on the festival circuit from the summer before. People knew; they told their friends. It was as if the smoke signals went out. But Michael should talk about the advertising, because he knows that.

Michael Lang: We didn't do a lot of regular advertising except for the ad in the *New York Times* when we got kicked out of Wallkill. We had Wartoke, who was our PR agency. They were very dedicated to the idea of Woodstock

---

[43] Harold Cohen (b. 1944) worked for Hanley Sound from 1966-1973 and was one of its longest-serving employees. In a private communication with the editors, he stated that he served as a backup engineer for the festival, arriving during the first night's performances. He was responsible for mixing Jimi Hendrix's closing performance, among others.

[44] The first article in the *New York Times* on Woodstock appeared on June 27, 1969. The headline "Peaceful Rock Fete Planned Upstate" betrays the early desire to disassociate Woodstock from the violence that had marred other large-scale festivals (see the sidebar in chapter 2).

and what it was going to be about, and they created this network of all the underground press around the country, and all the college press. And through that system, word got out. I think what kicked it up to half a million people showing up, and a million and a half people being turned back on the roads when they closed the thruway and closed the Canadian border, was when we got kicked out of Wallkill. I think we became a cause, and there was a lot of press around it, and then we moved and there was a lot of press around that. I think that just really galvanized people into thinking that they really had to be there, that this was some kind of a seminal event for our generation.

Rona Elliot: Also being someone who grew up a great deal of my life in California in addition to New York, the East Coast kids look at the summer in a different way. It's a time to go do things. You get in your car and you go places. If you're from the West Coast, it's always warm, and you don't have to go anyplace. So I think it became a thing where you got in your car or your van or the Peter Pan bus or the Trailways, and it became a thing to do as a summer adventure.

Michael Lang: But you know, it drew people from all over the world and all over the country. I think it was the only event to ever have been promoted nationally at that point.[45]

Moderator: And the diversity of the acts, with Ravi Shankar, Sly and the Family Stone, [Jimi] Hendrix, Janis Joplin. You really had a wide range of talent. Who decided?

Michael Lang: I did. It was people that I liked. You know, musicians and bands in the 1960s were very much a part of the counterculture, and a part of our message and the way messages get spread. And so everybody was kind of in this together, discovering people like Joe Cocker and Santana. That was part of the fun.

Audience: One of you said you had to coax Richie Havens on stage because he wasn't supposed to be the opening act. Who was supposed to be the

---

[45] Woodstock was not the first event to be nationally promoted. John Phillips of the Mamas and the Papas wrote the song "San Francisco (Be Sure to Wear Flowers in Your Hair)" in part as promotion for the Monterey Pop Festival. However, Woodstock was one of the first music festivals to benefit from a formal national advertising campaign.

13. Black and white photograph of Janis Joplin performing. Photograph by Henry Diltz.

opening act?

Michael Lang: I think Bert Sommers [*sic*] was supposed to open, but his band wasn't there. Tim Hardin was there: he could have gone on solo, but his band was also there, and I think their equipment was also there. He had just come off heroin; he was on the methadone program, and he was just not ready to do it. I didn't have the heart to push him. So Richie was my obvious target. I worked on him for an hour and then finally got him to go on.

Moderator: How many encores did he do?

Michael Lang: He ran out of songs! And I kept pushing him back on stage. He kept trying to come off, and I kept pushing back. "Freedom" was

14. Black and white close up of Richie Havens singing and playing the guitar. Photograph by Henry Diltz.

unwritten. He wrote "Freedom" on the spot out of desperation, I think.

Audience: Did any bands decline your invitation to play at Woodstock?

Michael Lang: Yeah, Led Zeppelin declined; they had been booked somewhere else. The Moody Blues were booked, but they weren't able to finish their album and they had to stay in the studio. I got a letter from them three weeks after the festival saying, "We kind of blew it, didn't we?" I wanted John Lennon to be part of it, but he couldn't get into the country; Nixon was not permitting him in because of his antiwar stance. The Beatles had broken up by then.

Interesting story: I was dealing with Apple [Records], their company, in corresponding back and forth, and they had sent me a letter the day that we got kicked out of Wallkill. It was offering us James Taylor and Billy Preston and the Plastic Ono Band. I never saw that letter until I wrote my book forty years later![46]

I wanted Roy Rogers to close the festival with "Happy Trails." We had

---

[46] Michael Lang, *The Road to Woodstock* (New York: HarperCollins, 2009).

grown up with *The Roy Rogers Show* every Saturday morning. At the end, Rogers would sing "Happy Trails," and I thought it was a perfect ending. His manager didn't think it would be such a perfect ending.

Rona Elliot: Dale [Evans] wanted to come, though![47]

Elliott Landy: Just to talk about Richie Havens and "Freedom": He described it when he was looking for what to sing. He said, "I was just looking at all those people, and all I saw was freedom. That everyone there was free; experiencing being themselves and experiencing what life should be about." He was saying "freedom, freedom, freedom." That's what he was saying.

Audience: First, I'd like to thank Chip Monck. One of the reasons we got involved in the rock and roll business was that we got the chance to work with Chip. I also have a couple of different comments. We're in the middle of the Vietnam War, and most of these people were against it. I was at Woodstock, and one of the interesting things about Woodstock is that not a single person died because of drugs, and one of the reasons for that was—there were plenty of drugs, all right—but there was a huge rescue operation in terms of helicopters, but there were nowhere near enough civilian helicopters. What you had at Woodstock was not shown in the film. You had armed military helicopters flying in, and the pilots were doing the peace signs, and the kids were waving at them, and it was just an unbelievable experience.

And the other thing you were asking about was what happened during the day. We were woken up on Saturday by Wavy Gravy of the Hog Farm saying, "What I have in mind is breakfast in bed for four hundred thousand people." That's when we began to realize what this was. So thank you all, and thank you Mike [Lang].

Audience: Earlier, Chip was saying something about the mindset behind being able to pull off something like this. And I'm wondering what anybody else might have to say about what you learned from actually pulling

---

[47] Dale Evans (1912–2001) was an American singer and actress, and the third wife of actor and singer Roy Rogers (1911–1998). Evans is credited with writing "Happy Trails," the song that Evans and Rogers sang over the end credits of *The Roy Rogers Show* (1951–1957).

this thing off. And whether it's life lessons, or lessons about putting on a festival or an event like this, and to what degree it still applies today.

Rona Elliot: That's a really big question. I'll do a short philosophical thing and then defer to our fearless leader here, because as a journalist I've covered Woodstock 20 [1989], Woodstock 25 [1994], and I did a big book on Woodstock 40 [2009]. I really think that Michael [Lang] had this idea, he had a vision, and a community showed up. It took a village to manifest his vision, and that included peace, love, and rock and roll. And to a lot of people then and now, that just sounds like so much malarkey, and for me then and now, and for my fierce dedication to music, that's always what music was. It's the power of love and the power of peace.

In contemplating what happened at Woodstock, and the little window that I think opened and then quickly closed due to the circumstances that happened, it demonstrated that people could get along. You could just do whatever was required to make it work for the person sitting next to you. And I really believe that's true, and I don't think it's airy-fairy or anything like that, and I don't expect anybody to believe me or agree with me about it. But I think that's really what happened, and it has continued to be sort of a guiding principle for what I have done in my life, that doing it on a team is better than doing it alone. Doing it in a community is better than not doing it in a community.

To appreciate and respect the other people in my personal case: Michael is always very mellow, and I'm not very mellow, and I've seen Michael under a million pressured situations, and he has the capacity to let things roll off of him. And the situation was extraordinary, as you can see in the pictures by these two very weird dudes. [*pointing to Henry Diltz and Elliott Landy*] They were perfectionists. Elliott and Henry were able to capture out of their perfectionism, and I've sort of ended up being the keeper of a certain kind of journalistic information.

For me, what happened was that this was real, and the "peace, love" part was real. Today's youth have the music and the technology to connect to people, and to manifest "peace, love." For me, that's real, and if I sound like an old hippie, it's because I am one.

You know, over the decades I've asked Michael, "What were you thinking? How were you thinking? How did you think about it?" Because this is not a guy that takes credit for what happened; that's just not in his nature. But he shifted the world, and he created an environment that shifted the world, so for me that's been my lasting thing as being a part of that. [*to Michael Lang*] How about you?

Moderator: Lessons learned?

Michael Lang: I've always been of the school that if you have a vision for something, you can figure out a way to manifest it. Woodstock, for all of us, was the kind of thing where you would wake up in the morning and there would be a hundred insurmountable problems, and you would surmount them by the end of the day, and the next morning you would wake up and there would be another hundred. And you would just keep going, and that's kind of your commitment.

And there are disappointments along the way, just as there is with the fiftieth [anniversary concert] that we're doing now; there's huge things to overcome. But if you're committed, you don't get affected by the ups and downs. It's just part of what happens; it's just part of how it is. It is expected. You just keep going, and you just keep solving everything you can solve. What you can't solve, you put aside until you can solve it. And I think that if something really is meaningful to you, and it's something you're willing to commit yourself to and it's worth the effort and worth going through the ups and downs, that there is no reason why anyone should feel that something isn't possible.

Chip Monck: Michael is willing to face it that way.

Henry Diltz: Yeah, I remember Michael being the calm center of the cyclone. Because he would be on stage or I'd see him all day, and people would come running up to him with a problem. "This is happening!" or "That is happening!" He would smile and say, "Okay, we'll deal with it." It was a very Zen kind of approach.

Bill Hanley: Water off a duck's back!

Henry Diltz: That's right! Water off a duck's back! [*laughs*]

Moderator: We have another question.

Audience: Thank you. My name is Walter, and we came a long way, from Denmark, in Europe, to be here. I couldn't make it for Woodstock fifty years ago; my mother and father wouldn't let me. I was nine years old! So, I apologize.

Moderator: [*jokingly*] That's no excuse!

Audience: I have two questions, actually. Joni Mitchell, wasn't she invited?

Michael Lang: Actually, she wasn't invited. She was coming with Graham Nash, and she would've been wonderful to have had.[48] It's just we hadn't booked her. And her manager, David Geffen, had booked her onto a TV show on the Monday morning, and so didn't want her to come up because he thought she might miss the show, and then she sat at home and wrote that song.[49]

Audience: Fantastic song! My second question: the Incredible String Band from England. I tried to go to the rare concerts of Robin and Mike, whenever they did one.[50] I understand they were at Woodstock, but they declined to play on Friday night—I think that's right—and they came on Saturday night together with the rock and roll bands.

Michael Lang: Yes.

Audience: Can you elaborate a little bit on that?

Michael Lang: Yeah, I think it had to do with—Chip, correct me if I'm wrong—but I think it had to do with not having the ability to do a sound check, and they were not prepared to just come out and play, so they deferred.
Chip Monck: Yeah, it's kind of a difficult position. Sound checks are usually

---

[48] Graham Nash (b. 1942) and Joni Mitchell (b. 1943) lived together for several years in the late 1960s, and Nash cites this relationship as the impetus for the Crosby, Stills, Nash & Young hit, "Our House."
[49] Joni Mitchell's song "Woodstock" was released on Mitchell's third album, *Ladies of the Canyon* (1970). It later became a big hit when Crosby, Stills, Nash & Young included a cover of it on their first album as a quartet, *Déjà Vu* (1970).
[50] Led by Robin Williamson (b. 1943) and Mike Heron (b. 1942), the Incredible String Band was a British psychedelic folk group that played at Woodstock. The group's third album, *The Hangman's Beautiful Daughter* (1968), was their most experimental, and it was their highest-charting album in both the UK and the United States.

something where the bugs are weeded out or the levels are set, or EQs or things like that.[51] They are a private thing; it's kind of difficult when you just move yourself into a site and don't have the opportunity to try and do your very best, often which has to do with either audio or even light. We all have to have some sort of grand meeting to get it together, and people are kind of stuck in that. It's not a haphazard industry by any means. Everybody needs the acceptance of perfection, or near to, as best they can.

Audience: I'd like to ask about Native Americans in this festival, or lack of Native Americans at the festival. I heard about some Hopi artists. And I remember, of course, Jimi Hendrix's costume, but that's all.

Michael Lang: You mean performers? Well, there weren't a lot of—or any that I knew of—Native American bands at the time. But we did bring a group of artists from New Mexico and flew them in to be a part of Woodstock. It wasn't just a music festival: it was a music and arts festival, and we were celebrating all of the countercultural arts. And so we had a broad program of the arts from kids from inner cities and Native Americans. Because we had to move, we lost some of that part of that plan. We had a lot of sculpture on site. We created this amazing children's park, and so we included people from every place we could, given the time we had. But in terms of Native American musicians, I wasn't really aware of any then. In our next festival, Woodstock 50, there's an incredible band, a guy called Nahko, and you'll get to hear him.[52]

Moderator: So, tell us quickly about Woodstock 50.

Michael Lang: Quickly? [*laughs*]

Moderator: Quickly! As quickly as you can.

Rona Elliot: It's happening.
Michael Lang: It's happening! [*laughs*]

---

[51] Equalizers, or "EQs," are pieces of audio equipment used to adjust the balance of frequencies in a recorded sound.
[52] Nahko Bear (b. 1986), an Oregon-born singer with Puerto Rican, Native American, and Filipino roots, fronts the band Nahko and Medicine for the People. Their musical style blends the musical genres of rock, hip-hop, and alternative music.

THE ART CREW

The landscape art and architecture scattered throughout the festival grounds was produced by the art crew, a collection of art students led by Bill Ward, a faculty member at the University of Miami in Florida. Mel Lawrence invited Ward to Woodstock after the two had collaborated on the second Miami Pop Festival with similarly successful results. Bill and Jean Ward, along with Ron and Phyllis Liis designed the large, abstract structures made from local organic materials that dotted the landscape, including a large area known as the Playground.

Moderator: It's happening!

Michael Lang: Woodstock 50 is a continuation of the 1969 ethos. It's really about sustainability and activism and engagement; that's kind what it's being built around. A lot of the talent, a lot of the acts are also committed to those issues and are a part of that. If you look at the way it has been booked, it's really some of the legacy acts, and the rest are very contemporary. There's nothing from the 1970s,—well, late 1970s or 1980s or 1990s. It really is a continuation of that intent.

Moderator: Good thinking. We're almost out of time, and I wanted to thank these folks. But before I do, I want to read a quote that I think is appropriate. It's from Margaret Mead, who was a famous American cultural anthropologist. It's from a *Redbook* article that was written in the early part of 1970, and she said:

> I do not think the Woodstock festival is a miracle, something that can happen only once. Nor do I think that those who took part in it established a tradition overnight, a way of doing things that sets the pattern of future events. It was confirmation that this generation has, and realizes that it has, its own identity; no one can say what the outcome will be, it's too new. Responding to their gentleness, I think of the words: "consider the lilies of the field" and hope that we and they themselves can continue to trust the community of feeling that made so many of those three days, it was beautiful.[53]

---

[53] Margaret Mead, "Woodstock in Retrospect," *Redbook*, January 1970, 30.

So thank you to Bill Hanley, Elliott Landy, Henry Diltz, Michael Lang, Rona Elliot, and Chip Monck. I'm Bob Mulvey, thanks a lot for coming out—I really appreciate it!

Rona Elliot: Thank you, Berklee, for recognizing the importance and giving us a platform to discuss this and reconnect and be together and re-examine these things that were so important to so many of us. So thank you, everybody here at Berklee!

WOODSTOCK 50

Michael Lang had long hoped to host a festival on the fiftieth anniversary of the original Woodstock. Planned for August 16–18, 2019 in Watkins Glen, New York, Woodstock 50 had booked a mix of pop and hip-hop stars such as Miley Cyrus and Jay-Z alongside a variety of legacy bands, including John Fogerty and Santana. But a series of problems, eerily similar to those that plagued the original festival, ultimately brought about the dissolution of Woodstock 50. Just like the original festival, Woodstock 50 lost its initial venue (at Watkins Glen), and faced opposition from other potential sites, including a last-ditch effort to move the festival to Columbia, Maryland.

With all of this turmoil, artists began jumping ship, with the departure of Jay-Z serving as the final death knell for Woodstock 50. In a personal communication with the editors, Michael Lang added, "The Festival was illegally cancelled by financial partner Dentsu. The court found that Dentsu did not have the right to cancel but the damage had been done and Woodstock 50 was unable to recover."

CHAPTER 2

WOODSTOCK FIFTY YEARS LATER

Saturday, April 6, 2019, 5:00–7:30 p.m EDT
David Friend Recital Hall at Berklee College of Music
Boston, Massachusetts

Participants:
Henry Diltz, photographer
Rona Elliot, public relations
Michael Lang, cofounder
Chip Monck, lighting designer and emcee
Gerardo Velez, percussionist

Moderated by Alex Ludwig, assistant professor of liberal arts, Berklee College of Music

Moderator: Welcome back. From stage right to stage left, we have the voice of Woodstock himself, Chip Monck.

Chip Monck: Good afternoon.

Moderator: To his left we have Rona Elliot, who worked on public relations. Sitting center stage we have Michael Lang. And to my immediate right we have Henry Diltz, the official photographer at Woodstock.

The earlier roundtable was a behind-the-scenes look at Woodstock. That was billed as "Woodstock Then." For tonight's roundtable, we're thinking more along the terms of "Woodstock Now." So I imagine we'll be talking a little bit about Woodstock 50, if Michael Lang feels up to it.[1] And I really wanted to frame it around questions of how Woodstock is thought of today versus how it was thought of fifty years ago. We also have some footage that is premiering later this summer at the Tribeca Film Festival, so will share a sneak peek with you today. And then we also have a special surprise, a video message that one of our guests on stage doesn't know anything about.

Rona Elliot: [*interjecting*] They do now.

Moderator: Stay tuned for that. So my questions are for everyone; I'm not really going to specify for a while. My first question is, in the documentary, in the *Woodstock* original documentary, Michael Lang, you're quoted as saying, "This festival is not the end but a beginning." And Michael can answer this, or all four of you can take a crack at this. I'm just curious: has the perception of Woodstock changed for you in the fifty years since you started to now?

Michael Lang: Has the perception changed? I don't think it has changed that much. I think what it stood for then is pretty much what it's remembered for. You know, the movement, the music, the issues. It was a completely peaceful event in the midst of a lot of turmoil that was going on in the country and in society in general, and pretty much around the world. I think it stood for a kind of a moment of hope that the world could actually maybe heal itself a bit and become a kinder, more gentle, better place and, shall we say, more compassionate.

Rona Elliot: In my travels as a music journalist, and particularly going to communist countries, if I was working with acts, I would talk to the kids and I would tell the kids that I worked at Woodstock. They would always say, "We want our Woodstock," wherever I was, in Poland, or the former Czechoslovakia, or USSR. That was the late 1980s or early 1990s. Whatever

---

[1] For more, see the sidebar in chapter 1, "Woodstock 50."

STAN GOLDSTEIN, IN AN INTERVIEW CONDUCTED BY RONA ELLIOT ON NOVEMBER 14, 2008

Stan Goldstein: The concept of the show was implicit in the language we used to attract our audience. We offered to present three days of music in a peaceful atmosphere, and we wound up presenting three days of music in a peaceful atmosphere . . . . At the time, there were no shows like Woodstock . . . . and Woodstock was different from the other festivals to the extent that we offered the situation out of an urban environment. We offered camping, we offered something that was not surrounded by concrete and hard barbed-wire fences. We offered respite, and that was what we wanted to offer. In the 1960s at that time—this was following the assassinations, the burning of cities, the Democratic Convention—the country was in absolute turmoil. And what we offered was something out of that, something different, something other.

it was that was put into motion traveled around the world sufficiently so that that idea, whatever Woodstock was, was something that those kids held up as an aspirational idea.

Moderator: I'm just curious if you all thought fifty years ago that you were working on something that you would be honored [for] fifty years later.

Michael Lang: We didn't think we would be around—

Chip Monck: [*interjecting*] Luckily.

Michael Lang: —fifty years later, frankly.

Rona Elliot: We didn't know we would get through August!

Henry Diltz: I think Woodstock set the tone for how to celebrate your generation in music and in people who listen to music. So there was Woodstock '94, which was great, great music, '99 was great, and 50 will be great. It's [a] different mix of groups, it's a different generation. The crowd acts

15. Black and white photograph of a woman crowd surfing at Woodstock '94. Photograph by Henry Diltz.

differently. There was no crowd surfing in 1969: it hadn't been invented. But in '94 there were thirty to forty people at a time being lifted by the crowd. So we'll see what happens this time. But it's always a celebration of that generation's music and the people. But '69 set the tone for it all, because it was the first one.

Rona Elliot: I don't think that people knew that we'd be sitting here on a stage talking to people about something that happened. I think I certainly was, and I think the crew was aware that something unusual was going on. There was no way around that.

Moderator: Chip, do you feel that—

Chip: It remains to be seen. [*laughs*] Basically when you come down to it, all the plans are laid as best as Michael can, and as we all think about it. Give the opportunity for something to happen and the void is usually filled. We don't know how it's going to happen. It was skillful tooling; there's a possibility of taking the entire audience on a long ride. Strangely enough, though, in a previous interview with Michael, when the interviewer was given a day's look at the activity for them to try and place it in the order they wanted to see it was intriguing. This person went through it two or three times saying, "Ooh!" and "What's going to happen?" "How do you put these acts into position so that there's a highlight for most people every time?" It's a great puzzle.

Moderator: I'm curious. There were a number of these festivals that resulted in violence: Denver Pop and Altamont, obviously. Woodstock '69 was pretty immune to these problems. What do you think, the four of you who were on the ground working, what do you think were some of the factors behind that?

Michael Lang: I think it was our preparation and our plan. I went to most of the festivals. I went to Denver Pop. I saw the violence at the gate because people were trying to crash to get in because—I think I said this before—there was this sense even among the counterculture that music should be free, that it belonged to the counterculture, which was a novel idea, but not practical. But we thought if we did everything right and people got more than they were expecting, and the price was right, that people would be happy to pay it, and we made allowances for people who would come who couldn't afford, or didn't have the money. They could come in. There were free campgrounds, free stages, free food, and it turned out everything was free. [*laughs*]

Rona Elliot: And I would say—Michael won't pat himself on the back—but Michael was deeply committed, and I think remains committed, as we do, and much of the staff, to this real vision of peace and love and music, Michael used to say this, sitting in the sun outside in the country, listening to music, and I think that really imbued the staff. I think it was an authentic sensibility for Michael, and the people that gathered around him wanted that. We wanted a peaceful thing. We wanted the best of the music and the best of everything else. And I think he set the tone. I really mean this, he set the tone. The rest of us, the people who gathered around him, were very committed to that as well, and I know that sounds airy-fairy and hippie-dippy but I think that's really what happened, and it didn't happen later at different places. And it wasn't about the money, sadly, and it didn't result in being about the money. But it was where he came from in creating this event.

VIOLENCE AT FESTIVALS IN THE 1960S

Although multiple violent riots occurred at pop music festivals in the 1960s, the Denver Pop Festival and the Altamont Free Festival were two of the most infamous. The former festival, held at Denver's Mile High Stadium on June 27–29, 1969, saw violence on two different occasions. On the second night, a large crowd charged the gate, gaining entrance for free. Police in riot gear arrived, provoking a different group of turnstile jumpers. The police then fired tear gas into the crowd, which soon drifted into the stadium causing a panic and forcing Barry Fey, the producer, to open the gates. The third night replayed events from the prior evening, with both sides seeking revenge.

No casualties were reported at Denver Pop, whereas multiple audience members died at Altamont, a festival held just east of San Francisco on December 6, 1969. Altamont's violent conclusion was described by *Rolling Stone* as "rock and roll's all-time worst day," and its similarities to Woodstock, which occurred less than four months prior, are relatively few. Taking place at the Altamont Speedway in Livermore, California, the festival was designed to feature Jefferson Airplane, the Grateful Dead, and the Rolling Stones. But above all else, Altamont is known for the decision to hire the Hells Angels as a "security" force. By all accounts, they escalated the situation, instead of defusing it.

The Grateful Dead, the coheadliners of the festival, refused to play, and left upon hearing of the chaotic security. During the performance by the Rolling Stones, the final set of the festival, an audience member, Meredith Hunter, was stabbed to death by Alan Passaro, a member of the Hells Angels. Passaro was charged with Hunter's murder, but was acquitted after footage from the documentary, which was later released as *Gimme Shelter* (1970), showed a plausible claim of self-defense.

STAN GOLDSTEIN, IN AN INTERVIEW CONDUCTED BY RONA ELLIOT ON NOVEMBER 14, 2008

Stan Goldstein: We anticipated that there would be people who would show up without means. They would be attracted simply because we were presenting it. In legal parlance sometimes they speak of things as "attractive nuisances," which means you are responsible for the people who are attracted to whatever you have created, whether you intend for them to be there or not. And so we anticipated there would be a lot of people there who would come without tickets, without means, without shelter, and that we had a responsibility and an interest in providing for them.

So the campground areas were set up. There were designated people in each of the campground areas to be there as information centers. Not quite as administrators, but for oversight in case of emergency conditions. [They] were part of our inner circle, not in terms of the festival, but inner circle in terms of the campground's organization and operations. We were feeding these folks. The Hog Farm kitchens were set up, [and] we were providing shelters. As people who came, whatever their conditions, they became part of this greater operation. They were enfolded into the organization.

Rona Elliot: Let me get this straight: when you were sitting with Michael [Lang] or whoever, you knew fifty thousand people were going to show up. They'll be stoned, they won't have tickets, and we're going to have to take care of these people, so that planning was in place?

Stan Goldstein: Absolutely.

Rona Elliot: So do you think that is a reflection of the culture as it was then?

Stan Goldstein: It was unique then and it has been considered only rarely in the years since. Our sense was that we had to have a link to the audience, that most of the audience at that time would be college age, and if not politically active, politically inculcated, and so the attitude that people would be coming to the show with [was] a sense that we the promoters were capitalist, motherfucker, rip-off pigs, and that whether that was right or wrong, we were stealing the people's music and that we were somehow profiting unjustly, and so on.

From the very beginning, we considered it necessary to create a communications link to the crowd so that we were not in a "versus" atmosphere. That there was an interface between the promoters and the crowd that had integrity; the crowd could accept us as the promoters, but would be knowledgeable enough about us to tell the truth to those who came and who could be trusted to tell the truth.

Henry Diltz: I agree. Michael's balance, his laid-back attitude, just his aura is what made Woodstock what it was. His calmness, all of that. I mean, when they talk about Altamont as a comparison . . . I heard somebody say, "Yeah, you know the way that happened, they hired the Hells Angels and paid them with beer."[2]

Henry Diltz: Was it you that said that? [*pointing at Michael Lang*]

Michael Lang: Probably.

Chip Monck: Send a bushel basket full of pills. . . .

Henry Diltz: That's the other way to do it.

Rona Elliot: Chip was finishing the sentence.

Henry Diltz: Did I steal that from you? [*asking Chip Monck*]

Chip Monck: Send a bushel basket full of pills?

Michael Lang: Yes.

---

[2] This is a reference to the unorganized approach to producing the Altamont Free Festival (see sidebar above).

MEL LAWRENCE, IN AN INTERVIEW CONDUCTED BY RONA ELLIOT ON NOVEMBER 14, 2008

Mel Lawrence: [My interest] was in all the other stuff beside the stage and the show itself. It was creating paths through the woods, creating places where people could sell arts and crafts. It was producing the parking areas and signage. One of my favorite things was naming the streets and roads that went through the woods. I loved doing that. . . .

One of the things that I think is probably emblematic was that one of the hard-and-fast rules was that you can't drive your car, your truck, your motorcycle or your anything across the area where the people were going to sit in the bowl. That was supposed to be kept just beautifully and pristine, and I think that gave us a feeling of treating this site with respect to the nature of it, and this feeling that we had I think permeated through the festival. When I set up the systems to create all of these things—a playground, pathways through the woods—there were certain rules that I felt were important, and principally that we respect this place, respect this land that I felt was heaven-sent by Max Yasgur.

16. Black and white photograph of Mel Lawrence in an office trailer at Woodstock. Photograph by Henry Diltz.

Chip Monck: That's the way of Rock Scully and Emmett Grogan, and that's the way they were.[3] [The first person I think of is] Denver's Barry Fey.[4] Delicious promoter. Now has left us. They didn't follow the rules of the stadium. That was the problem.

Rona Elliot: Elaborate.

Chip Monck: The cops were outside, they saw a problem on the inside, they tossed tear gas from the outside into the inside, and they thought they were going to solve the problem.

Moderator: This was at Denver, Denver Pop.

Chip Monck: Yes, Denver, at the stadium, Mile High Stadium.

Moderator: And Chip, do you think there was something about the physical layout, the geometry of Woodstock, that bowl on Yasgur's farm, that—

Chip Monck: Yes, it was a fortification. It was a fortification to keep people out and let the paid come in. This [Woodstock 50] is going to be moderately different. It's in a massive amount of acreage and it's got three units, three stages, plus smaller intermediary stages or advisory positions or product positions, or representatives of what we think is of importance.

Moderator: So my next question is a general one. Can you think of an unsung hero, someone who obviously is not here, that played a vital role in Woodstock '69?

---

[3] Both Rock Scully (1941–2014) and Emmett Grogan (1942–1978) were known for their prodigious drug use. Scully was one of the managers for the Grateful Dead. He signed them to their first recording contract and booked them into the Monterey Pop Festival and Woodstock. Grogan was the founder of the Diggers, a combination of street-improv actors and community activists, based in the Haight-Ashbury district of San Francisco. Their most visible action was handing out free food in Golden Gate Park.

[4] Barry Fey (1938–2013) was a rock concert promoter whose most notable events were presenting Led Zeppelin's first American concert (in Denver, December 26, 1968), and producing the Denver Pop Festival, which featured the final performance of the Jimi Hendrix Experience. For more on Denver Pop, see the sidebar above.

17. Black and white close-up photograph of the stage being built at the base of the sloping field, with scaffolding in place. Photograph by Henry Diltz.

Michael Lang: There's a lot of them. Stan Goldstein was critical. I mean, it all started with Stan. Stan was the first person I hired. He was just this bottomless resource for personnel that fit the right mold. And from Stan to Wes Pomeroy, head of security.

Rona Elliot: Mel Lawrence. . . .

Michael Lang: Don. . . .

Rona Elliot: Don Ganoung. . . .[5]

Michael Lang: Mel Lawrence. I mean they're lots of them that are gone, but they're all why Woodstock worked.

---

[5] Head of community relations at Woodstock, Don Ganoung (1929–1973) was a former minister that Wes Pomeroy recommended. Ganoung frequently attended town council meetings in Wallkill, and more than one of the Berklee participants noted his frequent cigarette use.

Moderator: So, Rona, who else were you working with?

Rona Elliot: Well, I mean they're just [*sighs*] Bill Graham, Mel Lawrence, Don Ganoung, Peter Goodrich, Lee Mackler, Allen Ford, half the musicians.[6] You know. . . .

Michael Lang: [*interjecting*] John Roberts.

Rona Elliot: John Roberts. . . .

Michael Lang: Without John Roberts, there would be no Woodstock. Joel Rosenman.

Rona Elliot: Well, Joel's alive.

Michael Lang: Artie Kornfeld. . . .

Rona Elliot: Artie's alive.

Chip Monck: Well, Joel and John did this magnificent trip up the hill and overlooked the first—

Rona Elliot: Max Yasgur. It took a village.

Moderator: So in this vein, I would like to actually play this clip that we have. This is very raw footage from PBS's *American Experience*. They have a new documentary coming out that's premiering at Tribeca later this summer, and then we'll see it on PBS as well.[7] Half the names that were just mentioned appear in this video, and it concludes with a name we haven't

---

[6] Peter Goodrich (1928–1974) was in charge of concessions at Woodstock. Friends with Michael Lang from his time in Miami, Goodrich was tasked with overseeing the Bindy Bazaar, where all kinds of countercultural goods would be sold. Lee Blumer (born Mackler, 1945–2015) was the assistant to Wes Pomeroy in charge of security and administration at Woodstock. John Morris, the head of production at Woodstock, knew Blumer when they both worked together for Bill Graham. Allen Ford (1944–1976) worked on the stage crew at Woodstock, especially on building the stage itself, designed by Steve Cohen.

[7] *American Experience*, "Woodstock: Three Days That Defined A Generation," directed by Barak Goodman, aired August 6, 2019 on PBS.

WAVY GRAVY AND THE HOG FARM

Born Hugh Nanton Romney Jr. in 1936, Wavy Gravy was a key figure in the counterculture of the 1960s. Ostensibly a poet and entertainer, Romney befriended Bob Dylan and Lenny Bruce. But Wavy Gravy was most visible as the leader of the Hog Farm, an activist commune that was brought to Woodstock at the behest of Stan Goldstein. Affiliated with Ken Kesey and the Merry Pranksters before splitting off on their own, the Hog Farm is generally recognized as one of the longest-running communes in the United States. At Woodstock, they were tasked with multiple jobs, including creating trails and campfires, setting up free kitchens for the distribution of food, and maintaining security and order, ostensibly in tandem with Wes Pomeroy's ad hoc police force. Wavy Gravy jokingly referred to the role of the Hog Farm as the "please force" because of their polite manner of interacting with the attendees. Michael Lang hoped they might also help exemplify how to live outdoors for the duration of the festival.

Given his nickname by B.B. King, Wavy Gravy and his outsized personality were put to good use making announcements from the stage, including his most famous statement: "Good morning, what we have in mind is breakfast in bed for four hundred thousand." Wavy is a cofounder and board member of the Seva Foundation, a charity focused on restoring eyesight in underserved communities around the world.

mentioned yet: Wavy Gravy and the Hog Farm. So this is about a four-minute clip, and then we can talk about it.

Chip Monck: May I ask a quick question?

Moderator: Absolutely!

Chip Monck: You said, is that the WGBH?[8]

Moderator: Yes, correct.

Chip Monck: Neat.

Moderator: Again, they wanted us to stress this is pretty raw. We're going to have time stamps on it and everything, but it still gives us some really great footage that has been locked away in the Warner Brothers archives essentially since 1969.

[*clip from the film with a focus on Wavy Gravy and the Hog Farm plays*]

Rona Elliot: I just want to say it's really, really emotional for me to see that. First of all, this shit really happened! This was—I mean, this happened, half of these people are dead, but this actually happened.

Michael Lang: You know, this notion of the Hog Farm being security was a mistake. Somebody said something about it and the press picked it up, and suddenly they became security. When I first met with Wavy, we were talking about security, and I said, "Well, what would you guys do?" and he said, "Well, you know, if there's something going on, we have a lot of cream pies," and I knew that we needed to have him there. But they were never security; they made *me* feel secure.

Moderator: So, my next question: is there a Wavy Gravy, is there a Hog Farm equivalent at Woodstock 50?

Michael Lang: There will be a Wavy Gravy!

Moderator: Wow, fantastic! So can we talk about Woodstock 50 a little bit?

---

[8] WGBH (FM) is the call sign for a public radio station in Boston, Massachusetts. Its first broadcast was a performance of the Boston Symphony Orchestra in 1951; twenty years later, it was a charter member of National Public Radio (NPR). Founded in 1955, WGBH-TV is the oldest public television station in Boston. Some of its original programming includes *This Old House*, *The French Chef* with Julia Child, and the documentary series *American Experience*.

Michael Lang: A little bit!

Moderator: A little bit! So is it just serendipity, or do you think there's a larger power at work here that in 1969 we had a fractured political environment, and we have very similar conditions fifty years later?

Michael Lang: I mean, I think it would take someone with a weird sense of humor to arrange that but—

Rona Elliot: [*interjecting*] That's why we have Wavy Gravy.

Michael Lang: —it's true that a lot of the conditions that we were facing in the late 1960s and a lot of the issues that we thought over the decades had been dealt with have come back to haunt us. A lot of that comes out of politics and the present government [the Trump administration]. When we started, we were involved in the early days of the environmental movement. And because things didn't move fast enough, and now there's this denial of the fact that we may be facing annihilation unless we deal with it, and we have a government that's either ignorant or deviously cruel. We were coming out of the civil rights and women's rights movements, and the movements against the Vietnam War.

Now we're dealing with Black Lives Matter and the Me Too movements, and things seem to have sort of backed up on us, the pendulum seems to have swung back.[9] We thought that the generations in the interim, who had prejudice, would have died off by now, and that young people wouldn't be sort of saddled with those issues. Now it looks like we have them back in full force. So it's bizarre, but it is timely to have another reminder of what we're dealing with, and to engage people and to encourage their voices and their votes, to get involved in these issues and help save the planet.

[*brief silence*]

---

[9] Founded in 2013, the Black Lives Matter movement was a response to the murder of Trayvon Martin and the subsequent acquittal of his murderer, George Zimmerman. Its founders are three Black activists: Alicia Garza, Patrisse Cullors, and Opal Tometi. Today there are more than forty BLM chapters throughout the world. The Me Too movement was founded by Black activist Tarana Burke in 2006, and is intended to support survivors of sexual harassment and assault.

THE ENVIRONMENTAL MOVEMENT

While most of the counterculture's energy was focused on ending America's involvement in Vietnam, it also pursued equality for all, especially in the push for civil rights and women's rights. Prior to Woodstock, sensational news reports of smog in Los Angeles, fires on the Cuyahoga River in Cleveland, and pollution throughout the Great Lakes were held up as warnings of a dire environmental future. The year 1968 saw interest in environmental policies break through to the mainstream: the crew of Apollo 8, the first crewed spacecraft to orbit the moon, took the famous photograph known today as *Earthrise*, and Stanford University professor Paul Ehrlich published his book *The Population Bomb*, in which he tied Earth's dwindling environmental resources to its growing population.[10] The nascent environmental movement quickly coalesced at the end of the decade, celebrating the first Earth Day on April 22, 1970, and finding purchase in the administration of Richard Nixon, who in 1970 created the Environmental Protection Agency and signed into law the Clean Air Act.

Chip Monck: All I can say is, vote!

Moderator: Chip, are you registered to vote in the United States?[11]

Chip Monck: I am indeed!

Moderator: You are, okay!

Moderator: So I have a larger question related to this, thinking about fifty years now and then. I've seen Woodstock '69 described as a sort of cathartic moment for that counterculture. Do you think of it more as a cathartic moment, or a crucible through which we came out on the other end changed? And after you have thought about that, do you think the same terms can be applied to Woodstock 50? Either catharsis or crucible?

---

[10] Paul R. Ehrlich, *The Population Bomb* (New York: Ballantine Books, 1968).
[11] Chip Monck has resided in Australia since 1988.

Rona Elliot: Well, I might not say either of those, but all of us growing up in households that went through the experience of World War II and coming out of that experience, our generation said, "We don't want any of that. We don't want the Nazis, we don't want all the killing. We want peace, love," and something shifted. It might have been cathartic for us; for some people who had a bad trip that day, maybe it wasn't cathartic. I think that anyone who was part of it had an experience, and whether or not they reflected on it for the next fifty years is something only they know. I'm sure there were people there who went and said, "I'm never going to sit in the mud again," and they went and became a banker.

So crucible, catharsis, clearly it shifted everyone, some more than others. I believe in the karmic reality for me that had we done this for the fortieth anniversary of Woodstock, ten years ago, the situation wouldn't have been the same. The importance of the politics, the relevance of social justice wouldn't have been the same. So I welcome the opportunity for those of us who have been there to wave the white flag and to provide the direction on how to participate. So I just think it's influential. I hope it is.

Chip Monck: Attagirl!

[*applause*]

Moderator: Henry, you've been chronicling the counterculture for it seems like fifty years. Do you have thoughts on this transformation or lack thereof?

Henry Diltz: Gosh. Oh boy. You know, look: to me life is a big adventure. That guy who led the morning wake-up thing, Swami Satchidananda, is a guru that I read a lot.[12] One of my favorite things that he says is, "Look, we're all here to learn. We know that and therefore we're all students. But you should think of yourself as the only student. And everybody else is your teacher." And that's the way I try to live my life. So I mean I don't know what Woodstock 50 is going to be. It's going to be great. It's going to be an adventure. We're going to learn, we're going to be with each other, there'll

---

[12] Known as the "Woodstock Guru," Swami Satchidananda (1914–2002) was a yogi who spoke at Woodstock. After Richie Havens' opening performance, Satchidananda opened his invocation with the line, "I am overwhelmed with joy to see the entire youth of America gathered here in the name of the fine art of music."

be music! There'll be all kinds of things to deal with, but we'll just march along enjoying the adventure. It's as simple as that. [*laughs*]

Moderator: Well, while we've got Henry talking a little bit, I have another question targeted for him, but something about which I think all of us should be thinking. This will be the first Woodstock with cell phones in pockets. Or at least cell phones with good quality photos. What are your thoughts on—

Henry Diltz: Yeah, what's that going to be like, right? Everybody holding their things up like that? [*mimics holding a phone above his head*]

Michael Lang: Look, cell phones are a part of our lives. Hopefully it's not going to be Coachella, where cell phones are pointed at yourself.[13] But it's a part of our reality, and it would be nice if people were in the moment. We're hoping that they will be. We're hoping that it's a learning experience, that it has an impact on their view of the world and their view of their ability to make changes in the world, and that they listen to unbelievably good music and become close with new people and new friends, and share in kind of a revitalized will to make their thoughts and their dreams and their concerns heard and known, and hopefully we'll shape a better tomorrow.

Moderator: Henry's nodding.

Henry Diltz: What he said.

Rona Elliot: I'm going to cry.

Moderator: I definitely want to leave time for more questions. I do have a few other questions to go. Just prior, I would like to mention that Henry Diltz is here in his capacity as the Herb Alpert Scholar-in-Residence for

---

[13] Commonly known as "Coachella," the Coachella Valley Music and Arts Festival is a music festival held annually in California. It is one of the largest and most profitable music festivals in the world. Located at the Empire Polo Club in the Coachella Valley, the festival has run almost every April since 1999.

18. Black and white photograph of Swami Satchidananda on stage, flanked by associates. The photograph is taken from the stage, showing the back of Swami Satchidananda and the vastness of the crowd. Photograph by Elliott Landy.

2019 and 2020.[14] [*applause*] He has been visiting classes, speaking with students, and giving lectures and talks along with Chip and Rona, who have been here as well. It's been a wonderful addition to the college community for the week, and we're looking forward to having Henry back next year. And it turns out you had a fairly important birthday sort of recently, is this right? We have a video message brought in that Henry doesn't know anything about. So please join with me in wishing Henry a happy birthday. Let's get the lights down please. Henry, are you ready for this?

[*Video plays, showing an image of a cake with candles reading "29,200 days," with "Birthday" by the Beatles playing. Ringo Starr appears and says, "Happy*

---

[14] The Herb Alpert Visiting Professor Program was established in 2000 to bring practicing scholars and musicians to Berklee. Every year, each division at Berklee hosts a guest artist or scholar, such as Henry Diltz. Previous visiting professors include John Oates, Janis Ian, Bernice Johnson Reagon, and Pat Metheny.

birthday to you, Henry Diltz, as I like to call you, the last hippie standing, though I'm not looking too bad myself. Anyway, I'm only here to wish you a happy, happy birthday, Henry, to tell you I love you, and I saw the shots you took of us early in the year, you're still doing great. Peace and love, peace and love. And maybe I should say it louder now that you're, you know, you know what you are. [whispering] *You know, eighty! Eighty!*]

Rona Elliot: Henry is sufficiently beloved that Ringo agreed to do that video.

Henry Diltz: My birthday was a few months ago but, yeah, Ringo is a beautiful guy.

Rona Elliot: They said yes immediately. I called, [*whispering*] would you do something?

Moderator: Ringo's always on time, right, as a drummer?

Henry Diltz: Yeah! I got a call one day from somebody at a rehearsal who said that Ringo was with his group rehearsing. It was his first All Starr Band in LA, and the person said they needed a photographer to take a photo of each person in the group for the tour book. And I said, "Okay, I'll come down." So I met Ringo for the first time and I said, "Look, Ringo, do you mind if I get up on the stage while you are rehearsing? Because I have to get the drummer, and I have to get a good shot of everybody." He said, "Look, I'm the drummer, you're the photographer, it's as simple as that."

So you know Ringo always calls me to take his picture because I just come in with my camera, and I don't bring an entourage, and I don't bring lights. And he called me two weeks ago. Not him, but his person called me, and said "They're down in San Diego and they've just changed somebody in the group"—[*aside*] you know he tours with an all-star band. They're people from very famous groups so each one of them can sing three or four hit songs. So if you ever go to his concerts, it's amazing. It's all hits and then he sings his songs in between. But they called me just two weeks ago to say he needed a new group shot because they changed somebody. So we have become good friends over the years.

Rona Elliot: And he quickly said yes to doing a video—

Henry Diltz: [*interjecting*] Of course, yeah.

Rona Elliot: —for Henry, which lets you know how beloved Henry is.

Henry Diltz: I just do—the phone rings, and I just do whatever they want, you know, whatever. Somebody says, "We need pictures," "Fine." It's all a new adventure.

Moderator: So as a way of closing here before we open up to questions from the audience, I would like to ask each of you, do you feel like your Woodstock experience was the defining experience of your lives, or was it a launching pad into greater things?

Michael Lang: I mean, I don't know about greater things . . . In my life, it's always been the elephant in the room, but as I have written, I've made the room bigger.

You know, after Woodstock, I had to get away from it for a while. It was so overpowering, and at that age it was survival. But it's always been a pleasure. One thing that always pleases me, and it's happened repeatedly over the years, is that people will come up to me and say, "Aren't you that guy?" "Yeah, yeah." "Well, you know, Woodstock changed my life," and they tell me the story about how, and it's always positive and it's always very rewarding to hear those things.

Moderator: Rona?

Rona Elliot: I had three defining music experiences, and Woodstock was the crowning jewel. I saw Bob Dylan plug in in 1965, I saw the Beatles perform together, and then I worked at Woodstock. So for me it was, obviously this is what you're supposed to be doing. But Woodstock colored my entire career and created a community, which . . . We haven't seen each other in fifty years. It's pretty amazing.

Chip Monck: A launching pad.

Moderator: A launching pad, bigger and better. [*Chip nods*] Yeah. Henry?

Henry Diltz: For me, I mean, Woodstock was a step along the way. I mean, it was wonderful to be there, and it was the best music festival I ever went to, but I've been to many more since. This year it's made a big change in my life because I have all these pictures, and I keep getting calls from all kinds of people who want to have them in videos and books. I got a call from a Chicago advertising agency, saying, "Could we use that picture of John Sebastian out in front of the crowd? We want to use it to sell Jimmy Dean sausages." [*laughs*] So I called Michael to ask him, and he said, "Well, you better ask John's permission." I called him and he said, "Yeah! Oh, I love Jimmy Dean sausages!" So it's happening. So this year more than ever, Woodstock has been a big thing in my life.

Audience: What's the connection? I don't get it.

Michael Lang: I didn't really get it either but John got it, so. . . .

Henry Diltz: The connection of him and Jimmy Dean sausages, or my answer?

Audience: The sausages.

Henry Diltz: Well, John said, "I have a friend who works at Jimmy Dean sausages," and I said that it's probably why it all happened. But I'm just saying that for me; all these people keep calling me about Woodstock all the time. We're sitting here right now talking about it.

Moderator: Well, and that's what's been so wonderful about this week and today, is getting these four and all of our luminaries together in the same room for the first time in fifty years.

Rona Elliot: We've seen each other in different combinations.

Moderator: But not all together.

Rona Elliot: It's fairly shocking.

Moderator: Yeah it's wonderful. And to see everyone interacting together, that you are still so friendly with each other after all you've been through.

Chip Monck: It's because we're sitting in front of you. [*laughs*]

Rona Elliot: [*at the same time*] Speak for yourself!

Michael Lang: You know that's true pretty much about everybody who worked at Woodstock. We've all sort of remained as this extended family, even when you don't see someone for thirty or forty years. It's just amazing.

Rona Elliot: I also want to say, Michael, that there are a lot of us that have left already, and they're really present for us because we couldn't have done it without Stan [Goldstein] and Wes [Pomeroy] and all of these giants who worked with Michael and Chip and Bill [Hanley], who really held the gravity of the place. Wes Pomeroy came from the Department of Justice, Don Ganoung was a minister who ended up sleeping with the mayor's daughter, and—

Michael Lang: [*interjecting*] Over a brothel.

Rona Elliot: —right. But there's all those other people who are still present with us, and I just really want to make sure they know we're still thinking about them.

Moderator: Well said. On that note, I would like to open it up to the floor once again. We have microphones floating around and hands up already.

Audience: Hi and thanks again. I'm wondering: for all the music that you all have seen, who were some of your favorite performers or concerts that you've been to? What music has kicked your ass?

Henry Diltz: Today you mean?

Audience: Since you were born!

Chip Monck: Felix Pappalardi and Mountain.[15] [I] went to Japan to do a tour with him, and later he was shot in the head by his wife. That ended a glorious career, but he was actually a very close friend, and [it's a] shame they couldn't get in the [*Woodstock*] film. It just ran out of space.

---

[15] Felix Pappalardi Jr. (1939–1983) was an American singer and bass player in the band Mountain from 1969 to 1973. At the same time, Pappalardi produced for various artists, including the Youngbloods, Joan Baez and, most famously, Cream, including their second album, *Disraeli Gears* (1967). Pappalardi was shot and killed by his wife in 1983.

Rona Elliot: What do you say after that? The Stones, Marvin Gaye, Tina [Turner], the Beatles, [Paul] McCartney. I mean they're all great shows. I've seen the Stones, U2... They're all legacies of Woodstock. Everything, all the lighting, all the staging, all the sound systems... But great rock and roll is great rock and roll. I've seen a lot of great rock and roll with people in this room. But you know, it's whatever rings your bell. Some people go and have that experience at a Britney Spears concert. But great rock and roll.

Michael Lang: Most of mine are related to things that I was involved in, so many of the performances at Woodstock were things that I'll never forget.

Moderator: We seem to have another visitor on stage. This is another first time.

[Gerardo Velez enters, hugs Michael Lang and Rona Elliot, and takes a seat]

Chip Monck: I must tell you, not as an answer to what I said just before, but I don't go to concerts under any circumstances. As a person who's hung up on visuals, anytime you go and see a concert you walk away with—possibly intrigued by one cue that you saw and you cannot help but duplicate it in your future work, and I think that's theft. I work basically on intuition. That's what—some of us do that. We don't go to see other people's work. It just comes. Just a statement.

Michael Lang: So the other one that from what things that I've been involved with that has always stayed with me, is the Miami Pop Festival. Jimi Hendrix was our closing act. Jimi and his band arrived at Miami International Airport and missed their pickup. Consequently we had to make arrangements with Gerry Stickells to fly them in by helicopter, which meant that they came and landed backstage.[16] It was very dramatic, and I didn't realize how dramatic it was going to be, because it turns out that at the airport they ran into somebody who gave them some STP.[17] STP is like acid on steroids—

---

[16] Gerry Stickells (1942–2019) was the tour and production manager for the Jimi Hendrix Experience until Hendrix's death in 1970. Stickells later worked with Queen, Elton John, Paul McCartney, and many others.

[17] STP is a psychedelic drug with strong stimulant qualities that can manifest intense feelings of energy. STP stands for "Serenity, Tranquility, Peace."

Rona Elliot: [*joking*] Isn't that motor oil?

Michael Lang: —and so they played their set as Mitch Mitchell describes it, from thirty feet up in the air.[18] But it was one of the best performances of that band ever.

Moderator: Speaking of Jimi Hendrix, we have an additional body up on stage. This is Gerardo Velez from Woodstock himself.

Rona Elliot: Well, since we're talking about the greatest performances, and some of you won't be here tomorrow, [the moderator] had asked what were the greatest performances we've seen. Since you're here, why don't you tell us about that performance [playing with Jimi Hendrix at Woodstock]?

Gerardo Velez: Thank you for having me, it's a pleasure to be here. I started playing percussion and dancing and singing when I was six to nine years old. I was a dancer my whole life, and I started playing percussion at nine. I was self-taught. Jimi was self-taught. When he and I got together, we were trying to do something different. Something we were hoping that would kind of change the flow of music, which eventually happened with my original band, Spyro Gyra.[19] That's when we were a jazz fusion band. I'm one of the original members of that group. But we [Gypsy Sun and Rainbows] were trying to do a fusion sort of band. Miles Davis was doing *Bitches Brew*, he was in the studio. We were working on that [jazz fusion] the whole time. We were trying to come up with original material that we could perform at Woodstock that would be uniquely Jimi's, uniquely ours, as the Band of Gypsys, Gypsy Sun and Rainbows.[20]

To me that's really what it was about. Everyone was exploring, everyone was trying to figure out something new, different. Crosby, Stills, Nash &

---

[18] John "Mitch" Mitchell (1946–2008) was a British drummer best known for his work with the Jimi Hendrix Experience. After Hendrix's death, Mitchell also played with Jack Bruce, Jeff Beck, and many others.

[19] Spyro Gyra is an American jazz fusion band formed in 1974 by Jay Beckenstein and Jeremy Wall, featuring a variety of musical styles and musicians, including Gerardo Velez.

[20] For more on Gypsy Sun and Rainbows, see the sidebar in chapter four on Hendrix's various ensembles, "The Jimi Hendrix Experience, Gypsy Sun and Rainbows, and Band of Gypsys."

Young, they covered Joni Mitchell's "Woodstock," and everyone was trying to come up with something interesting.

We would sit in the house that we had, and Jimi had trunks of albums, and we would go like this—[*moves forward and gestures pulling something out*]—take out an album, put it on the turntable, and we would play to that record. And then we would try to come up with some ideas off of classical, didn't matter, just grab a record. [*repeats the motion of pulling out a record*] And we would just go about the business of trying to come up with something new. To me, that is what Woodstock is all about. Turning the table, turning the next page of time, and that's what we were trying to do. Eventually, with Spyro Gyra, I kind of did that, but that's what we were going after, that's why we added Larry Lee, because he was a rhythm guitar player, and Juma [Sultan], another percussionist, and myself, and we were trying to come up with something original and different.[21]

Rona Elliot: Could you talk about the performance?

Gerardo Velez: Now the performance, yes. I got to the stage and I looked out into the audience, and it was my first professional gig. [*laughter from the audience*] Yeah, and it was also my birthday, August fifteenth.

Henry Diltz: Wow, wow.

Gerardo Velez: So, you know, I just wanted to go sideways from there. But anyway, the performance to me was more. Jimi always stood next to me and we had a good rapport. If you look at the video you'll see that. We had an excellent rapport between us, and it was always like that because we hung out together, we lived together, we partied together. But on that stage he was the commander. He took full control of everything. That stage is the altar to me, and he was the one who kind of described it to me. He said, "Listen, forget about everything else that happens out there; when we get on that stage, it belongs to us. The world belongs to us. These vibrations belong to us. Let's go out and kick some butt." And that's what we did. And we played.

---

[21] Larry Lee (1943–2007) was an American guitarist and friend of Jimi Hendrix. He joined Hendrix's Gypsy Sun and Rainbows one week before Woodstock, which was their biggest show. Juma Sultan (b. 1942) is an American percussionist known for playing with Jimi Hendrix at Woodstock. His avant-garde jazz drumming includes many musical styles, including rock, blues, and jazz.

I look at myself back then and I say, wow, did I overplay. If I could play with him today I would feel an accomplishment of sorts. So, full circle, here we are fifty years later, and I have a band with his second cousin, Hendrix by Hendrix.[22] We're doing some of Jimi's material, but we are doing our own material. Because it's a different time, it's time for change, but it's time to remember the past, so I'm very happy to be here, thank you.

JIMI HENDRIX AND "THE STAR-SPANGLED BANNER"

Jimi Hendrix's performance of "The Star-Spangled Banner" at Woodstock is certainly one of the festival's standout moments both because of Hendrix's technical virtuosity and also because of the political context in which the performance took place. Despite its iconic standing, Hendrix's "Banner" performance at Woodstock was not a singular event: Hendrix had been performing versions of the "Banner" for more than a year prior to Woodstock, and he would continue playing it up until a month before his death.

Given Hendrix's brief stint in the Army (1961–1962) and his inclusion of a portion of "Taps" in this rendition of the "Banner," it is easy to connect his performance with the politics of the Vietnam era, even more so when you note that Hendrix's first performance of the "Banner" aligned with the deployment of his former unit, the 101st Airborne Division, to Vietnam.[23]

Rona Elliot: I can't help the music interviewer in me. Would you talk about rehearsing "The Star-Spangled Banner" with him when you were roommates?

Gerardo Velez: [*laughs*] So here's what happened with that. We were the counterculture, right? He kept saying, "I want to do something really different. I'm going to do 'The Star-Spangled Banner.'" And I looked at him and I

---

[22] "Generation H: Hendrix by Hendrix" is a collaborative concert performance featuring Gerardo Velez and Jimi Hendrix's second cousin, Regi Hendrix.

[23] For more on the fascinating story of Hendrix's "Banner" performances, see Mark Clague, "'This Is America': Jimi Hendrix's Star Spangled Banner Journey as Psychedelic Citizenship," *Journal of the Society for American Music* 8, no. 4 (2014): 435–78.

said—[*aside*] because we were hanging out in the living room—I said, "'The Star-Spangled Banner'? Let's do something else, you know? We're the counterculture, man, let's do something else! Let's figure out something else!" "No, I want to do this." And he just kept working on it and working on it and working on it, and then he put it to the side, right, went away from it for a while.

He would go up against the wall with his electric guitar and feel the music coming off the wall, he would be like this. [*mimes leaning forward and playing guitar*] And he'd feel the music coming off the wall, and he'd say, "I have another idea!" And he'd run back and he'd start to play with the amp and he'd start to do some stuff, and we'd start jamming. And then when he did "The Star-Spangled Banner," it was like we all kind of stepped back and said, "Let the brother rip." And we just stood back, because if you notice, we were on stage, we were like, "Ta-na-na-na-na-naaa wo-wo-wo-wo-wo-wow," [*singing the first phrase of the song*] and I'm going like, "Whoaaaaa."

It was fantastic, looking out into the audience and being an American kid growing up in New York—[*aside*] my parents are from Puerto Rico, and they were always very proud. "This is America, this is your land, this is your opportunity, my son." And I took that to heart always. And for him to play "The Star-Spangled Banner," and to achieve what it achieved over the years . . . Everybody remembers that moment as the most iconic moment, I believe, at the festival. You may have a difference of opinion, but to me that's the most iconic moment, when Jimi played "The Star-Spangled Banner." Do you agree with me?

Audience: Yeah!

Gerardo Velez: Those of you who saw the video, right? Okay! So that's the kind of person he was. The performance was amazing, because we didn't know what the heck we were doing. It was the first time we ever really played out together. We did a couple of things in the town of Woodstock: we did the playhouse, Tinker Street Cafe, all those wonderful places that were just filled with culture and music, and we brought that to the stage.[24] We

---

[24] Located at 59 Tinker Street, in Woodstock, New York, Café Espresso was the center of folk music in upstate New York during the 1960s and 1970s. Everyone from Bob Dylan and Rick Danko to Joan Baez and Peter Yarrow (of Peter, Paul and Mary fame) played there, and Dylan is rumored to have stayed in the White Room upstairs, writing material for *Another Side of Bob Dylan* (1964) and *Bringing It All Back Home* (1965).

19. Black and white photograph of Jimi Hendrix playing guitar. Photograph by Henry Diltz.

performed our music, and we didn't know what was happening, and when we left, we just took a deep breath and looked back, and I said, "What just happened, Jimi?" And he would answer, "I don't know man, I don't know, but we have to rehearse." [*lots of laughter*] "I thought we were improvising a bit!" "We have to rehearse."

So that was the amazing experience, my first experience on a stage, so I have nothing else to relate it to. From then on, I've been very lucky, very fortunate. I've had a wonderful career in music, but that was my first professional experience as a musician. I was doing dances since I was six, but that's different from getting up in front of thousands of people and performing. But for me it's my life, and so has been a natural way of doing things.

Moderator: You mentioned that iconic performance, and I'm sure much of it is iconic because it was in the documentary that we can still see it fifty years later. Can any of you—would any of you like to speak to some of those moments that are not in the documentary that were iconic to you, that you would like to sort of fill us in on?

Audience: Gerardo, tell the story about your pants!

Gerardo Velez: I'll do that. My girlfriend and I, we were on our way to Woodstock, and Jimi had given me a limo to drive in, so I brought all my friends, of course. That's the way it was back then. So we're all in the limo and my girlfriend was putting these clasps onto my pants—you know, you put them in and then you clamp them on the back because they have little sharp points, right, they have little sharp points, four of them. You're supposed to clamp them together. She did an excellent job up and down here. [*gesturing to the sides of his legs*] But on my glutes, my buttocks, they were still open. So as I'm playing and performing, I'm moving along and I'm sweating now, and I'm feeling like, "This is a little weird," you know, and I'm pulling my pants up my butt—excuse the expression—and I'm wondering what the heck is going on, and then I realize they're stabbing me in the butt, all these various . . . And I just kept playing because, you know, I was on a few things, a few mood-altering—

Everyone on stage: Yup.

Gerardo Velez: —yes, a few of those, so I didn't really realize what was going on. The colors were happening, rainbows were happening, and my ass was on fire!

Rona Elliot: I'll pass on a story. So one person who can't be here is one of the women who prepared lunches at the beginning. It was one person at the end, and there were three women who delivered I think four hundred lunch bags, and she had been living in the abandoned hotel, the Diamond Horseshoe, which they opened for the crew.[25] It had running water, but that was about it. And they were unable to get back from the site to the Diamond Horseshoe. When Carol [Green] got back to her hotel room after the festival, there was a hatchet in the door of her room, and a couple from India had moved in, which still—it just raises too many questions. But that was a

---

[25] Located in Bethel, New York, the Diamond Horseshoe was an abandoned hotel near Max Yasgur's farm that housed close to two hundred of the festival's workers. On the night before the festival, the hotel had a massive fire, but no one was injured because almost everyone was still working at the festival site in preparation for the opening the next day.

kind of a Woodstockian experience. But it just sounds fantastic. One of the things that happened was—[*aside*] I don't know if you were involved in this, Michael—everyone was very tired, and there was a guy named Dr. Abruzzi. Do you remember him?[26]

Michael Lang: Yes, of course.

Rona Elliot: He was arrested in the late 1980s or early 1990s for being a molester of patients, but in the 1960s he would give us B12 shots and we would line up for them. [*looking at Michael Lang*] I don't think you were there, and he would just shoot up the whole crew, because nobody had slept. I mean, it wasn't drugs, it was B12. You know, when you think about this, and you go, did I make this up? Did this really happen? So I don't mean to sound like I'm telling tales out of school, but so many unbelievable things happened.

Moderator: Chip, can you think of one of those performers? You were there calling them out.

Chip Monck: It's very difficult. Because there are twelve arcs, carbon arcs that have to be trimmed and they each have forty-two minutes, and I don't have time to do anything other than deal with them as shapes.[27] I'm listening to the music in reference to count. I'm not allowed to necessarily get excited or move myself from that position because if I get excited, right, something won't happen or won't happen on cue. I'm structured that way in my craft.

Michael Lang: For me, it was Artie Kornfeld.

Rona Elliot: Oh, yeah.

---

[26] Dr. William Abruzzi (b. 1925) was the official festival doctor at Woodstock. He became known as the "Rock Doc" after treating hundreds of people who experienced bad trips after taking drugs at Woodstock and other festivals in the 1960s. In 1976, he pled guilty to the sexual abuse of one of his patients.

[27] Chip Monck is describing a specific type of lighting instrument called a carbon arc lamp. Light is produced by an electric current arcing between two carbon rods, which are slowly vaporized. Because the rods are constantly getting shorter, the distance between them must be adjusted (trimmed) by the operator and eventually they burn out. In this case, Monck is saying that each carbon arc lamp can run for forty-two minutes before burning out.

"A WHITE LAKE HAPPENING"

On September 2, 1969, Dr. William Abruzzi submitted a report on the medical care provided at Woodstock to the New York State Department of Health. Titled "A White Lake Happening," the report describes what had been Abruzzi's initial plans for the event, including the hiring of eighteen doctors, thirty-six nurses, and twenty-seven assistants who could work around the clock in eight-hour shifts. Once Abruzzi realized the crowd would be much larger than the anticipated fifty thousand, he called for reinforcements from neighboring towns and as far away as New York City.

Two pressing medical concerns were drug overdoses and so-called "bad trips." Although the standard medical treatment for such trips was the administration of Thorazine, Abruzzi embraced the Hog Farm's technique of talking down patients instead of adding a potent tranquilizer to the drugs already coursing through their systems. But according to Abruzzi, the greatest number of casualties involved foot injuries, of which he reported "938 lacerations, 135 punctures, and 346 other foot injuries." Abruzzi's report not only includes incredible details, but also rather florid language: "Not a knife wound was sewed, not a punch wound was treated. This might very well have been an example of the first time that a large number of people have come together, lived together, suffered together, and given to the rest of us an indication that it can be done in love and peace."[28]

Michael Lang: Artie was tasked with walking the bands to the stage and trying to get them to sign releases for the film. To his credit, I think he got about half the bands to sign and the rest were sort of negotiated afterwards. But on the second day, Artie came walking across the stage. I forget who he was with, but I noticed that his eyes were sort of spinning in his head. I walked to the side, and he had been dosed and he didn't know where he was or what he was doing. I sat with him at the side of the stage for about twenty minutes trying to—as you do with somebody who is going through that trip—

---

[28] The full report is in the New York State archives with the title, "A White Lake Happening," New York State Department of Health, Executive Division, Commissioner's Office, Subject Files of the Commissioner's Office, 1952–1977, Mass Gatherings file.

Rona Elliot: [*interjecting*] He's the associate producer of Woodstock.

Michael Lang: —"It's going to be okay. Time will, you know, time will heal this and you'll be fine," and then I realized this was not going to be over in twenty minutes, and so I walked him up to the trips tent where the Hog Farm took care of him. And that was the last I saw of him pretty much for the festival.

Rona Elliot: But there are pictures of Henry's of Michael sort of standing by Artie, and you can see that Michael is just being gravity near Artie. There's one particular picture with Gabe Pressman, and Artie looks like a wild man, and Michael's just standing there really calm, next to him, and Artie was one of the four guys.[29]

Henry Diltz: Very quickly: I already told my moments of seeing Jimi play and thinking, "Why is he playing that song ["The Star-Spangled Banner"]? That's their song. No, wait! That's our song! We're taking it back!"[30] But an odd thing for me was that I had an all-access pass, so I could be on stage, anywhere, and all the other photographers were down in the pit, as they called it, kind of looking up at the stage. Right below the lip of the stage was a little boardwalk for the film crew, the guys that were filming the movie. Since I had an all-access pass, I would jump down on that so that the stage would hit me right in the chest, so I had the best seat in the house!

Moderator: Is this what we're looking at here? [*pointing to the photo of John Sebastian that was used in the sausage ad*]

Henry Diltz: Yeah. You see those guys down in the pit? They're looking up. See the guy with the camera? I was up there, up higher, and so at night I would be up there, like shooting Janis [Joplin] and the film people, you

---

[29] Gabe Pressman (1924–2017) was a correspondent at WNBC-TV in New York for more than six decades and one of the few television journalists to report live from Woodstock.

[30] When Henry refers to the national anthem as "their" song, he's setting up a binary opposition between the mainstream, as owners of the anthem, and the counterculture, as protesters of what it symbolizes. Ironically, Hendrix's performance itself tries to split the difference by including "Taps" and his virtuosic fireworks as allusions to both sides. For more, see the sidebar above on Hendrix's "Banner" performances.

know, the production assistants would come up and say, "You can't be here. This is just for the film crew."[31] And I would answer, "No! I have an all-access pass! I'm shooting for Michael Lang!" But it wasn't a major thing, with a couple of little shoving things that happened. But in later years, I met those same people in LA and we became friends and laughed about it.

Rona Elliot: But it was that way.

Henry Diltz: Yeah, that happened.

Moderator: I think we should open it up to the floor again. I'm sure there are lots of questions. I saw Bill [Hanley] actually had his hand up as well, so let's get to Bill.

Rona Elliot: Would you reintroduce Bill?

Moderator: Yes! So Bill Hanley was here earlier this afternoon, "Father of Festival Sound." He did sound for the Beatles and then here at Woodstock. So, Bill!

Bill Hanley, from the audience: Hi! I just want to go back to Denver Pop and how I tried to get Barry Fey to be able to get paid, get the police to slow down, and give tickets out to the kids to get them inside so they wouldn't be fighting and they wanted to make a fight out of it. They were the biggest obstacles of all the people that were there. Thank you.

Audience: This is for Michael Lang. How did you decide to put Woodstock 50 in Watkins Glen rather than Bethel? And for everybody else: what effect do you think that different venue will have on the way the festival develops?

---

[31] Janis Joplin (1943–1970) was an American blues and rock singer, noted for her distinctive and captivating voice. She made her mark on public consciousness first at the Monterey Pop Festival, singing with Big Brother and the Holding Company. Her most famous songs include "Me and Bobby McGee," a cover of Kris Kristofferson's original, and her original song, "Mercedes Benz." By most accounts, her performance at Woodstock, backed by the Kozmic Blues Band, was hampered by her growing reliance on drugs and alcohol. On October 4, 1970, she died of an accidental overdose of heroin.

20. Black and white photograph of the back of John Sebastian, who is onstage facing the audience and holding a guitar. Photograph by Henry Diltz.

Michael Lang: So, Bethel. Well, it's sort of home ground for us, but it is too small a venue now for the Woodstock we have in mind. They are limited to about fifteen thousand people in their shed, and so it just wouldn't work and the town would completely . . . I don't know what they'd do if they thought they were getting another influx of the same kind of people. There's a big paranoia about that in Bethel. And we wanted to keep it in New York State, because it's really the home of Woodstock, and like [Woodstock] '94 which was in Saugerties, and [Woodstock] '99 which was in Rome, this one is in Watkins Glen because it's a big facility with a thousand acres of green field, some infrastructure, parking, and all of those other essentials.

Chip Monck: It's a great relief to actually get into a working facility that is appropriate to the event. To have all of those things available to you rather than worrying about standing on the four-inch PVC water pipe because that's everybody's drinking water.

Moderator: Other questions?

Audience: How would you say Woodstock influenced the business of the music industry, and can you give some specific examples of the influence Woodstock had on the music industry over the past fifty years?

Michael Lang: Sure. Before Woodstock it wasn't an industry, it was a business. After Woodstock, it was an industry. Suddenly everybody realized the power of these acts to draw people. For example, we paid Jimi Hendrix $32,000 for two sets: $2,000 for expenses and $15,000 per set. Three weeks later at Madison Square Garden he was paid $150,000, and it went on from there. And then came, kind of, the 1970s and music labels, record companies, who had been kind of small businesses, but very creative people were starting to be bought up by big public companies, and suddenly the music was due on the third quarter or the fourth quarter because they needed it for the end-of-the-year results. And suddenly, if something was a hit, there were eighteen more records that were done exactly the same way, and it became an industry. I think that's pretty much been true until the record business fell apart a few years ago when they ignored the digital world.

Audience: How about with concert production?

Michael Lang: Concert production just grew technologically. People figured out how to make great sound, and the kind of thing that Bill had to invent became kind of commonplace. Lighting is the same, although the person that's behind it, the creative, is still what determines how great it is or isn't. But just in terms of the technical aspects of it, it's become a real sort of grown-up industry.

Gerardo Velez: I'd like to comment on that as well. As a musician, at the beginning, we didn't get any respect, not that we get much respect now, but we didn't get much respect. After Woodstock, and the feeling of concept albums and that we were a group, we were a force together, and you had to reckon with this force that was now changing things, and music allowed people to live vicariously through other people that they admired, and they admired their work, album after album after album. And what Michael said is exactly what happened. They took this creative place that people had all the time, because we were all trying to work together.

Back then, you'd have a concert just like Michael put together: you'd have jazz, funk, R&B [rhythm and blues], rock, psychedelic music all together, because it was all music, and we all wanted to hear variations on the theme of music. So as we went along as musicians, we realized we were being boxed in and boxed in.

At first we were given a lot of money. Money was thrown around. Record deals were like, "Hey, you want $100,000? Go, and we'll do something, we'll put it on a shelf for you." That's how they were using the money that was coming in, so they would continually control the money, and the artists weren't getting their just due. That's what was happening to us during those times and into the 1980s. Then certain acts after that realized, wait a minute, we don't have to give these promoters all the money, we'll do our own thing. Of course when Napster happened and the music business went into the toilet, so did everything else.[32]

I know from the jazz idiom, it just turned the corner and then, like Michael mentioned, music's all syndicated, so whatever they agree on in Los Angeles happens across the country. So you don't get people really being creative and developing careers. It took Bruce Springsteen four albums before he had a hit, because they believed in him. No one believes in musicians anymore the way they did back then. But it's a level playing field now because of the internet.

Audience: I just wanted to thank you all for being here. It's probably one of the coolest events I've ever attended. So one of the pictures that really struck me was seeing Bill Graham sitting on the side of the stage with Jefferson Airplane. As a huge Allman Brothers fan, Bill Graham has kind of played a big part in my musical upbringing. I was just wondering if you could speak on your relations with Bill Graham, whether he influenced Woodstock or you guys influenced him, because, I mean, Bill and Michael come to my mind as the two best concert promoters I've ever heard of. Thank you.

Michael Lang: So I'm sitting in my office probably sometime in April or May. We had just finished most of our booking, and—

Rona Elliot: [*interjecting*] 1969.

---

[32] Napster was a peer-to-peer file sharing service that completely upended the music publishing industry. Released in 1999 and created by Shawn Fanning and Sean Parker, Napster quickly laid the foundation for streaming media services. Early legal challenges to Napster, first by the heavy metal band Metallica and rapper Dr. Dre, were followed by a lawsuit from the Recording Industry Association of America (RIAA) that alleged massive copyright infringement. Napster lost, and by 2002 it was completely bankrupt.

21. Black and white photograph of members of Jefferson Airplane – Sally Mann, Paul Kantner, and Grace Slick, with a cigarette in her mouth – seated on the side of the stage along with Bill Graham, who is kneeling. Photograph by Henry Diltz.

Michael Lang: —1969. And John Morris came running into my office saying, "We're fucked![33] We're fucked!" "What do you mean, John?" "Bill's going to buy out our show." [*laughs*]

Chip Monck: That's his usual approach.

Michael Lang: Yeah. And I said, "What do you mean he's going to buy out our show? We already paid for our show." There are radius clauses in contracts where you can only play—if you're playing Bill's club, you can't play within fifty miles of the club or something like that. And we were well beyond the radius. And so I said to John, "Set up a meeting with Bill," and

---

[33] John Morris (b. 1939) was the head of production at Woodstock. Prior to that, he was the stage manager at Bill Graham's Fillmore East. At Woodstock, Morris took on the position of stage manager and shared emcee duties with Chip Monck, among others. In fact, Morris was the speaker that announced the changing status of the festival, declaring "It's a free concert from now on."

he did. We met at Ratner's,[34] which was a restaurant right next to the Fillmore East, and I wondered, what had I done?[35] Was this just his ego, or how was I going to deal with this? You know seeing him eat the pickled herring sort of helped me calm down a bit, and I relaxed.

And so I said, "What is it? What is it?" He said, "You booked my entire spring and summer shows, and who's going to come to the Fillmore when they can see everybody for six bucks at your show?"[36] So we came to an understanding, and I said I wouldn't advertise the acts until they played the Fillmore, and then I'd put them on the bill, and he was like, grudgingly, "Well, yeah, okay, that kinda works." And then I invited him to come up and emcee one of the days, and his line to me was, "We can't both be God on the same day!"

Rona Elliot: There is only one God! And you know Mr. Mellow here [*referring to Michael Lang*] [wasn't going to play God].

Michael Lang: So we later became friends, and he sent me the Santana tape, which was an amazing discovery for us. It was a local band that he was working with in San Francisco, and then when he came to the festival he sort of tried to give me his insight into how to handle things. He asked me, "What are you going to do with all these people here?" And I said, "Well, we're going to take care of them, Bill," and I walked away, and then he famously made that comment about how do you sort of control a crowd of this size, and he described what they do with ants in India: you dig a big trench around everything and you fill it with oil and light it on fire.

Rona Elliot: Different philosophies!

---

[34] Ratner's was a famous kosher restaurant. After operating for nearly one hundred years, Ratner's closed in 2005.

[35] Located at 105 Second Avenue and East Sixth Street in New York City, the Fillmore East was the East Coast counterpart to Bill Graham's first venue, the Fillmore, located in San Francisco. Opening in March 1968, the Fillmore East quickly became a hotbed for rock, with notable performances by Jimi Hendrix (on New Year's Day, 1970), the Kinks, and Led Zeppelin. The Allman Brothers Band played so often that they were informally called "Bill Graham's House Band."

[36] The first mail-order tickets for Woodstock were sold for six dollars each. Woodstock Ventures quickly raised the prices to seven dollars for one day, thirteen dollars for two days, and eighteen dollars for three days. By the end of the first two weeks after opening the sale, they had sold $169,388 worth of tickets.

Michael Lang: Yeah, different philosophies.

Rona Elliot: Peace, love!

Michael Lang: But he really created the music business as we knew it, and was a giant in that way.

Rona Elliot: Bill Graham was a polarizing figure!

Michael Lang: Certainly.

Rona Elliot: You loved him or you didn't, you were loyal to him, or you weren't. You walked away damaged, or you were really loyal to him. Right. But Michael is the antithesis of Bill Graham.

Michael Lang: I did steal a lot of personnel from him.

Moderator: Pugilistic?

Rona Elliot: Pugilistic is an understatement.

Moderator: Okay! And Michael Lang has never been described as pugilistic.

Rona Elliot: And never will be!

Chip Monck: Graham was an entirely different animal. It was like approaching one nation. We built the Fillmore [East] and I took all the crew and put them into Woodstock, right? And closed his doors. Michael had booked them and I sucked the place dry. We had occasional punches and one day an off-duty cop stood in between the two of us and took the punch, which was very nice of him, you know. Because I would just stand there and he would punch me, and then I would raise my price.

Moderator: So good lessons for our students in production! All right, other questions?

Audience: This question is for Michael Lang. With so many legacy bands dominating the concert sheds each summer, some with even just one original member, what's your view on this new and evolving technology of holograms, kind of bringing the dead rockstar back as a—there's no better way to say this, I guess—bringing these since-past legends of rock back.

Michael Lang: I think when it's used properly and judiciously and you don't try to take them on road and tour them, I think it's fine. The Tupac thing at Coachella was kind of interesting.[37] It's a little bit gruesome, in a way. I don't think it's got a big future in terms of touring bands.

Rhoda Rosenberg, Bill Hanley's wife, from the audience: This is more of a comment, maybe, than a question, but I'd like to contribute it. One of the words that I think comes to my mind when I hear many of these panels is the word "responsibility." There is this sense of responsibility that I think all of you seem to have: responsibility to the audience, responsibility to the musicians, and responsibility to the community that you work together, as a crew. And one of the things that I have always felt from this group is that there isn't this sense of enormous ego. That somehow or other I think one of the things that I came away from is maybe this festival worked so well because from the top down and all along, it wasn't about you, it was about the event, it was about the people, it was about the music.

You also worked tremendously hard. I mean, I remember . . . I teach, and one of my students once said to me, "Oh golly, what was it like, you know, dating Bill [Hanley] back then?" And I said, "Dating? We didn't date! It was like, 'Get in the truck, let's go! We're late!'" It was just getting the job done and doing the job right because there was that responsibility to the event, to the music, to the musicians. And sometimes, I don't know, but a lot of times, Bill never got paid for the work he did either, but he did it, and I think today I'm not so sure if that happens.

Michael Lang: It doesn't.

Chip Monck: The responsibility is still extreme. We don't have a job unless we do it correctly. We don't have a life. How do you live with yourself after you fucked up forty times, you know? You can't!

---

[37] On April 15, 2012, a hologram of rapper Tupac Shakur (1971–1996) "performed" onstage at the Coachella Music Festival alongside Dr. Dre and Snoop Dogg. The hologram was created using a digital projection system based on a technique called "Pepper's Ghost," named after the English scientist John Henry Pepper (1821–1900).

Rona Elliot: It was never about Michael. It just never was about Michael. And when you're around some musicians it's always about them and only about them. And I'm not saying this—and [*to Michael Lang*] I'm sorry if I'm embarrassing you—but that sense of responsibility was there throughout the crew, and we were on an adventure together, and he may have been our fearless leader, as I have been calling him for a day or so, but it wasn't about him and his accomplishments, and it never has been. And I think that's a very, very important distinction. It was about something he created, but it took all of us to create, and if you look out at many of the acts now, and the promoters and the managers who all think they're important, and they think it makes a difference that they're famous or a celebrity, that was just never what was going on over there, so it's great to see that it's recognized, so thank you.

Chip Monck: The purpose of management in the eyes of the artists is that they say no on behalf of the artist. The artist always answers a question with, "Yes, I would be delighted." Beyond that, I forgot what the rest of it was going to be. Oh yes! As we spoke about it once a couple of times before in our presentations, the performers in general—no, most all—require acceptance from you, as the audience. Basically, they almost can sustain and live upon it. It becomes not necessarily an obsession, but it's very similar to a drug. They have to be—they have to get your approval. It is absolutely necessary that they walk away owning you.

Gerardo Velez: To answer your question before, what you said, it was youthful exuberance. If you try to do this when you're forty or fifty, you go, "I'm not going to attempt this!" But at twenty-two, twenty years old? "We're going to conquer the world! There is nothing that would stop us." And anybody that's here that's over twenty years old will agree with me that that is in your spirit and in your heart. Don't try to do this when you're even thirty years old or forty years old, because you have a cycle of experiences already that says, "Mmm, I don't think so," but that was what happened back then. When you see Michael and these young guys, you see all of us, and I look back and I go, "Wow, I was twenty years old?"

Chip Monck: Charlie Watts terms it as "youthful arrogance."[38] What he actually said was, "We get out of the limo, we do our forty-five minutes, we get back in the limo, we don't do an encore, and we leave." Bill Graham and

---

[38] Charlie Watts (b. 1941) is best known as the drummer for the Rolling Stones.

myself gave us the opportunity to learn how to get more from you if we gave more. It's a two-way street.

Moderator: We have time for one or two more questions.

Audience: As someone who was there, what I didn't realize then that I do now, is how much of the accidents that happened were well thought through. And I think, Michael, it sounds like they stem from who you are or who you were at that time. But for me, going there, the music was the reason I went. But leaving, yeah, I was introduced to music I hadn't heard and people I hadn't heard, but what happened there was not really about the music. It was much more about all of a sudden realizing there are all these people who think and want the same kind of things that I think and want, but at that time I only knew about twenty other people who felt that way. And all of a sudden there were five hundred thousand of us at the same place.

For me, in that experience, the windows were blown wide open. It was like, "Oh my God." So I kept waiting the last fifty years for that to happen again. Not for me, so much, as for society. I kept looking for those experiences twenty years later, thirty years later, now, where people could have that experience, where the windows could be blown open and people could say, "This is the way we want to live." So I don't know if that's what it was like for you, but that's what it was like for me, and where do we find those windows now?

Michael Lang: One of those windows was [President Barack] Obama's inauguration for me, frankly. You know those rare moments when people sort of get control of what happens in the world.

Rona Elliot: I think I have always remained very hungry to have that experience, and having young kids around, I want them to be able to have that experience now as well. But I think as Gerardo just pointed out, for one reason or another, it is in their hands to create that. We can open the door, they have to walk through. Not to be too serious.

Moderator: On that note, I would like to thank all of our participants here today. We have Chip Monck, Rona Elliot, Gerardo Velez, Michael Lang, and Henry Diltz all together for the first time in fifty years.

WOODSTOCK IN THE NEWS

On August 16, 1969, the front page of the *New York Times* contained a report from the first day of Woodstock. Under the headline "200,000 Thronging to Rock Festival Jam Roads Upstate," Barnard L. Collier's report initially focused on the traffic. Collier interviewed Wes Pomeroy, Woodstock's director of security, who is quoted as saying "Anybody who tries to come here is crazy. Sullivan County is a great big parking lot."

Collier also spoke to Sullivan County Sheriff Louis Ratner, who reported that an estimated fifty arrests had been made for drug possession. However, according to an unnamed state police sergeant, none of the drug arrests had been for marijuana. The sergeant is quoted as saying, "As far as I know the narcotics guys are not arresting anybody for grass. If we did there isn't enough space in Sullivan or the next three counties to put them in." Collier went on to specify that John Roberts, one of the four co-organizers of the event, estimated the crowd to be as large as two hundred and fifty thousand in the presentation area by the stage and another one hundred and fifty thousand in the hills and surrounding farmland.

Collier ended the article by noting the controversy surrounding Woodstock's last-minute move to Max Yasgur's dairy farm near the town of Bethel, New York. Collier pointed out that when citizens of Bethel put up a sign protesting the festival, some festival attendees responded with a sign of their own: "Don't bother Max's cows. Let them moo in peace."

But by no means was Collier's article the first reference to the festival, nor was the *Times* the only paper to print articles about it. An earlier reference to Woodstock in the *New York Times* appeared on June 27, 1969, under the headline "Peaceful Rock Fete Planned Upstate." Written by Louis Calta, the article accurately described the festival, listing performers such as Janis Joplin, Jefferson Airplane, Blood, Sweat & Tears, and the Grateful Dead. Calta listed Michael Lang and Artie Kornfeld as the promoters, and Wes Pomeroy was identified as the director of security, who noted that "None [of the policemen] will be in uniform and none will carry weapons."

Issues surrounding the festival might not have caught the *Times*'s attention until two weeks before opening day, but for smaller upstate newspapers in the vicinity of the festival, the imminent arrival of thousands of music fans was already a concern fully one month before the festival was to be held. On June 17, 1969, the *Poughkeepsie Journal* published an article about the concerns of residents in the nearby town of Wallkill had about the upcoming festival. This article, "Wallkill Aroused by Folk Festival," stated that "public alarm at the prospect of having 50,000 young music lovers invade this small Orange County community could bring about the relocation of a massive rock and folk festival scheduled for August." Wallkill's concerns included how the traffic caused by the festival might impact the opening of a new Sears Roebuck scheduled for the same time, and also on ongoing construction on one of the roads leading to the festival site. Of course in the end, the festival was moved to a different location, and approximately ten times the number of people reported by the *Journal* were in attendance.

The *Journal* continued to report on conflicts between Wallkill residents and the festival organizers, printing an article titled "Woodstock Rock and Folk Festival May Face Ban in Court" on June 23, 1969. According to the article, four Wallkill residents were seeking an injunction from the State Supreme Court, claiming that there would "not be enough police to maintain order" and that "lives and properties will be endangered."

In the end, Wallkill successfully forced the Woodstock organizers to find a different venue. This change was seen as newsworthy by the *New York Times*, which reported the move on July 17, 1969. The article, titled "Woodstock Pop-Rock Fete Hits Snag," details the Wallkill Zoning Board of Appeals's rejection of the festival. In an article published by the *Times* the next day ("Woodstock Festival Vows to Carry On") festival organizer John Roberts is reported to have said "that his group did not recognize the board's authority and that the festival would be held as promised."

One week later, on July 23, 1969, reporter Richard F. Shepard wrote an article titled "Pop Rock Festival Finds New Home," announcing the move from Wallkill to Bethel, New York. When this article went to press, the new location, Max Yasgur's farm, had already become the focus of protests: the article quotes a sign in Bethel that read "Stop

Max's Hippie Music Festival. No 150,000 hippies here. Buy no milk."

Journalistic interest in Woodstock did not cease once the festival was over. On August 18, 1969, the day after the festival ended, the *Times* published an op-ed titled "Nightmare in the Catskills." In this piece, the editors harshly criticized both the organizers of the event, "who apparently had not the slightest concern for the turmoil it would cause, [and therefore] should be made to account for their mismanagement," and also the culture at large, exclaiming, "what kind of culture is it that can produce so colossal a mess?"

However, the editors had to admit that things had gone more smoothly than anyone could have hoped. They concluded the op-ed with several positive comments, including praise for local residents, "who boiled water and made thousands of sandwiches for the hungry, thirsty hordes of youngsters," and the festival attendees, whom they described as "freakish-looking intruders [who] behaved astonishingly well, considering the disappointments and discomforts they encountered. They showed that there is real good under their fantastic exteriors, if it can just be aroused to some better purpose than the pursuit of LSD."

Similar articles appeared in newspapers across the country. The *Daily Herald* from Provo, Utah, published an article titled "Thousands Leave Overcrowded Woodstock Music and Art Fair" on August 18, 1969, in which the reporter lists the myriad challenges that faced the festival, including two deaths (one from a youth being run over by a tractor and another from a drug overdose), three thousand injuries, four hundred "unfavorable reactions to drugs, including three young men in critical condition in a hospital," two births, and four miscarriages. The reporter also describes how rain converted "the large pasture in front of the stage to a slippery brown quagmire."

An article published on August 19, 1969 in the *Leader-Times* of Kittanning, Pennsylvania, reported different numbers of casualties, stating that there were three deaths and five thousand injured, including "those [suffering] from bad trips on LSD." According to the article, the third death occurred on Monday, August 18, "when an unidentified young pedestrian was struck by a car on route 17B just east of the fair grounds." Although the reporter focuses on the festival's misfortunes, they also specify that despite the rain and lack of food and shelter, "both the festival crowd and local residents were enthusiastic about each other in most cases."

One week later, on August 25, 1969, the front page of the *New York Times* featured another Woodstock article, titled "Woodstock: Like It Was." Members of the *Times* staff, including Mike John and Richard Reeves, gathered "five young men and one young woman" for a wide-ranging conversation, divided into sections under ten headings: "Motives Are Explored," "Group Is Described," "Sharing Was Common," "A Question of Fear," "Drug Use Frequent," "The Essential Ingredient," "Parents' Views Studied," "The Way of Youth," "Sex Part of Scene," and "A Return of Sorts." Comments by the interviewers appeared in various places throughout the article, including:

> The conflicting themes of alienation and commitment were threaded in and out of the conversation. Some of the young people had taken part in the political fervor that culminated in last year's Democratic convention in Chicago. Some had been in peace marches and campus protests. . . .

> The search for new experiences—exemplified in the widespread use of drugs—gives the youth scene an aura of promiscuity in the minds of many adults. The participants in the discussion were quick to point to the new standards of sexual conduct that their generation accepted.

On September 9, 1969, *New York Times* reporter Barnard L. Collier published yet another Woodstock article, this time investigating the financial problems faced by the festival's four co-organizers. Titled "Woodstock Fair's Staff Parting in Dispute Over Future Control: Split of Organizers Reflects Difference of Ideas Among Entrepreneurs on Mining the Youth 'Underground,'" the article looks at the delicate conversations between Michael Lang, the "baby-faced promoter with a Shirley Temple hairdo," and his financial backers, Joel Rosenman and John Roberts, the latter of whom was the twenty-four-year-old heir to the Polident fortune. Roberts and Rosenman maintained control of the Woodstock Ventures brand, while Lang and his partner, Artie Kornfeld, retained credibility with the youth market that had driven Woodstock's popularity. The article notes that the inherent conflict between John Roberts's practical goal of "mak[ing] money off the kids," and Artie Kornfeld's vision of selling a rock festival as "a groovy meeting of the tribes" was too difficult to repair.

Observers quickly recognized the long-lasting impact of Woodstock, despite the challenges everyone involved had faced. An article by reporter Jackie Ross published on December 27, 1969 in the *Hartford Courant*, of Hartford, Connecticut, says that 1969 "was characterized by something that didn't happen until August." Ross notes that one of the festival managers [John Morris] got on the stage and announced to the crowd that "there are a lot of us here, so you damn well better remember the person next to you is your brother." Ross refers to this as "the spirit of Woodstock," and notes that people who were there "glowed just to remember what a nice feeling it was to share your half sandwich with the guy who just squished down next to you. . . . You just figured things were so bad they were good." Ross concludes the article by saying that the festival gave a name to a feeling that many had, the "concern young people had been expressing for the poor, the uneducated, the discriminated against." It is "the spirit of Woodstock."

CHAPTER 3

WOODSTOCK'S STARDUST

Thursday, April 4, 2019, 4:00–6:00 p.m. EDT
David Friend Recital Hall at Berklee College of Music
Boston, Massachusetts

Participants:
Henry Diltz, photographer
Rona Elliot, public relations
Chip Monck, lighting designer and emcee

Introductions by Alex Ludwig, assistant professor of liberal arts, Berklee College of Music
Moderated by Gretchen Moore, assistant professor of liberal arts, Berklee College of Music

Alex Ludwig: Welcome. All the way on stage right is the infamous Chip Monck. He was the lighting designer for Woodstock who got pulled into being the voice of the festival at the last second. So if you've seen the *Woodstock* documentary, you've heard his voice; his voice is the one telling people not to take the brown acid.

To his left is Rona Elliot. She was responsible for community outreach at Woodstock, and at the last second they needed to find an entirely new town for the festival. Rona was one of the people in charge of helping grease the skids, shall we say.

Rona Elliot: [*interjecting*] I spoke to the Kiwanis Club, yes, but in my real life I'm a music journalist.

Alex Ludwig: And finally, we have Henry Diltz here today. If you've seen pictures from Woodstock, you've seen Henry's pictures. He was the official photographer. Can we say "the official photographer?"

Henry Diltz: [*nodding his head*] Yes, I worked for the producers.

Alex Ludwig: He has fantastic stories. You'll know every single person that he's going to be talking about. At this point, I want to hand it off to our moderator, Gretchen Moore.

Moderator: Thank you so much, Alex. Welcome everybody! The first question I wanted to ask you is I think a question that you may have heard before, and that is, how would you say that Woodstock changed the trajectory of your life and your work?

Rona Elliot: I'll start.

Henry Diltz: [*interjecting*] Take it away, one of you guys.

Rona Elliot: I had three music events. I wasn't a musician, and I longed to be in the world of music. In 1965, I saw Bob Dylan plug in;[1] in 1966, I saw the Beatles;[2] and then in 1969, I worked at Woodstock. And I realized

---

[1] On July 25, 1965, Bob Dylan (b. 1941) changed the course of music history when he "plugged in" and played an electric guitar at the Newport Folk Festival, eschewing the acoustic folk style that had brought him to prominence and ushering in the new world order of rock and roll. According to legend, Pete Seeger (1919–2014) was so furious about Dylan plugging in that he attempted to stop the performance by swinging a pickaxe at the power lines. Despite the colorful nature of the story, it has not been corroborated. Seeger has denied having any violent intentions toward Dylan and has stated that he had no philosophical objections to the fact that Dylan was playing an electric guitar.

[2] In 1966, the Beatles were touring America for the third time, playing nineteen times during the month of August.

that was my path. Those were the three seminal events of my generation, in terms of defining what a musical experience would be. And at the time, there were no places for women. Women were not on television; they weren't on the radio. They were girlfriends or they were back-up singers. And the badge of Woodstock for me—and probably I think for the others here—those three credentials, in particular Woodstock, allowed me to move into public relations and then finally get on the air, and then finally get on TV at the *Today Show* for a decade. Because it gave me a certain credibility that I don't think I would have had otherwise, because everybody wanted to be at Woodstock.

I did many, many other things to build my skills along the way. But Woodstock, everybody knows what Woodstock is. They're like "Oh, Woodstock," "Oh, the Beatles," "Oh, Bob Dylan."

Rona Elliot: Henry?

Henry Diltz: It's a hard question.

Moderator: I'm sure!

Henry Diltz: Woodstock changed me more from being there and seeing it. Somebody said, "We didn't know there were so many of us, which was amazing," and that's what amazed me. I am very interested in people, and there were a lot of people there. I mean, it was a milestone, I guess, in my career. I had just done Crosby, Stills & Nash's first album cover and they came and played [at Woodstock].[3] As a matter of fact, the night they played, I was way up at the back of the hill photographing from far away, and I heard Chip's voice say, "Ladies and gentlemen: Crosby, Stills & Nash." I went, "Oh shit! I've got to get all the way down the hill!"[4] They were my friends, and I had to get down there. [After Woodstock] I went home and did The Doors' *Morrison Hotel* album (1970), so that was a time when I was shooting a lot. But Woodstock, it was the festival itself that affected me.

---

[3] *Crosby, Stills & Nash* (1969).

[4] Crosby, Stills, Nash & Young performed two sets at Woodstock: an acoustic set and an electric set. Neil Young, the newest member of the group, joined part-way through the acoustic set. His dissatisfaction with the performance led to the removal of his name from the film and the soundtrack.

Chip Monck: [*interjecting*] Your library is essential.

Henry Diltz: Ooh. . . .

Rona Elliot: His catalog? Archive?

Chip Monck: Okay, the catalog. . . .

Henry Diltz: The library is good, yeah. You mean, of Woodstock?

Chip Monck: Oh, indeed.

Henry Diltz: Yeah, I'm so glad I got there. Actually I got there because I got a phone call from Chip, whom I had known for years in various—

Chip Monck: [*interjecting jokingly*] Moderately reputable.

Henry Diltz: —places. I was in LA, and he called and said, "Henry, we're going to have a huge concert out here this summer. You should be here." And I said, "Chip, I would love to. I've heard about it, but I don't know those guys; how am I going to get a photo pass?" And he said, "I'll speak to the producer," and the next day, Michael Lang called me. He said, "Chip says we need you. I'm going to send you an airline ticket and $500." Click!

Rona Elliot: I want to add something, because that reminded me so much of the flow of which door you go in. I was in Algeria visiting a friend of mine whose boyfriend was sort of in the Peace Corps, and I was planning on staying for the Pan-African Cultural Festival, which was going to be that August with Eldridge Cleaver and Timothy Leary, if you know who those people are. And I got a telegram that said—from a mutual friend of ours—"Come home. Festival in upstate New York." And I remember weighing the options: Algeria festival, or the Catskills? And I decided on the Catskills. So sometimes it's just intuitive, it's that same thing.

Moderator: Speaking of intuitive: Rona, did you ever think, did you imagine in your wildest dreams the impact of getting that phone call?

Rona Elliot: The telegram?

Moderator: Oh, the telegram, rather!

Rona Elliot: Should we go to Chip first to finish?

Moderator: Yeah, absolutely.

Chip Monck: You will have to repeat the question for me.

Moderator: How do you think Woodstock impacted the trajectory of your life's work?

Chip Monck: I must tell you that from then on it was three or five contingency plans for everything. At Woodstock, we never had a roof; we never had any hanging space for lighting, draperies, light show, anything like that; so it was kind of touch and go on the production side for us. The turntable didn't work, which was a blessing. Meaning that if we were to turn acts over as quickly as we had thought, we would have left the audience unentertained for approximately eight hours.

Our major concern at Woodstock, necessarily, was how the audience would work with the property holders, adjacent tenants, and the landowners. It's a difficult area for us, in as much as production was demolished, and it was an embarrassing event for me because I couldn't do what I wanted to do. There were six hundred thousand watts under the stage just rusting: I was unable to hang it because the roof load was insufficient. The light show couldn't perform because of the roof load. So you adapted as best you could.

We managed to get a total of twelve follow spots, and that lit the entire performance for everything. It was dark, it was very touch and go, but it turned out well for the film, and that was important, I suppose, because the film generated income in the future. So it was a success in its own right. But the thing that was very peculiar for me was the fact that we were led by something else entirely, which is not necessarily my program. Rona can tell you far more about the value of what we left behind for four hundred and sixty-five thousand people. To me, I would have wished to have been able to complete what I had committed to, and then Michael tapped me on the shoulder on Friday morning and said, "Oh, by the way, we haven't yet had the pleasure of hiring an emcee, and you're it!" The wonderful part about it was that I didn't have the time to prepare anything. It was such a moment that I just wondered what I was going to do with the mess.[5] And we can

---

[5] Given the tight window of less than three weeks to build and prepare the stage for performers, it is no surprise Chip Monck wondered if they would finish.

22. Black and white photograph of Chip Monck working with cables under the stage. Photograph by Henry Diltz.

get into that later, because there were relationships that were formed, and people that understood where it was important for me to lead them, or assist them, in getting what they wanted from this event. It's about the way it worked, in a nutshell, which chipmunks like a lot.[6]

Rona Elliot: Do you want to toss me that earlier question?

Moderator: Yeah, sure! So, you know, the telegram that you received.

Rona Elliot: Well, um, how many of you are musicians? [*asks the audience and sees many raised hands*]

Henry Diltz: It's a music school!

Rona Elliot: Yeah, but some people are engineers, some are lighting people . . . At age ten I was a musical maniac, but I knew I wasn't a musician,

---

[6] Known familiarly as "Chip," Edward Herbert Beresford Monck (b. 1939) earned his nickname at a summer camp at Lake Winnipesaukee, New Hampshire. Apparently, the -munk/Monck rhyme was too much for the campers to ignore.

and it drove me insane. I decided then that I would be someone who would meet the greatest people in the world, I would travel around the world, and I would see the greatest musicians in the world.

Chip Monck: And give a service that was impeccable.

Rona Elliot: [*parroting Chip*] "And give a service that was impeccable," says Chip. So I had to figure out that path. At the time, there were no women on television, and there were no women on the air. And the word "career" didn't really exist. So what I had to do—and this goes back to the telegram—was make it up. I knew I wanted to speak to musicians, because I wanted to try to decode what they did and share that powerful experience with other people who might not have felt what I felt when I heard Bob Dylan or the Beatles. So during the course of the years, I just put one foot in front of the other and tried to find my way, and navigate a way to be more and more involved in music.

I went to see the Rolling Stones in LA [Los Angeles] at the Long Beach Civic Center. No one would go with me in 1965 because the ticket was too expensive: it was five dollars. The Rolling Stones' fiftieth-anniversary concert in 2012 was $835 at Madison Square Garden. I was willing to drive and go see the Stones alone in 1965 because I was going to see the Rolling Stones. So the telegram about Woodstock, fitting into a long line of things that appeared musically in front of me, was like Eldridge Cleaver and Timothy Leary: very countercultural, very important. "Festival in upstate New York": that just spoke to me. And I had to go and introduce myself to Michael and tell him a position I thought I could have. I knew it would get me closer to the music, and that's where I wanted to be.

But you know, part of the secret of Woodstock is that it took a village. Chip has become one of the shining stars of Woodstock. Everybody knows you. The first line in your obituary will be "Chip Monck, who said 'Don't eat the brown acid.'"[7] It won't be about your lighting rigs, I'm sorry to say. I'm sorry. [*laughing*] It took a combination of people working together, and that

---

[7] Chip Monck's famous quote has been distilled down to "Don't take the brown acid," but the full quote captures his verbose way of speaking: "To get back to the warning that I've received, you may take it with however many grains of salt you wish, that the brown acid that is circulating is not specifically too good. It's suggested that you do stay away from that; of course, it's your own trip so be my guest, but please be advised that there is a warning on that one, okay?"

was one of the lessons of Woodstock. So that's the story about the telegram. I'm only sorry I didn't keep it.

Moderator: Nowadays, all of our students use social media to tell each other what's happening. I'm wondering how you think social media might have affected Woodstock? Do you think it would have been a benefit? Do you think it would have been a harm? Just curious what you think about that.

Chip Monck: As a prelude to Ms. Elliot, I can't imagine how it could have been dealt with on a social-media basis. We would have had excessively more of an audience, possibly, if the transit availability were possible.

Rona Elliot: Okay, so, first of all, I would change the question a little bit. I have twenty-two-year-old twins who are the same age as you guys, so they're obviously involved in social media. I want you to imagine for a second that you are in a field, in Max Yasgur's farm, without your phone. You've driven on [Interstate] 87, or wherever you've been, and you've gone with your friends to hang out. And that's it. Very few people have a camera. There are six payphones. The idea of being at Woodstock was to have an experience. It wasn't about sharing the experience. The experience ended up being shared inadvertently through the film. It was about being there, having that experience, and I make that distinction because like these guys, I use social media, and I have kids who use it. But it's inconceivable what would have happened then if everyone had cameras. The things that happened at Woodstock were direct experiences.

On the other hand, when Bonnaroo, Coachella, or Burning Man happen, it's posted within two seconds.[8] The people who are there are not in the experience, from my point of view. They are in there with their telephones. They are not with Jimi Hendrix and that remarkable performance. I'm not dissing social media, I am just saying that when an event happens and social media is part of it, it is a different kind of an event.

You can't ever recreate anything anyway, but the experience of telephones in general at concerts, when people are sending up their recording like this—[*mimes a person holding up a cellphone over a crowd*]—from my point of view, they are not being with the artist on stage. They are being with their telephone, which is fine if you want to go be with your telephone, but I honor musicians, so it's an issue for me. It's also a problem for me if I spend

---

[8] Bonnaroo Music & Arts Festival.

$200 on a ticket and there is some jerk in front of me standing up with their phone. So I think the question is different, and it's something each of you, both as artists and musicians and people in the audience have to ask: What is the role of the artist? What is the role of the observer? What is the experience that you want to have? Do you want to be with the artist? Or do you want to show your friends that you are at a concert?

And I think this is very fundamental. It's fundamental to me, because my most transformational experiences in my life, other than having children, were in concert settings, listening to a musician, whether it was Marvin Gaye, Otis Redding, the Beatles, or Jimi Hendrix. The thing that connected me to other people throughout the course of my life has something to do with being with another person.

In an interview setting, when I was interviewing Paul McCartney or George Harrison, I wouldn't have picked up a cell phone. I wouldn't have left to go to the bathroom if I had to; I was going to sit there and have that experience. I'm not taking away technology because it's your future, it's the way you are going to connect with people musically, but there is a time and a place. If Jimi Hendrix were sitting here now, do you think you would be taking a picture of him? You would be hanging off of the guy!

Particularly as artists, what is the role of the artist in communicating to the person out there? What is the responsibility of the fan or the member of the audience who is trying to absorb something from that artist? For me, social media in general takes away from that experience. And again, I'm not trying to sound like a Luddite.

Henry Diltz: Lucky we didn't have to deal with that at Woodstock.

Rona Elliot: And there were six pay phones. But I think the fact there was no place to go, no one to call, nothing to do. . . .

Henry Diltz: I was just going to say, even if they did have cell phones, they would have gone dead after a day because there was nowhere to plug them in, right? Nobody would have been able to film Hendrix Monday morning because they would have run out of juice. Anyway, good thing we didn't have to deal with that. [*turning to Rona*] I agree with you.

Rona Elliot: Well, I'm just very passionate. When I think about you guys [*speaking to the students in the audience*] and the struggle that you go through to try and succeed in this business, and that there's some jerk in the front row with the phone up, it takes something away from me, and of course that's my opinion. I know I sound like a dinosaur, but I have a deep respect for what you do.

I was at the funeral of a very famous tech guy and not a person had their phone out. And I thought there was a sufficient amount of respect in the room that people put their phones away. So people are capable of doing that, but they just generally don't. And there's a certain lack of consideration about the people around you, which is also very, very important for me. Music is a connector for me. So when you're there and have your cell phone up, you're not respecting the person who bought the ticket next to you.

Chip Monck: Point well said.

Rona Elliot: Sorry if I sound. . . . [*trailing off*]

Moderator: I was reading that many journalists wrote about Woodstock as [though] it could be compared to living through a war. Would you agree with that comment, or disagree?

23. Black and white photograph of the crowd and some of the scaffolding, with rain clouds and muddy ground. Photograph by Dan Garson.

MEDICAL ISSUES AT WOODSTOCK

Despite the preponderance of drugs at the festival, only twenty-eight of the reported seven hundred and forty-two drug overdoses required medical attention. Three deaths were recorded: an eighteen-year-old Marine on leave, named Richard Bieler, died of a suspected heroin overdose; another person died from a burst appendix; and Raymond Mizsak, a seventeen-year-old, was killed when he was run over by a tractor while sleeping on the side of the road.

Chip Monck: The point about a war is somebody lost and somebody won. A war wasn't what Woodstock was. Everybody walked away with something, and something that cannot be replaced. Henry's visuals are a courageous attempt, even when he went to fisheye [lens], because there was beauty in the structure.

Rona Elliot: Let me clarify the part of it that was a war for me. Well it's really what Chip said, "Everyone walked away with something good." But I was on the staff, and there was a young man off the property who went to sleep under a tractor and died. The tractor driver took the tractor away.

Chip Monck: [*interjecting*] Because the guy needed the tractor the next day.

Rona Elliot: As a staff member, my sense of responsibility for the people who were there, who came as young kids just like me, was enormous. And my sense of responsibility in terms of being an adult. What else could I do to make sure that that didn't happen again? And in that sense I became extremely vigilant. So, yes, I agree completely with Chip. But in terms of how I process this after the level of responsibility that you have to have when you undertake mounting something, whether it's a convention or a Rolling Stone [*sic*] show, you have to take it extremely seriously. You have hundreds of thousands of people's lives in your hands. So that's all.

Chip Monck: [*turning to Henry*] Henry, will you please say something?

Henry Diltz: What was the question?

Rona Elliot: Was it a war?

Henry Diltz: Oh. gosh, no. There was an ordeal part to it, but it was peace and love and brotherhood, and everyone dealt with the weather and the lack of food and stuff, and had a great time. There wasn't a winner and a loser; everybody left with something. Chip answered that question perfectly. I can't really add to that. I mean it didn't seem like a war to me.

Rona Elliot: Could you tell the story about Pete Townshend and Abbie Hoffman?[9]

Henry Diltz: Oh, there was a funny incident where Abbie Hoffman wanted to get on stage to say something.

Rona Elliot: [*interjecting and addressing the audience*] Do you guys know who Abbie Hoffman is, Chicago Seven?[10]

Henry Diltz: One of the Yippies.

Rona Elliot: Political protester.

Henry Diltz: Anyway, he wanted to jump on stage and grab the mic and tell the crowd that they should let the Chicago Seven out of jail or something like that, and he wanted to do that, and he wasn't going to be allowed to do it.[11] So one afternoon, they were introducing the Who, who would go on later at night, but I remember the Who were standing right at the front of the stage; I was right behind them.[12]

Rona Elliot: [*interjecting*] Michael Lang finally told Abbie Hoffman he could talk.

---

[9] Pete Townshend (b. 1945) is an English guitarist, songwriter, and cofounder of the Who, a highly influential rock band in the 1960s.
[10] For more, see the sidebar in chapter 1, "The Chicago Democratic National Convention in 1968."
[11] Henry Diltz is conflating John Sinclair (b. 1941) with the Chicago Seven, likely because both parties were victims of politically motivated arrests in the late 1960s.
[12] The Who did not take the stage until daybreak.

Henry Diltz: Abbie ran out and grabbed the microphone and started saying, "Remember the Chicago Seven," and I was right behind Pete Townshend, who just very calmly picked up his guitar—it was resting on the ground—turned it over, and went *boom* right in the back of Abbie's head. [*mimics Pete Townshend stabbing Abbie Hoffman with the neck of a guitar*] You know, like, "Who is that guy? I don't know." Pete Townshend wasn't going to take that kind of shit from some mad crazy guy running out there.

Rona Elliot: [*aside*] He also won't talk about Woodstock.

Henry Diltz: So I thought he took care of it very neatly.

Rona Elliot: [*joking*] So it wasn't all "peace and love."

Henry Diltz: I was standing there with my camera, but it happened so fast I didn't take a picture. Years later Abbie Hoffman always used to say, "That never happened. If it happened, where's the photo? There were so many photographers." And I'm thinking that I'm the guy who didn't get the photo because I was standing right there. It was very dramatic.

Chip Monck: Did anybody to your knowledge take that photo?

Henry Diltz: No, I don't think there's a picture of it. It's in my head.

Moderator: Rona, why do you think Pete Townshend doesn't want to talk about Woodstock?

Chip Monck: He knew what the event was. It was not to become a political escapade.

Rona Elliot: Well, yes. And listen, these are just opinions, but I covered the twentieth anniversary of Woodstock for the *Today Show*, and I did a Woodstock 40 book. And every year it's like, "Hi Pete! Do you want to go do an interview?"

Henry Diltz: [*to Rona*] Did you ask him about Woodstock?

Rona Elliot: No! He doesn't want to talk about Woodstock.

Henry Diltz: Any part of Woodstock? Not just that incident?

Rona Elliot: None of it.

Chip Monck: Well, he walked out of his transport and stepped in cow shit up to his knees. A shame, but then he just turned to Michael Lang, and said, "I'll take cash, thank you," and he sat down. John Roberts called the banker; the banker arrived with a bag full of cash, and handed it to Mr. Townshend. And then Pete Townshend said, "I'll now consider whether I'm performing music or something else."[13]

Rona Elliot: Welcome to our world. These are the stories behind it. I do a lot of interviews. Maybe he's tired of talking about it. Maybe he wants to say crappy things about it. Maybe he's not interested in saying anything about it.

Chip Monck: It's just another gig. He's got a huge overhead.

Rona Elliot: Right, and you know there are people that are generous with their time. There are people who want to talk about things. There's no rhyme or reason to it. I certainly wouldn't try to get into Pete Townshend's head. But—

Chip Monck: [*interjecting*] You'd certainly not!

Rona Elliot: No, no! But always the way the conversation goes, someone will say, "I want to do something on Woodstock. I'm going to call Pete Townshend and get an interview." I say, "Good luck, okay, great, go for it." So I don't know the answer, but whatever it is, it's really irrelevant because so much of this is documented.

Chip Monck: Well, Roger Daltrey said it could be too warm for him to

---

[13] Michael Lang provides a different version of the story in chapter 1. According to him, the Who demanded to be paid upfront but were informed that was not possible. When they were given the options of either waiting until Monday to be paid or having a formal announcement made to the crowd about why the Who would not be taking the stage, the band changed their mind and agreed to perform.

perform. So we know when they ended up performing.[14]

Moderator: I have a question for you, Henry. How do you think being a musician helped you to be the photojournalist that you became?

Henry Diltz: Okay, not necessarily Woodstock but just . . . ?

Moderator: No, your career in general.

Henry Diltz: It helped a great deal, because I was a folk musician for five years before I ever picked up a camera, and I think musicians know how to hang out. When you're a musician, you work a couple hours in the evening, maybe. Maybe you go to bed at three or four, get up at noon. You don't have a nine-to-five job, so you know how to hang out. You hang out backstage, you hang out at recording studios, you hang out at the airport, you hang out in the van driving eight hours; you have a lot of downtime.

A lot of photographers are professional photographers. I didn't ever consider myself a professional, because I never went to photo school. I never meant to be a photographer. It was just something I liked to do, and still like to do it. But a lot of those guys were kind of pushy. They'd say, "Okay, I'm here to take the picture; stand over there, let me do my job."

Once, a record company said, "We want you to shoot the Red Hot Chili Peppers," but I didn't really know them. They gave me an all-access pass, and the guy from the record company said, "Just go in the dressing room. Just go in, and shoot." So I walked in the dressing room, and of course everybody stopped and turned around because they didn't know me. They're looking at me, and I just very quietly put my cameras down and sat down on the couch and didn't do anything. In a couple of minutes they were all doing what they were doing. And I could pick up my camera and take a picture. If I'd been another kind of photographer, I would've said, "Hey! The record company said I could come in here!" You get in their face. You have to be respectful of people's space, that's all. I like to be a fly on the wall. My Chinese animal is the tiger; the tiger in the bushes. I like to look at the other animals.

---

[14] Roger Daltrey (b. 1944) is an English singer who is a cofounder and lead singer of the Who. The Who started playing around 5:00 a.m. on Sunday morning (August 17). The full lineup from midnight Saturday until early morning Sunday was quite a murderer's row: the Grateful Dead, who finished around midnight; Creedence Clearwater Revival; Janis Joplin; Sly and the Family Stone; the Who; and Jefferson Airplane.

Rona Elliot: For Henry's book, I've interviewed about a hundred people that he took pictures of, and they all talk about hanging out with Henry, so that's one thing.[15] And to think that Henry is not a professional photographer, I beg to differ!

Chip Monck: Because it's not done the way it is professionally done, which is an invasion! On the other hand, Henry will say, "I'll sit there until such time as you ask me why I'm here. And then I'll tell you, 'I'd like to get a few snaps if it's possible. Would you prefer it on stage or may I do it while you're relaxing?'"

Rona Elliot: This is very important, what he's saying. There are a lot of photographers whose work you see, and you see the photographer in their work. And you don't see Henry, you see those people and their work. Henry does not insert himself into the picture.

Chip Monck: That's a blessing!

Henry Diltz: Thank you, thank you! I'm more interested in hanging out with people. I'm very interested in people, so having a camera is like a passport into people's lives for me.

Chip Monck: Well, you already have the visual in your head of what you think is possible?

Henry Diltz: Well, when I see it, you know? I don't have a preconceived notion of anything, ever!

Chip Monck: Attaboy! That's it! That's the thing that allows you entrance and accessibility.

Henry Diltz: That's right. Whatever happens!

Chip Monck: It's a polished way of life for you.

Rona Elliot: "Polished"?

---

[15] Henry Diltz, *California Dreaming: Memories & Visions of LA 1966–75* (Guildford: Genesis Publications Limited, 2007).

24. Black and white photograph of the stage at the base of the sloping field, showing the landscape of the area. Photograph by Henry Diltz.

Moderator: My next question is for Chip. What did it feel like for you when you took those steps out onto the stage and made the announcements in the beginning? What was that like? How did you feel at that moment?

Chip Monck: Horrified. My knees were knocking together. If I had the opportunity to think about the position that I was going to be given, the whole interaction between me and the audience would've been completely improper, inappropriate. This was, "Okay you are going to do this now," so I just started out quietly. The first thing I'd been asked to do was ask the audience to move. I said, "Even though you're settled in the mud nicely"—[*as an aside, jokingly*] or the cow shit, whichever you choose to call it—"we're going to ask you to pick up your things and I'm going to move you back ten major steps, because when the rest of the crowd arrives, you're going to find that the pressure moves you forward because we're on a downhill. . . ."

[*aside*] On that kind of ramp, it's like a raked theatre. "You're going to be pressured forward and you're going to spend your three days viewing a piece of plywood which is not exactly what I thought you would like, so let's

see what we can do about this. Would you mind picking everything up, and I'm going to count the steps backwards I'd like you to take. Then we'll take the two fence posts and the piece of clothesline that is your demarcation line, and ask you to stay behind that and fortify that for me." [*counting the steps*] "One, two . . ." [*adding what he was thinking at the time to himself, jokingly*] Holy fuck, they're doing it!

All of a sudden they became easily persuaded when it was something for their benefit, and that kind of became the whole thread of my relationship with them. I was paid $7,000 for my three months's involvement in 1969.

Rona Elliot: You see, many of the people here at Woodstock who worked on the crew had unusual personalities!

Chip Monck: Mainly fucked!

Moderator: So, many of our students here are enrolled in a course called Professional Development Seminar, and we talk a lot about learning from our challenges. I was hoping that you might share with our students what have been some challenges in your careers, and what you have done or what you've learned from those challenges.

Rona Elliot: I could start out because I have some practical things. As I said, there were no women on the air. I was working in the PR department at a fantastic radio station, the first underground station in San Francisco, KMPX.[16] There was this fantastic event that was going to be held at Goddard College, in Bennington [*sic*], Vermont, with [Ram Dass].[17] It was called the Alternative Media Conference, and I went to my boss and said, "I've been invited to the Alternative Media Conference and I'm going to go." He said, "We don't send girls on trips like that," and I said, "It's not a problem; I

---

[16] Run by Tom "Big Daddy" Donahue (1928–1975), KMPX (FM 95) was San Francisco's first freeform radio station. It began with just a few hours of rock programming, but as the spring of 1967 turned into the Summer of Love, KMPX quickly became a full-time rock and roll radio station, one of the first in the nation.

[17] Held in June 1970, the first Alternative Media Conference began as a class project at Goddard College in Plainfield, Vermont. It was the brainchild of Larry Yurdin, who invited over one thousand people working in the fields of alternative radio stations, newspapers, and video, in hopes of sparking a new free-form radio movement. Sponsored in part by Atlantic Records, the conference featured performances by Dr. John, Cactus, and the J. Geils Band, and a keynote speech by longtime Timothy Leary collaborator, Ram Dass (born Richard Alpert, 1931-2019).

don't work here anymore. I'm gone!" And as you can see, I am not shy, and I never was. I took a stand for myself, if I was passionate about it, but it wasn't always warmly accepted. But if my driver was music or something I believed in—I will get to professional development, but this is a story I want to tell because it's so critical to my personal development and my professional development.

So I faced many challenges. I finally got on the air and moved to New York. In 1984, I was working for NBC Radio in the entertainment division and on a network radio show. I did a daily show, and I was producing monthly shows and live satellite shows. Tina Turner came into my studio with her manager, Roger Davies [*glances knowingly at Chip*] an Australian. Fantastic people! And I was beside myself. When I was a young teenager, Tina Turner was my hero. I went to the people I was working with and I said, "I've never seen such a relationship"—this was at the beginning of her comeback—"between an artist and manager; there's something magical going on there." And I always knew—and this is something very important—when the magical parts of me were working, I always knew when it was the right thing.

So as the months went by, Tina was starting to have a comeback. I stayed in touch with her, she would come into 30 Rock, and *SNL* [*Saturday Night Live*], and I would always interview her and I would always promote her.[18] And I went to my bosses at NBC, and I said—and everyone please forgive me, this is what really happened—I said, "Listen, we're on the ground floor here with Tina Turner, and we should do an hour-long show with her and she'll do this with me because we have this relationship now." And my boss—and please forgive me, this is what he said—"She's old, she's a has-been, and she's Black." She was forty-five years old, and I was so fucking flabbergasted! All I could say was, "You didn't listen to the record." I mean, there were so many other things I could have said, but it was all there in the music.

I could see that in my foresight and my understanding of the direction that music was going, I was working around people who didn't have creativity and breadth of knowledge. They were in a structure at NBC, and a few months later they passed on the opportunity with Tina Turner, and that was a big mistake.

---

[18] "30 Rock" is shorthand for the address of the National Broadcasting Company, located at 30 Rockefeller Plaza in New York City, not to be confused with the television show of the same name starring Tina Fey.

Later I was doing a live show from Abbey Road with Duran Duran, a live radio broadcast, three days after "Do They Know It's Christmas?" came out, if you guys know that song by Band Aid. I got a glass pressing of the record, and I was in the ending-hunger community, so I knew a lot about the famine that they were singing about. At the end of the show, I asked Duran Duran to sign the record, with the idea that I would take it back to New York and somehow auction it off. This was before celebrity auctions. And their publicist was very concerned that this might look like Duran Duran was trying to take advantage of the situation. I said, "No, I'll find other people to sign this." And who was on the plane home with me? Larry Mullen [Jr.] and Adam Clayton of U2. So they signed and then I got Bono and The Edge to sign it.

So we held a press conference at the Hard Rock Cafe in New York with Bob Geldof, and I heard that Live Aid was gonna happen. I went back to my bosses and I said, "We can buy the rights; NBC can buy the rights to Live Aid. They're not even going to announce it for six months." And here's what they said, same guy: "People who don't have business cards won't be able to produce this show."

It blows my mind telling this story thirty years later, because I was working with people who didn't have a vision and who were working inside an institution in which they weren't willing to take a chance. And that day, I said to myself, "That's it for me." And I was in a rage, and I went home. I was in such a rage that I had a vision that night. I said—because I had a show at the Hard Rock [Cafe] with Paul Shaffer—"I'm going to ask Isaac Tigrett, the owner of the Hard Rock, 'Let's put the Hard Rock backstage, in Philadelphia and in London.'"[19] So I had lunch with Isaac the next day in New York, and I said, "Isaac, I want to go call Bob Geldof; it's going to cost you a half a million bucks." And he put the Hard Rock backstage at Live Aid in Philadelphia. For me. I could broadcast from there. ABC couldn't shut me down when they bought it.

The main lesson that it taught me was to follow my own lights, because those things, especially about Tina, then about Live Aid, these were the things that were important to me in my life. Her comeback story wasn't just her story: it was everyone's story of transformation and regeneration, and she was a woman who came from the bottom of the heap. Live Aid was people getting together to help other people; that's what Woodstock ended

---

[19] In both London and Philadelphia, the atmosphere of the Hard Rock Cafe was recreated for the backstage area of Live Aid. The walls were covered with guitars and papier-mâché gold records, helping the artists to relax before and after their sets.

BAND AID AND LIVE AID

In 1984, Bob Geldof, an Irish singer-songwriter, and Midge Ure, a Scottish musician, laid plans for a musical charity endeavor that was prompted by a BBC report about starving children in Ethiopia, which at the time was in the midst of a severe famine that lasted from 1983 to 1985. The resulting charity event was termed Band Aid, and the featured performers comprised a supergroup that recorded the single "Do They Know It's Christmas?" Geldof and Ure invited performers like Bono, Phil Collins, Boy George, George Michael, and Sting, among many others. The song was the number-one single of 1984 and raised more than $24 million toward famine relief.

The popularity of Band Aid spawned Live Aid, a dual concert held on July 13, 1985 and televised around the world. One concert took place at London's Wembley Stadium, and the other at Philadelphia's JFK Stadium, since demolished. The event is thought to have generated upwards of £150 million. The Wembley portion is most associated with a set by Queen, often labeled as the greatest live performance on record, while the JFK concert featured a number of band reunions, including the original Black Sabbath with Ozzy Osbourne, the Beach Boys with Brian Wilson, and the surviving members of Led Zeppelin.

---

up being. So in terms of my path, if it doesn't feel right, I don't do it. When I work with people who I know have a different way of looking at things, I recognize them, I can respect them, but often, I can't quite fit in.

[*addressing the students*] So I would just say to you going out there: at the beginning of your careers, you have to do everything. You have to do the filing, you have to clean the toilet, you have to do this, and you have to get the coffee. Whatever it is you have to do, you have to do it all. And then as you refine what your own personal skills are, make sure you use those. And make sure you love what you do, right? So those are my two really deep stories.

Moderator: Thank you!

Rona Elliot: You're welcome!

Moderator: How about you, Henry? Challenges?

Henry Diltz: Challenges?

Moderator: Any challenges in your career that you would like to share with our students?

Henry Diltz: You know, as a photographer in rock concerts, I am usually working for my friends, and I get an all-access pass and stuff. The biggest challenge I usually face is the security guys, because they're local wrestlers or something. So we had a big concert at the Forum [sic] called Peace Sunday, and all these groups were playing: Tom Petty, Jackson Browne, and Stevie Wonder. So many groups were playing this one afternoon.[20]

    I had an all-access pass and I was shooting, but I went backstage and I heard this announcement that coming on stage were Bob Dylan and Joan Baez, and I thought, "Wow! We need a picture of that!" I ran up front with my camera ready to shoot, and a big guy came up and said, "No photos!" I said, "Well, no, I'm the photographer, I've got the pass." The security guard said, "We were told no photos." Meanwhile, Bob Dylan and Joan Baez are playing up there and I said, "Look! This is Peace Sunday; we're talking about peace all over the world, and we want this message to get out all over the world. I'm the guy. There's Bob Dylan and Joan Baez singing about it."

Chip Monck: [*interjecting with an ominous voice*] No photos!

Henry Diltz: Yeah! "I'm the guy who's going to take the picture for other people to see, and you're the guy keeping that from happening!" You know? And he finally said, "Well okay. . . ."

Rona Elliot: I've never seen the picture!

Henry Diltz: I have a picture of Dylan and Joan! Anyway, for me, that's it. We're talking about how to overcome obstacles, right?

Moderator: Yeah! Any challenges you faced? What have you learned from it?

---

[20] Subtitled the "We Have a Dream" concert, Peace Sunday took place at the Rose Bowl on June 6, 1982. Performers included Gil Scott Heron, Stephen Stills, Stevie Wonder, Joan Baez, and Bob Dylan.

Henry Diltz: I read the Indian gurus, like [Paramahansa] Yogananda's book called the *Autobiography of a Yogi*, and now I read a guy named Swami Satchidananda.[21] In fact, he was at Woodstock! The guy in the orange robe and the white hair. Friends of mine were devotees of his, and they gave me a book of his sayings. Three hundred sixty-five sayings, and you read one each day. My favorite one is, "We know we're here to learn," speaking generally of course; [*pointing to the audience*] you're all here to learn. In life, we're all here to learn. Therefore, we're all students.

But you should think of yourself as the only student, and everybody else is your teacher. So everybody you ever see is really your teacher. If you just allow that to happen, it kind of changes the valence of things; it changes your life. And the people that give you the most hassle and the most trouble are your biggest teachers, because they're making you respond, they're making you learn, so really, when you think in your life of all the friends you've had in elementary school, in high school, in college, all those people have kind of been your teacher, they make you who you are. A little bit of—I am a little bit of you, Rona!

Rona Elliot: I'll tell you a story about this! Henry is my teacher. So I'm working on Henry's book, and I'm interviewing all these musicians, and this one famous musician won't give me a quote about Henry. It is somebody Henry has worked with a lot. Henry could care less; he's so mellow. Henry says, "It's okay. . . ." I said, "Henry, you shot a million of this guy's album covers. I'm not asking to interview him." I am in a rage ten years later. This guy wouldn't give me a quote about generous Henry, and Henry is like "It's okay, just let it go!" So Henry is my teacher, right?

Henry Diltz: You have to let the universe decide.

Rona Elliot: Right!

---

[21] Paramahansa Yogananda, *Autobiography of a Yogi* (New Dehli, India: Global Vision Publishing House, 2021). First published in 1946, *Autobiography of a Yogi* describes Yogananda's (1893–1952) path to becoming a notable Indian guru. He was especially influential in the United States. The book has sold more than four million copies, and Yogananda was hosted at the White House in 1927.

Henry Diltz: My friend Stanley Moss is a lovely fellow.[22] At one time, I was saying, "Stanley, what if we go there and they're not ready, and then this doesn't happen?" And I'm kind of all in a flutter, worried about something. And he said, "Henry, why don't we just let the universe decide?" And you know, you've heard that before, but at that moment I just went, "Ahhhh . . . Of course!" And those words echo in my head. "Everybody is my teacher" and "just let the universe decide." And we're all different. Chip, you're a guy who is very . . . I mean, you have a contingency plan. You're very detailed.

Chip Monck: [*agreeing*] I delight in nuts and bolts because they don't talk back.

Rona Elliot: And that's why you want him putting up the stage.

Henry Diltz: That's right, yeah! And I'll just be there taking pictures. Let the universe decide!

Rona Elliot: Introducing people to each other.

Henry Diltz: God made us all different, you know? And hopefully we'd share . . . So we are.

Chip Monck: So far, we're getting along.

Moderator: Love it!

Chip Monck: It's been fifty years now!

Moderator: Before I turn the mic over to the students for questions: Rona, did you want to say something else about professional development?

Rona Elliot: Well, I would just say—The reason I'll say something is it's been harder for women along the way, particularly women in the music business. As I said before, women were usually girlfriends or groupies or backup singers, and I think even in the last year of the Me Too movement,

---

[22] Stanley Moss (b. 1948) is an American author, poet, and publisher. His book, *The New Wave Cookbook*, published in New York in 1980, is part of the permanent collection at the Museum of Modern Art in New York City.

and all the things that have happened with the many many record producers and film producers, I think you just have to be very firm and take a stand and keep your eye on the ball about what you're there for.[23] It used to be when I was on the *Today Show*, that people would say, "Oh, have you slept with any musicians?" And I said, "No, I am really happily married." Actually, today is my thirty-eighth anniversary, and I'm with you! Thank you!

I was there to find out about the music. So once you can focus in, just stick to your guns, and along the way, I've had to do many many things I haven't loved. But I think in the end, I have had a number of dream jobs. For instance, I am on the board of the Rock & Roll Hall of Fame. I am really interested personally in imparting wisdom and information, as all of us are, including Michael Lang and the other people that will be here for the conference. If you need guidance, email me.

I think it's hard now, I think the situation is different; you put your resume up on Indeed and you never even get an interview. I always felt that if I could meet somebody in person I could sell myself, but you may not even have that opportunity, so you have to be very vigilant and very consistent, and remember what you're there for. Give it a shot, and give yourself a couple of years to find your dream and express it, and see what the universe returns to you. I tell my children the same thing.

Moderator: Thank you! Let's take some questions from the audience.

Audience: Hi! This question is directed to Mr. Diltz. I read that you were involved in the Eagles' first album photography, where the guys went out to the desert. And I read that it was pretty chaotic. At the time that you were shooting the picture, did you realize that something amazing was happening? Because that is a very beautiful and very famous picture, the one in the inlay of the Eagles album. It's like this magic, iconic photograph that comes out of chaos. Did that happen frequently in your career? Did you know it was happening at the time? Can you give us any other examples?

Henry Diltz: You're talking about Eagles' first album? In the desert?

---

[23] The Me Too movement gained attention in the fall of 2017 when accounts of sexual harassment and assault were published, centering on Harvey Weinstein and Kevin Spacey. These reports inspired other victims to speak out with new allegations coming in the fields of politics, entertainment, news, and sports, among others.

25. Black and white photograph of the Eagles standing beside a cactus in Joshua Tree National Park. Photograph by Henry Diltz.

Audience: Yes! That's the one I'm talking about.

Henry Diltz: That wasn't chaotic. I work with a graphic designer and between us we agreed we should always try to take the group on an adventure to get them away from town, away from their managers, and away from their girlfriends so we could have their attention. And so we decided to take the Eagles out and spend the night in the desert so we could shoot all that stuff around the campfire and shoot the next morning. We were there a day and a half. Chaotic, I don't know; I'm not sure what that means!

Audience: I did read that there were some hallucinogens involved.

Henry Diltz: Oh, yeah, we had peyote buttons![24] The Indian medicine man had given us a whole bunch of dried peyote buttons which we made tea out of, and drank the tea. It wasn't chaotic: we kind of laughed. We were laughing at everything, and we had a pretty good time. Peyote buttons in

---

[24] Peyote buttons are found on a small cactus plant native to Mexico and the southern United States. The top of the shoots, known as the "button," is traditionally used for religious purposes, but in the 1960s they became popular as a hallucinogen.

the desert are good because they are desert plants. I remember at one point sitting as the sun was setting. The sun was setting, and next to me was a cactus plant, the kind with all those little tails and little things sticking up.

Chip Monck: [*interjecting*] Saguaro.

Henry Diltz: And I looked at him [the saguaro]—it's a living thing, I could feel the life of this plant—and I said, "Wow, you guys are so lucky! You get to sit up here every day and watch the sun come up and go across the desert," [*mimes the sun rising and setting*] and I really felt a camaraderie because I was high on cactuses . . . And I think it was that way for everybody.

Rona Elliot: Who was there!

Henry Diltz: Yeah! Glenn Frey, who had his pants down doing something, saw an eagle and yelled "Eagle!" And he ran and he was pulling his pants up and running. And then Don Henley said, "No, it was a hawk." But my partner, my designer partner said, "It was a crow." [*laughs*] So my job was to take photos of everything that was happening, which is what I wanted to do anyway. Gary would say, "Just photograph everything that happens. Film is the cheapest part!"[25] I would photograph it all anyway. And then Gary would look through it all, and pick out the one that was used. He had an unerring eye to pick out the good photo.

Chip Monck: Depends what lens you're looking through, I suppose.

Rona Elliot: Yes, always.

Henry Diltz: Yeah, in life you mean? [*everyone laughs*]

Audience: Hi, I was wondering in terms of Woodstock 50, how much involvement you guys had, or [what] advice did the people who are in charge of it now asked you for? Do they come to you and ask your expertise on any of that?

Rona Elliot: They'll be here [at Berklee]! They're landing!

---

[25] Gary Burden (b. 1933).

Henry Diltz: Michael Lang, who is the producer of it, and also did one in 1994, one in 1999, he's doing this one. And I'm going to be there taking photos again!

Chip Monck: Yeah, I mean there are certain levels of our involvement. Some negotiated, some not, some hoped, you know? We'll see what happens. It really depends on Michael Lang, who is our leader this time as he was before. We'll see what happens.

Rona Elliot: We will!

Audience: And to follow up, what are your thoughts on the Watkins Glen location being added for this summer?

Chip Monck: Well, it's a reasonable choice. The best thing that you could do is go to a legitimate facility for plumbing, for toiletry, for accommodation, for the acreage that it has, for the permit that it has. You're not going to be interrupted by any number of different areas that could be.

Rona Elliot: Parking, safety, etc.

Chip Monck: Yeah, plus the fact that there was a six-hundred-and-sixty-thousand people adventure there with CSN [Crosby, Stills & Nash], the Allman Brothers, and The Band.[26] I mean, it's a tried and true adventure. A bit out of the way, though: you fly through Detroit or Rochester.

Audience: I'll be at Watkins though. I am very excited!

Chip Monck: Oh wonderful! It's a very diverse, fine lineup. We'll see how it is accepted by the people who buy tickets. We have no idea what the ticket price is. Michael has not decided to make that public yet. He's just signed a group that is going to do a Hendrix hologram—reasonably adventurous. We'll see what happens. It really is one of those sorts of

---

[26] It is estimated that over six hundred thousand people came to Summer Jam, an outdoor festival modeled on Woodstock that took place on July 28, 1973, at the Watkins Glen Grand Prix Raceway in New York. The festival featured the Grateful Dead, The Band, and the Allman Brothers, each of whom played multiple hour-long sets. The concert concluded with an encore jam with musicians from all three bands.

things. It goes on and on and on until somebody makes the decision, and it's not necessarily us.

Audience: Hi, my question is about drugs and alcohol, and whether you think that that has hindered you or informed your career?

Rona Elliot: I will answer because I have the least to say. I don't drink; never did. I had a beer once: it made me want to pee and go to sleep, so that was the extent of my drinking career. I wasn't much of a druggie. I mean, I tried all the drugs you were supposed to try, the mandatory drugs of the 1960s: grass and LSD. And by 1970, I was meditating, and that was the extent of my drug and alcohol career. [*looks at Chip and Henry*] Some of us have other answers!

Chip Monck: In Monterey, unfortunately, I asked for a purple tab, which is an upper, because that's what we were taking in London. When I was on the way to Monterey to do the lighting, I got purple haze instead, and that was a little difficult for the film, because for the next hour and a half, it was all red![27] So that was a bit of a challenge, and Art Garfunkel said, "Oh my heavens! We're going to do the next ballad in red!" It got in the way but . . . It just got in the way. Period. Usually does.

Any alteration from the program that you have set for yourself or for the adventure is problematic. You're not allowed to leave that, really, and that was totally unintentional, but Laura Nyro was to drop her wrist in order to cause a blackout and I said, "I was wondering what she is doing that for!" Doesn't work very well![28]

Henry Diltz: Drugs and alcohol haven't hurt the Rolling Stones . . . It depends on who you are, really! I mean, gosh, I would say in the 1960s, we

---

[27] Purple haze is a strain of cannabis. Chip Monck's reference is most likely to Monterey Purple, a form of LSD created by Owsley Stanley.

[28] Laura Nyro (1947–1997) was an American singer-songwriter who performed at the Monterey Pop Festival on June 17, 1967. The covers of her songs are better known than the originals, including Three Dog Night's version of "Eli's Coming," and Barbra Streisand's cover of "Stoney End." The motion referenced here, a sharp drop of her hand, was a signal to the light operator [Chip Monck] to turn the lights off at the end of her performance. Monck had trouble recognizing her cue because of the drug-induced haze he described above.

all smoked pot. We called it "grass." I call it "God's herb" now, because it's such a good thing and it makes you relax a little bit. I mean, the point is to expand your mind a little bit; it accentuates your senses a little bit. Seeing and hearing, it can do that. But like fine wine—I mean you can drink a glass of wine and feel really good, but if you drink a couple of bottles, you're not going to be very useful. Same with smoking! I mean, I hear the young kids now, or a couple years ago, saying, "We're going to smoke out" and get totally wasted. I think that is ridiculous and a waste of your time and energy. It can be a useful tool, just like wine.

Sometimes I say, "How do you think all that music happened in the 1960s and 1970s?" I have a photo gallery with some friends, and I had all my pictures in there one day, and a guy came in and looked through it and he said, "Did you ever smoke pot with any of these people?" I looked around and I said, "Every single one of them." We lived in Laurel Canyon; that was a part of being a musician; it was not a big deal! But then I watched some groups get really rich and famous and started using the white powders like cocaine, which I found was a terrible thing. That didn't increase your artistic feeling at all; it just made you rev your motor, and the next day you felt awful.

Chip Monck: Yeah, it's like a pattern of concentric circles. You just do it over and over and over again and it's very painful.

Rona Elliot: Well, I would also say if you look through the history of music, going back certainly into jazz, that drugs and alcohol have been an albatross around some of our greatest musicians. A lot of people our age, old hippies that we may be, they are pretty clean and sober. Mick Jagger dances four hours a day—not this week when he's having heart surgery—and drinks green juice every morning. Keith Richards, for the most part, is pretty sober. I'd say a great deal of the people we know are clean and sober. Everybody goes to AA [Alcoholics Anonymous] meetings in LA to meet famous rock stars.

I think there's a long history of abuse, but for me it goes back to a more spiritual place. If you don't know who you are, if you want to go unconscious, drugs and alcohol are a perfect way. I'm not in any way negating what Henry has said, but the abuse in 1971 with Janis Joplin, Jimi Hendrix, Jim Morrison, John Entwistle, Keith Moon, John Bonham... I mean, the list is endless!²⁹ So I think you have to look at the long-term effects and whose contribution, whose musical contribution sustains itself without that.

Moderator: All right! I think we have a question at the back?

Audience: I'm wondering about trends you've noticed in the past decades in festival and tour management, and whether you think the evolution is positive or negative, and how you expect to see it going in the future?

Chip Monck: To tell you the truth, I have no idea where it's going. I don't know if it's any better or if it's as stringent as it was for us. We had an advance trip, which is seldom done, I understand, these days. An advance trip was not only the hall, the placement of the stage, the rigging that would be necessary, the amount of power that you got to use, the division between the lighting and instruments so there wasn't any buzz . . . All of that sort of individual separation. Then you got to the hotel, and you got to the room assignments, and you got to the dressing room assignments and all of that sort of shit. I mean, we would do that in a period of maybe six hours per city, and we would go stringently through the entire listing or itinerary of the event.

I don't know if that's taken anymore, in that fashion, in that sort of pedantic method that we had. I have no idea what's happening presently. My present situation is that I'm doing the lights for a hotel in Melbourne, which requires me to interface with fifty-some-odd people, mostly architects that have no idea how to make something exciting as you walk into the entry of a hallway or into a room or a group of rooms. Basically not light the place you are in, but draw you into whatever section you wish to draw them into. I am doing the same thing: I'm taking people and moving them

---

²⁹ By 1971, rampant drug abuse had claimed the lives of many prominent rock musicians, the most famous of whom all died at the age of twenty-seven. Brian Jones (d. July 3, 1969), drowned in his pool after having been fired from the Rolling Stones one month earlier; Jimi Hendrix (d. September 18, 1970) asphyxiated while intoxicated from sleeping pills; and both Janis Joplin (d. October 4, 1970) and Jim Morrison (d. July 3, 1971) died from accidental heroin overdoses. Despite years of documented drug and alcohol abuse, the Who's John Entwistle and Keith Moon, as well as Led Zeppelin's John Bonham, all survived their twenty-seventh year but still died young. Moon and Bonham both died at the age of 32; Entwistle lived until he was 57.

to a place where I think they'll function realistically, if not comfortably. But I don't know how the music business and the actual touring works anymore.

Rona Elliot: Both Henry and I went to—I called it "Oldchella" or "AARP-chella"—the week that Bob Dylan got his Nobel Prize in Literature nomination [in 2016]; it was the Stones, and Bob, and the Who, and Roger Waters, and Neil Young.[30] I know because I've travelled and I've talked to people, that a lot of young people want "their" Woodstock, whatever that means. They want "their" Woodstock.

As festivals and events have unfolded, it's organized in a different way than before. You buy your tickets online, you buy your VIP parking passes, you buy your locker. Your tickets cost a fortune, but people go wanting to have a certain kind of experience, hence they bought tickets to the Fyre Festival.[31] But Bonnaroo, Coachella, Burning Man, Outside Lands, all of these festivals, because of Woodstock, people are going anticipating a certain kind of experience.[32] As the technology has gotten better—now you scan your ticket and your parking on your phone—it has a big role in it that it didn't before, and I think that technology will continue to play a larger and larger role. When I was at Oldchella, there were eighty thousand people behind me because we were in the front, and I was nervous because there were eighty thousand people behind me.

Chip Monck: [*interjecting*] Don't take a step forward!

Rona Elliot: No, I didn't take a step forward. And Bob Dylan that day wouldn't let anybody put his image on the video screens because he's Bob Dylan, and he said, "No video screens." So those poor people, eighty thousand of them behind me, they couldn't see him; they could probably barely hear him. So then I think to myself, "What is this about?" I had VIP passes,

---

[30] Rona Elliot is mocking the average age of Coachella performers during the week of October 13, 2016.

[31] Created by promoter Billy McFarland and rapper Ja Rule, the infamous Fyre Festival (2017) was meant to be a luxury event on a secluded island, but it turned out to be a massive fraud for which McFarland was sentenced to six years in jail. The supposedly luxury accommodations were actually FEMA-issued tents, and the "authentic Bahamian" food was merely plain sandwiches served in styrofoam.

[32] Bonnaroo Music & Arts Festival, in Manchester, Tennessee; Coachella Valley Music and Arts Festival, in Indio, California; Burning Man, in Black Rock Desert, Nevada; Outside Lands, in San Francisco, California.

along with Henry, and private toilets to go into. All those people in back, they had general toilets.

For me, it was a great musical show, and people want to be a part of that, and they wanted to be a part of a community. I wanted to be a part of it. I worked at Woodstock, and I wanted to be there with these six supergroups. But if Bob Dylan turned off the video—no one is going to tell Bob to turn on the video, believe me—then what is this experience? It's a little removed from the music; it is an experience, even though everyone still has their phones. But I think when you're in a field with eighty thousand people in that kind of setting, I think it's a little bit different now because the technology has kind of changed it. I think it'll continue to unfold in a way that the technology plays a larger and larger part, because now some people don't have to go at all, and you can stream the whole thing and sit in your living room.

Audience: I have a bit of a personal question for Rona. You've talked a little bit about the adversity you've faced as a woman, especially in this industry, and specifically as a journalist. Have you ever conducted an interview with someone who was blatantly dismissive of you because you were a woman?

Rona Elliot: I made a point of always letting the publicists and the people from the record companies know that this was a musical interview and that I wasn't particularly interested in asking anybody who they were sleeping with, what their drug problems were or weren't. I've interviewed some people who were just incredibly dull, believe it or not; it's shocking that they could sing, but be so dull otherwise. Not dismissive of me because I was a woman: there are people who are just dismissive of other human beings, and you wonder how can they sing such good songs when they're just such nasty human beings.

Actually the one that comes to mind was a woman who had a band member die, 'and she said, "It's so banal." And I thought, "What?" It was fairly shocking. But I can roll with the punches, I really can, and anything that anybody can come up with. I once did an interview with somebody who was so coked out that every ten minutes he'd get up and say, "I have to go blow my nose." He said he was sick, and I was so naive at the time, and he couldn't string together a sentence.

Generally speaking, I wasn't dismissed because I was a woman. At the time I was doing journalism that doesn't exist right now, except on *60 Minutes*. Most of it today is, "What are you wearing?" and "Who are your girlfriends?" That has nothing to do with the music. When I talked to Eric Clapton, I said, "How do you do that? Where does 'Layla' come from?" I try to remove any of the obstacles. As noisy as I am up here, when I do an interview I am almost silent, and I am just being. The people that were the problem were in the management, not the artists.

Audience: Woodstock seemed like really relaxed, chill people, and now in the music industry a lot of it doesn't seem to be people who are down to earth. What do you think about that?

Henry Diltz: What's not down to earth?

Rona Elliot: Is the music industry down to earth now?

Audience: A lot of people in the music industry now. It seems at Woodstock you really had the right purpose, and spiritual purpose as well. Ravi Shankar was playing at Woodstock.[33] [*to Henry*] You mentioned meditation and you mentioned reading a lot of Indian gurus. I don't see that as much in popular music right now, and I wanted to know what you think about that.

Henry Diltz: Once I asked Jackson Browne—we were talking about how everybody would ask me what was so great about the 1960s and the 1970s—and I asked Jackson that question once on the phone. He said, "Because it was new! It was new! There had never been a Woodstock before." A lot of that was new. The 1960s and 1970s were a big renaissance and a flowering of singer-songwriters. Before that there were songwriters and there were singers: Frank Sinatra never wrote any songs; Elvis Presley never wrote any songs. There were the people who wrote the songs and there were people that sang the songs. And then something happened in the 1960s with the Beatles and Bob Dylan. The Beatles didn't write their own songs at first: they sang "Roll Over Beethoven" and "Blue Suede Shoes," and then they started writing their own songs.[34]

---

[33] Ravi Shankar (1920–2012) was an Indian sitar virtuoso, whose influence on George Harrison, the lead guitarist for the Beatles, brought awareness of the sitar and Indian classical music more generally across the world.

[34] Both songs were covered by many artists, including the Beatles. "Roll Over Beethoven" was written and released by Chuck Berry in 1956; the Beatles later covered it on their second album, *With the Beatles* (1963). "Blue Suede Shoes" was written and recorded by Carl Perkins in 1955. Its most famous cover is by Elvis Presley, released in September 1956. The Beatles also performed it in their early stage shows.

26. Black and white photograph of Ravi Shankar playing the sitar. Photograph by Henry Diltz.

We were folk singers, and we saw them doing that, singing their own songs, and we said, "Why are we singing about the ox driver now? We could be singing 'She Loves You' [*sings the first few notes of the Beatles song*] or some original song like that. We loved their energy and the fact that they were singing their own feelings, rather than some one-hundred-year-old song. So that was a brand new thing; that was a big sea change in the industry. People like Joni Mitchell, Neil Young, Jackson Browne, James Taylor, and Paul Simon all started writing their own songs. That was different from the way it had been done before.

Rona Elliot: I'll give you my philosophical and spiritual take. For a lot of us, certainly for myself being brought up in a family after World War II and the Holocaust and all of those terrible things, our generation was the "peace and love" generation, and music was the glue that connected us. It was powerful; it was full of love. I think that someone like George Harrison, because he was a spiritual devotee, took the Beatles to Rishikesh, India, in 1968, hoping that they would learn to meditate, and he was a student of

Ravi Shankar's as well.[35] The way I see it is that George used his music as a pied piper to open the door to spirituality. Because George opened that door, and Swami Satchidananda the next year was at Woodstock, now fifty years later people walk down the street with their yoga mats and talk about mindfulness all the time. This is my particular take.

In my reality this is true, that this was George's soul's purpose, while he brought us "While My Guitar Gently Weeps" and some of the most exquisite music in the world. The Beatles moved our hearts and souls, and we came in to talk about peace and love. I appreciate that you can see us that way, but that was our generation's contribution. I've thought about this a lot, because I have kids who are your age, and I say, "if music was the glue that brought us together," however Chip expresses it in his perfect, intricate, engineering way. I want to share music and Henry can share his photography. Kids say to me, "Oh, we missed Woodstock; we don't have our Woodstock."

[*to the audience*] So what's your job? I think that what you have, what is particular to your generation, is this technology which connects you. When Steve Jobs died, there were flowers at his stores all over the world, and people posting pictures. And I thought, "What they have is that they're connected through technology." So this, I believe, is what is in front of you, to somehow use music and art, but technology is the way you guys are going to do it. We did it a different way; this was our way.

When I look out at the thing that dominates your lives now, the great part is the connectedness. And the fact that now, if something terrible is going on somewhere in the world, you can see it. It's instant. So something about that—the connectedness, the technology, the music—will be part of your healing process. Woodstock was ours. "Peace, love" was ours. It's outdated in a way, now. Not the ideas, but we're not going to manifest it. A half a million people at a concert. Now we're going to Watkins Glen because there are toilets!

If I were talking to you or my own kids, or my interns at home, I would say that considering that technology is a big part of your life, it is *the* part of your life, and you're artists and you're musicians and you're technicians, the

---

[35] The Beatles first met Maharishi Mahesh Yogi (1918–2008) in late August 1967 at one of his seminars on Transcendental Meditation. After a few additional meetings, the Beatles were convinced to visit Rishikesh, India, where the Maharishi kept his retreat. Although the visit was generally viewed as a disappointment by the Beatles themselves, they were nonetheless productive, writing most of the material that comprised their ninth studio album, known as *The White Album* (1969).

challenge is going to be the delivery system for the connectedness and the spirituality in some way. That's important to me; it may not be relevant to you. The biggest part of your life now is technology. So I don't know if that answers your question, but that's how I look at it. Don't mean to get heavy on you guys!

Chip Monck: I think that technology is a conduit, but I don't know if you are going to be able to express those feelings through that conduit. That's kind of up to you as individuals in how you treat it. I don't shy away from it, but I think that it is a very interesting question. You've got all of this available to you, and I'd really be interested in how you're going to use it. I've got no answers.

Rona Elliot: I didn't mean to get too philosophical, dudes and dudettes.

Audience: When Woodstock first happened, it seems like it was a largely counterculture movement of the time, and a lot of the essence of the message and the movement was rooted in that counterculture vibe. Now it has become something that is so widely nostalgic and very mainstream. How do you think that that has affected the message in the way that it is received by people who are getting this second-hand experience of Woodstock now?

Rona Elliot: That is a great question, and I've been living in that one for a long time, because people want "their" Woodstock, and they want to have that experience. They can't have that experience; that experience is gone. There are a lot of urban myths and legends. This is my experience, having spent many, many years thinking about Woodstock, and so they'll never go back and have that experience. And I've heard many people tell me what Woodstock was about before they ever knew I was there, and it has nothing to do with what happened. There were four hundred and fifty thousand people there who had different experiences. I think when something gets culturally appropriated, to use the current expression, it takes on a life of its own.

There's no question that people will go to Woodstock 50 having an intention to have a certain kind of experience, as Henry described, about being the "mud people" or this or that, or things that capture what they think is the spirit of what originally happened. And I think it's in Michael Lang's intention, and certainly mine and Henry's, and I am sure Chip's, to keep—and I know because Michael and I have discussed this at length—the actual spirit alive. It just so happens that because this is the fiftieth year and there is social activism because of the president that we have [Donald Trump], it mirrors the times of 1969 in a lot of ways. So Michael Lang is intending to put a lot of social justice issues in, to book different bands, and to make sure the spirit of the time mirrors what is appropriate for now.

If you look at the Woodstock audience, and I've had a lot of conversations about this, it looks mostly White but it's not completely White. There were a lot of diverse people at the original Woodstock, but you don't see them as much. If you think about what was going on in the tristate area and getting to the Catskills area in New York, you needed a car. Who had cars? Kids in the tristate area had cars. Not that many Black kids had cars at the time. It might have been more difficult to get to Woodstock. You could take a Peter Pan bus or a Trailways bus, so part of it was dictated by the times. All the women on the staff—the "girls"—we had secondary and third positions. That's the way it was.

I know that Michael is thinking about how to make it relevant for the issues of today and not make it a nostalgia show. None of us would want that. I certainly wouldn't want that. You cannot go back anyway; you can't ever go back. Half the people are dead, if not more than half the people are dead. And there are people who deserve a chance to take a stand and share their voice today, and that's what Woodstock was about: sharing your voice. So I think that is very much something that Michael Lang is in touch with. People will still have their preconceived notions: "I'm going to Woodstock," or "I bought a T-shirt," or whatever they do.

Chip Monck: It just seems to be an incredibly difficult booking situation, choosing artists on behalf of you with possibly not having any true indication of how you get your interest or how you secure your interests, and possibly arrive there with an interest in seeing an act or all of it. Most often I find booking to be sort of a catch-as-catch-can thing. I think this is going to be interesting in as much as seeing how Michael Lang is approaching this issue.

Rona Elliot: He got a raft of crap for some of the bookings he did last week, and everybody has an opinion.[36] "Why'd you book this one?" and "Why'd

---

[36] On March 19, 2019, Michael Lang and the organizers of Woodstock 50 announced an eclectic list of artists that were scheduled to perform. Rap artists like Jay-Z and Chance the Rapper and pop artists like Miley Cyrus drew mostly negative headlines. For more, see the sidebar in chapter one, "Woodstock 50."

you book that one?" and he just said, as Michael would, "You got to chill out." So nobody's going to be happy all the time; everybody comes to these things with their ideas about it, instead of being in the experience.

Chip Monck: That's the best way to entice people to come: "Chill out."

Rona Elliot: That's Michael.

Chip Monk: Yes, it's very much Mr. Lang. The only time you know that he's thinking is when he does this, [*mimes his hands shaking*] and that's a period when you stop talking and let him think.

Rona Elliot: I think that that question is really really relevant. It's a really good question—

Chip Monck: [*interjecting*] I don't know how you answer it.

Rona Elliot: —well, because people want a part of that experience, and that's not what this is; it's not what anything is. You know, *The Incredibles 2*, but it's not *The Incredibles*. *Toy Story 4* is not the original *Toy Story*.

Chip Monck: We'll be able to reminisce about what it is when it's finished, or while you make it. However you choose. It's very interesting.

Rona Elliot: It is.

Moderator: Thank you for this experience!

CHAPTER 4

PLAYING WITH JIMI HENDRIX

Sunday, April 7, 2019, 12:00–12:30 p.m. EDT
David Friend Recital Hall at Berklee College of Music
Boston, Massachusetts

Participants:
Gerardo Velez, percussionist

Moderated by Deborah Bennett, associate professor of liberal arts, Berklee College of Music

Moderator: I'd like to welcome to the stage Gerardo Velez, who many of you know was the percussionist in Gypsy Sun and Rainbows with Jimi Hendrix. But he has also played with a lot of luminaries in rock and jazz: Spyro Gyra, David Bowie, Elton John, Duran Duran, and my favorite, Chaka Khan! As a multiplatinum recording artist and seven-time Grammy nominee, he has a secure place in the pantheon of rock gods, and we are so glad to have him here with us today! *Bienvenido, Gerardo!*

Gerardo Velez: Thank you, *muchísimas gracias!*

Moderator: I don't know how many people know this, but your twenty-second birthday was very special; I'm wondering if you can tell us about it.

Gerardo Velez: So, I'm twenty and I meet Jimi Hendrix.[1] We're hanging out, playing music, recording every night, and we're jumping into his car. He had a beautiful, scalloped Corvette, but he only had a learner's permit. And he was like Mr. Magoo on the road.[2] I made it through the first two years with him, and then he started to discuss a new chapter of music for him and a new way of using his instrument, to change the sound that he made and did. And then he said, "I'm doing this show that they're going to have upstate. I'm getting a house; let's go up there and start to make music." It was at least six months before the Woodstock Festival. And my twenty-second birthday was at Woodstock, and it was also my first professional show.

Jimi always had ten thousand dollars in cash on him at all times. Back then there weren't credit cards, so either you had a checkbook or you carried cash. And he would—he had this thing with fringe on it, of course—and he would put it on the ground and then later ask, "Awww, where's my bag?" Sometimes he would lose his bag. To play with a guy like Jimi was very easy because he was a very easy-going guy.

My first professional gig was at Woodstock. It was my birthday, and I just wanted to go sideways. I wanted my career to just go to the left or to the right, but it went like, "Ahhhhhhhh. . . ." [*mimes looking over a cliff, then falling to the bottom*] and that's when I learned how to come back up and be a real musician, and I pride myself in learning that way.

When I was playing with Jimi, I learned how to play from playing with records. I was never really in an official band, and I'd jam with a lot of people, including my sister Martha Velez.[3] Martha had five records out, she was in the original cast of *Hair*, and her husband [Keith Johnson] was the musical director for a guy named Paul Butterfield, an incredible harp [harmonica]

---

[1] Gerardo Velez (b. 1947) met Jimi Hendrix two years prior to Woodstock.

[2] Mr. Magoo was a cartoon character who was a notoriously bad driver, owing to his extreme near-sightedness. Oblivious to the danger, he was frequently depicted weaving in and out of traffic.

[3] Martha Velez (b. 1945) is the older sister of Gerardo Velez. She is a singer, having recorded with Eric Clapton and Bob Marley, among others. She is also an actress on stage, having performed in the original Broadway production of *Hair*, and on television, most notably on the show *Falcon Crest* (1989).

player.[4] Keith was also Van Morisson's musical director. Martha's first album was with Eric Clapton, Mitch Mitchell, Brian Auger, and Jim Capaldi, I mean the best from England.[5] And her third album was produced by Bob Marley, and it's his only non-Jamaican production. It's called *Escape from Babylon*; check it out!

But anyway, my sister lived in Woodstock with her husband, and I used to travel up there, so I was going up to Woodstock before the festival happened. It was teeming with musicality and creativity because originally the town of Woodstock was an art community and not a music community. So that's how the town got its reputation. Then Michael [Lang] decided to do the Woodstock Festival and the town of Woodstock turned on him, which is why it happened at White Lake. But he kept the name and that's why it was called the Woodstock Festival at White Lake, in Bethel.

Moderator: Sounds like quite a birthday!

Gerardo Velez: Yes! It was a hell of a birthday!

Moderator: And you were conscious for the entire day?

Gerardo Velez: Here's what happened. My birthday is August fifteenth. We didn't go on until August eighteenth, and I didn't sleep the whole time. Because we were privy, we had a house, a special house for Jimi, up on a hill. He couldn't go out and be among the people, but I could, so I would take the limo and I'd tell him I was coming back with a party. I'd go down the hill and I'd say, "You! You! You! You want to come up to the house and hang out with me and Jimi?" They'd jump into the limo and we would go up there for a couple hours. Eventually we would have to say, "Okay, ladies, fellas, come on! We have to go back down!" And we would go back down the hill to be told that we were going to go on in another three hours. But we didn't go on. Then we would be told, "Another two hours." We didn't go on again. This happened for ten hours. Ten hours of delay, delay, delay, delay. That was on the eighteenth.

---

[4] Paul Butterfield (1942–1987) was a popular blues harmonica player. His band, the Paul Butterfield Blues Band, played at major festivals in the late 1960s, including both Monterey and Woodstock.

[5] Released in 1969, Martha Velez's first album, *Fiends & Angels*, featured musicians including Eric Clapton, Jack Bruce, and Mitch Mitchell.

And then, Santana—I mean in the town of Woodstock, Santana was playing in a place called Tinker Street Café, which I mentioned earlier, and I heard Santana, I heard this music, "Oye cómo va mi ritmo." And I said, "Oh my God! They're playing Latin music in there!" So we stopped the car, Jimi and I jumped out, and then when they started with "Oye Cómo Va," I said "Wait a minute! That's a Tito Puente song! I know that, I grew up my whole life listening to that song!" And I got up and I jammed with the guys. And then we left, and the rest is history, you know, because they weren't paid. I don't believe they were even paid.[6] Bill Graham, who was their manager, wanted to make sure that Santana performed at the show; he felt it was very important, and it certainly was very important for Santana, because that's how they broke internationally.

Moderator: We talk about Woodstock as being a countercultural experience, but it sounds like it was an amazing blend of cultures, actually, not counterculture, but a blending of cultures. Could you talk a little bit about all the different styles of music, your own background, and how that influenced the sounds that people heard there?

Gerardo Velez: Counterculture is a philosophy, it's a way of being. It was basically "We're not into greed, we're not into war." America has a war economy. We've been in wars for two hundred and twenty-seven years of our two-hundred-forty-whatever years we've been around. We are a war economy. "So what?" we said. "No! We don't want to do this, we don't want to be a part of that. I'm not going to Vietnam! They're not attacking me! Those people are trying to live, raise their kids just the way we're trying to raise our family. I'm not going."

I remember when Muhammad Ali stepped up, and we were . . . [*aside*] I was in the Young Lords, the Latino Young Lords, and we didn't take anything from anyone.[7] We were not at peace and love and Woodstock. We were like, "We belong, we're taking our rightful place here, and no one's going to stop us." And that was very important to me as a young

---

[6] Several unsubstantiated online sources state that Santana was paid $750 to perform at Woodstock. This aligns with Michael Lang's claim in chapter 1 that "everybody got paid at Woodstock." At the Berklee conference, Lang said that they paid Santana fifteen hundred dollars, claiming they were "the best buy of the festival."

[7] The Young Lords were a social and human-rights organization, based first in Chicago and New York, built on an activist model similar to the Black Panther Party. They aimed to improve the living conditions and social standing of Puerto Ricans in America.

27. Black and white photograph of festival attendees climbing and sitting on the scaffolding. Photograph by Dan Garson.

DAN GARSON

Woodstock is known today for the many indelible images that photographers and documentarians captured at the festival. Dan Garson (1952–92), at the time a seventeen-year-old Connecticut native, was one of the youngest photographers to attend. Garson arrived at the festival with a press credential to take pictures for the Trident, the high school paper of Amity Regional High School in Woodbridge, Connecticut. The press credential was supplied by Rod Jacobson, one of the media representatives at Wartoke Unlimited, the PR firm for Woodstock.

Over the course of the weekend, Garson shot more than two hundred and sixty pictures using two different cameras loaded with Ektachrome and Tri-X film. He covered the entire festival, capturing everything from the nude bathers in the pond, to the hippies at the Hog Farm, to the musicians on the stage itself.

Garson's photographs included here capture the raw and free-form nature of the festival. The visceral image of the attendees huddling against the dark clouds is iconic; Garson took it just prior to Joe Cocker's performance on Sunday, August 17 (see photograph number 23). Garson's photograph of the climbers on the scaffolding was taken during Jimi Hendrix's seminal performance on Monday morning (August 18). According to the edge numbers on the negative, we know that this is the last photograph that Garson shot at Woodstock.

Garson's photographs never ended up in the Trident; instead, he produced a slideshow, merging sound and image in an avant-garde style for Amity's students in the high school auditorium. A few weeks later, Garson set down some memories on paper from his notes at the festival: "I arrived at the campgrounds on Thursday, August 14. The place is just filled with acid heads, hippies, teeny boppers, and plain 'ole people (like me!)." Then the photographs sat in a box in his parents' basement for decades.

It was only after his untimely death from cancer at the age of forty that his good friend Brad LeMee had these photographs painstakingly restored to further Dan's legacy. They are a testament to Dan Garson's exceptional talent, captured at the age of seventeen.

man growing up, as a Latino, because we were at the bottom of the rung. There were Whites, Blacks, and then Latinos were all down there. So I was always trying to show that we were Americans and that's what America is all about.

You can go to Japan, you can go to England, but you'll never be English and you'll never be Japanese. They'll never bring you into their culture; you'll always be an outsider. The United States is the only country where you can come, become a citizen, and say "I'm an American," no matter what your background is. So we had a very important role in the world to take the music that we were writing at the time. "No, no, we won't go!" We're not going to go by what you're telling us to do, especially the regime that was in at that particular time. We had to make changes and eventually end the Vietnam War.

A lot of things happened in that disgraceful period of time in United States history. And we made music to say: "You see what's happening now? Don't let this continue to happen." And our songs meant something, albums meant something. Your artist that you love said those words and you would cry in your bedroom, or you would pick up a guitar, you would jump on your bed, and dance on your bed, and say, "Yeah, this is so cool. I love this, this is freedom, this is my people."

Back in the day, it was all about going to the club, being in the right space, and my bio is about being at the right place at the right time. And that's exactly what my career has been all about. When I had a drug problem and I relocated to Buffalo, New York, that's when we started Spyro Gyra. I said, "I can't take this. I'm either going to die or I have to go somewhere else and be reborn," and I went to Buffalo and I said, "I don't know what is going to happen in Buffalo," but I said, "I know I have to get out of New York City."

That's what happens: you never know where life and destiny are going to take you, and that was the beauty of the music. If you listen to Jimi's music, that's where everybody else went, "What is that guy doing?" Today's sound design is a field unto itself. Jimi was the master of sound design. Many times he left the stage in disgust. Today, it wouldn't happen, those things wouldn't happen. But to get the sound right, to get six amps working together on the stage all at the same time, allowing him to do his feedback and all the different things that he worked on in the house all the time. I mean, he gave me wah-wah pedals, he gave me guitars, he gave me basses. He said, "You want to learn?" I said, "Sure," because we're both lefties, and we always talked about how hard it is to be a lefty, and everything is made for righties. And you play the piano, left hand just plays the bass, everything's happening on the right side, you know? Left out? Leftover? Leftist? All negative terms. All negative terms to people who use this arm.

Audience: Sinister! Sinister!

Gerardo Velez: That's right! Yeah, exactly, you know? When I went to Catholic school, they said I would have to learn how to write with my right hand. My father, who's left-handed, came and said, "My boy's a left-handed person and so am I. He's not going to learn how to write with the right hand." My father was like six foot three and a big man, and that was enough for them to let me continue with my left hand.

Moderator: I'm wondering if you could talk a little bit about your education through this ensemble you were a part of. You talked about wanting to go left or right, but you went off a cliff. I'm wondering if you can talk a little bit about how you see your education as a musician.

Gerardo Velez: Right. I touched on that a little bit earlier and I'm going to do it again. When you're starting out in anything and you're a young person, the world is your oyster: you're the man, you're the woman, your destiny is beautiful, and that's the way you should think. That's how every musician should think. Otherwise, do something else. If you don't have the drive and the passion to do this, then do something else and enjoy playing your instrument. But you have to have the drive. I'd rather be with someone who has drive and desire more than the best players, because the best players, they kind of stay over there. They're not really a part of the chemistry that's happening in many respects. And I feel for a lot of people who are just virtuosos on their instruments but can't communicate. Music is all about communication, like what we're doing right now: we're communicating ideas.

To answer your question, I learned to play less. I learned how to play behind a singer, because an ensemble begins with the vocalist in the front and the accompanying musicians. And if the singer can't hear, then we're making mistakes. I learned that early on, from singers. I'd be playing and dancing on stage and they'd say, "I love you, G, but you better just back off a couple of notches, because you know. . . ." So it's a blessing and it's a curse when you're that type of person, so I learned how to be an ensemble player. That was very important to me.

I learned to do jingles, commercials, and all that. I went to college to learn how to read ten years after I was with Jimi. I went to college in 1975 and 1976, and I learned music theory. And then I took that and I threw it out the window. Because I learned how to play innately. You just have to play it once and I know it. That's how I did commercials, that's how I did jingles, that's how I did all that stuff. I hear it go by once and I have it.

Starting out from the beginning was actually learning how to play in an ensemble and quieting my role. Another thing I learned was the economy of sound and the economy of part playing. Miles Davis showed me how to do that. Not personally, but when we would jam, he would be like, [*imitating Miles Davis's voice*] "Hey, hey, man, you playing way too much, man. Yeah, I like what you doin' man, but, you know, man, yeah, but come on now, man." And I would be like, [*with a look of awe*] "Okay, Miles!" And you learn.

At first I would think, "This guy doesn't even know, I'm like a great player, man. This guy, he doesn't even hardly play, you know." That's how dumb I was. This guy is hardly playing! "I'm a virtuoso on my drums," I would think. "And he's hardly playing." You know Miles was a minimalist.

28. Black and white photograph of a road lined on both sides with cars, and with crowds walking down the middle to and from the festival site. Photograph by Henry Diltz.

[*imitates Miles Davis playing trumpet in a very minimalistic way*] And he made people concentrate, he brought us all into that space. [*imitates Miles Davis*] He showed me how to utilize space and drama. A lot of people come and bang right away. They bring it right up to here. [*gestures above his head*] Where do you go from here?

We have to be theatrical as well as musical, and that's what Jimi was. I mean the outfits, the playing between his legs, playing with his teeth, all the sexual innuendos in performing. That was when you're twenty or twenty-one, and your testosterone and hormones are going crazy, and you're the greatest person in the world, and the sexiest guy in the world, and so on and so forth. We had those robes and lights on us, and were playing music, and we were gods for the moment. It's not that we said that. It's not like we actually thought that. Maybe as a god is the wrong term. We felt freedom.

It was freedom from all the other crap that was going on at the time. The civil rights. Injustice all around us. It was musical freedom that we could all share. And that's what bands and musicians bring to the table and allow those who are not musically talented, because everyone has something to bring to the table. We're not all equal. We're not all equal, and not everyone's going to be great, and not everyone's going to be super successful, but everyone should find out who they are and what makes them comfortable.

Music is a kind of vehicle. We gravitate to certain music because that's the kind of music that makes us feel wonderful. And that's what we tried to do. We did psychedelic music because we were on psychedelics. And it was at the time we were experimenting. The jury's in now [on psychedelics], but back then it wasn't. We thought we were going to places that no one was going to go. When you take psychedelic drugs, that opens your mind. A universe opened up from it, we thought. Of course the jury came in, and there's too many complications with those drugs. But we thought we were experimenting, and we were going to go places that no one had ever gone before. And we certainly did that. But with that came a lot of complications.

What I'm saying is to just listen to that music. Even if you've never taken a drug in your life, listen to that music full blast and close your eyes. And if you're not going on the trip, you better make sure your heart's beating, because with that music, you can't help it. It's the vibrational energy of it. [*sings a riff from "Purple Haze" while gesticulating the chords with his left hand*] I mean, [*moves around in his seat as if he is floating*] your mind starts going and you feel like you're free-floating in the air. It's a totally magical experience to share that with other musicians on stage, and then to get the joy, when I see people really getting off on the music. Ahhh . . . that's like heaven.

Moderator: Can you talk a little bit about what it was like for you to transition out of that space, that headspace, when you started playing a different kind of music, when you went to Buffalo? What was the experience for you? If you weren't going on that kind of trip, what kind of journey were you going on?

Gerardo Velez: It was a flip journey. I was in a rock/psychedelic experience, and prior to that I mostly played Latin and rock. And then I played with Spyro Gyra, the first fusion band of rock, funk, and R&B. That's what we're trying to do with Gypsy Sun and Rainbows, and that's what Jimi and I worked on. And then Larry Lee came in.

THE JIMI HENDRIX EXPERIENCE, GYPSY SUN AND RAINBOWS, AND BAND OF GYPSYS

Over the course of his tragically short life, Jimi Hendrix (1942–1970) played with a wide variety of musicians and ensembles. Whether it was friends from his short stint in the Army, or backing artists like Wilson Pickett, the Isley Brothers, and Little Richard on the Chitlin' Circuit, Hendrix was comfortable with a rotating series of musicians. After moving to Greenwich Village in New York City, he quickly fell in with the city's burgeoning rock scene. Hendrix played with musicians like John Hammond Jr. and future "Spirit" guitarist Randy California at clubs like the Cafe Au Go Go, and Cafe Wha?, and soon befriended Linda Keith, the girlfriend of Rolling Stones lead guitarist Keith Richards.[8] With this connection in mind, Hendrix moved to London, where rock royalty including Eric Clapton, Pete Townshend, John Lennon, and Paul McCartney, soon flocked to see him play.

Backed by Mitch Mitchell on drums and Noel Redding on bass, the power trio known as the Jimi Hendrix Experience capitalized on their newfound fame by recording *Are You Experienced?* Released on May 12, 1967, this debut album, featuring the songs "Foxy Lady," "Fire," and "Purple Haze" on the US release, rose to number two in the UK and number ten in the United States. Hendrix's popularity in the UK notwithstanding, he was a relative unknown in the United States until his standout performance at the Monterey Pop Festival on June 18, 1967. This performance ended with the song "Wild Thing," near the end of which Hendrix famously destroyed his guitar by lighting it on fire. After Monterey, the Experience recorded two more studio albums, *Axis: Bold as Love* (1967) and *Electric Ladyland* (1968). The latter album was the only record produced by Hendrix himself, and it was Hendrix's final studio album to be released before his death in 1970.

---

[8] Founded in 1967, Spirit is an American progressive rock band best known for the song "Taurus" from their self-titled debut album (1968). The song includes an acoustic guitar solo that was reproduced almost entirely in the introduction to "Stairway to Heaven," by Led Zeppelin (*Led Zeppelin IV,* 1971).

After the Denver Pop Festival on June 29, 1968, Noel Redding left the Experience to form his own band, so Hendrix assembled a new group. He brought in two friends from the Army, Larry Lee on guitar and Billy Cox on bass, and he supplemented Mitch Mitchell's drums with two additional percussionists, Juma Sultan and Gerardo Velez. This ensemble was short-lived; they only played live four times, including their iconic performance at Woodstock, where Chip Monck introduced them as "the Jimi Hendrix Experience" and Hendrix had to quickly counter with the new name, "Gypsy Sun and Rainbows."

29. Black and white photograph of Gerardo Velez standing behind a conga, on stage with Billy Cox, Larry Lee, Juma Sultan, and Jimi Hendrix. Photograph by Henry Diltz.

Hendrix finished out 1969 by returning to his power-trio roots, most notably with his four-show set at the Fillmore East for New Year's Eve and New Year's Day, with a new group called the Band of Gypsys. This time backed by Billy Cox on bass and Buddy Miles on drums, the Band of Gypsys recorded a live album that was produced by Hendrix and Woodstock audio engineer Eddie Kramer. Later in the spring of

1970, Hendrix began a new tour with some familiar bandmates. The Cry of Love tour featured a reunited Jimi Hendrix Experience, albeit with Billy Cox replacing Noel Redding on the bass. This ensemble played with Hendrix throughout 1970, including at the second Atlanta International Pop Festival on July 4, and in Honolulu on August 1, which would be Hendrix's final concert appearance in the United States. Hendrix died in London on September 18, 1970, at the age of twenty-seven.

Here's what happened. There was a nightclub called Steve Paul's Scene.[9] Steve Paul was the manager of Johnny Winter, Edgar Winter, and several other artists at the time. He had a venue called the Scene, and it was downstairs. Now it's a Chinese restaurant. But it was on Forty-Sixth Street between Eighth and Ninth, and it was downstairs. It was just like the Cave in London: low ceilings and everyone sitting around. A dear friend of mine, Kenny Rankin, an amazing vocalist and guitar player, played there,[10] as did Dion DiMucci, who was Dion and the Belmonts.[11] I cut my teeth with those guys. And then we used to play at the Scene.

If you played at the Scene, you could go in every time for free. So I went in and I knew Rick Derringer,[12] who had "Hang on Sloopy" at the

---

[9] The Scene was a bar owned and operated by Steve Paul (1941-2012), the manager of Johnny Winter, among others. The Scene hosted many notable performances, including a three-week residency by The Doors, and the first New York City performance by the Jimi Hendrix Experience.

[10] Kenny Rankin (1940–2009) was a singer-songwriter from New York City, noted for playing guitar on Bob Dylan's album *Bringing It All Back Home* (1965) and befriending comedian George Carlin, with whom Rankin toured for over ten years.

[11] Dion and the Belmonts were a doo-wop quartet whose hits in the late 1950s, including "I Wonder Why," earned them a spot on the Winter Dance Party tour. This tour is infamous because of the plane crash on February 3, 1959, that killed Buddy Holly, Ritchie Valens, and the Big Bopper.

[12] Born Ricky Dean Zheringer in 1947, Rick Derringer came to prominence with his cover of the song "Hang on Sloopy," which peaked at number one on the *Billboard Hot 100*. He fronted the band the Real McCoys, and later worked with numerous artists, including Edgar and Johnny Winter, Steely Dan, and "Weird Al" Yankovic. Wes Farrell and Bert Berns are credited as the songwriters for "Hang on Sloopy." The first version of the song was recorded and released in 1964 by The Vibrations.

time. [*sings a line from the song*] And he's like sixteen or seventeen years old, and he's the band leader, and he and his brother, and their band, the McCoys, they were the band, and Jeff Beck was playing, and then Buddy [Miles] got behind the [drum] kit.[13] And I got up and I played two songs. I then took my drums, put them to the side, and went back and sat down with my lady and my lady, and my friends and my friends. [*gesturing to how people would have been sitting around him*] I lived with twins at the time. So they were living with me, and the other people were over there.

All of a sudden I got a tap on the shoulder and [*turns around to look behind him*] he [Jimi Hendrix] said, "Oh man that was some great playing. You want to come up when I'm playing?" "All right." And my friends were saying, "That's Jimi Hendrix! That's Jimi Hendrix!" But I was twenty-one years old; I was twenty years old going on twenty-one, and I said, "Ah, yeah, it's cool."

You know, I didn't feel. I didn't know what my destiny was going to be. When I felt it was right, I was going to take that opportunity. So I took that opportunity when he [Jimi Hendrix] said, "Let's get up and play." We got up and played, and then afterwards he said, "Hey, man, that was great. Let's go to the studio." And we went to the studio at four o'clock in the morning, and we played until four o'clock in the afternoon, and we did that for nine months, basically, going and jamming. Stephen Stills would come in and Buddy [Miles] would play organ. It was just magical. That was the beginning of fusion music.

Then there was a period of my life where I needed to readjust my values and get back on focus, and once I did that, I relocated to Buffalo, New York. We started Spyro Gyra, and it was a bunch of college kids, really. And it's funny, because we were categorized as jazz, but we weren't really jazz. The old jazzers, they liked us, but they were a little apprehensive because of the skills that they had, and they thought our skills weren't up to par. They also wondered what was up with the rock and roll and with the Latin, funk, and all that, putting it into jazz.

As I said, every generation needs their heroes, and we were the heroes for our generation. You know Return to Forever and John McLaughlin, and

---

[13] Buddy Miles (b. 1947) is an American drummer, vocalist, and producer known for playing with Jimi Hendrix in his Band of Gypsys, and as the lead singer of the California Raisins.

Al Di Meola?[14] I mean, these were amazing guys, and I played with all these guys. And that type of mixture of people is the essence of what fusion music is all about. So for me, I like to write a lot of music that has a montuno. [*vocalizes a montuno rhythm*][15] So you have the two and four [beats] so everyone can pick up on the two and four, but there's a lilt. [*vocalizes a lilting montuno, imitating the sound of an electric guitar*]

I like to stretch out my music in that manner. I'll come up with a particular rhythm, and then I augment that rhythm with the different instrumentation. It must come from a Latin R&B root, because I played with Nile Rodgers and Chic and a lot of R&B bands.[16]

The Black experience was my experience growing up. You can go to any community, but if you go to a Black community and you can do something well, they will accept you. I was a kid, I was an outsider, being Puerto Rican, and every time I went to the Black community they'd say, "Hey, man, come on, you can dance." And I was like, wow this is cool man, people accepting me. And then of course there's the legacy of Black entertainment and Black music. Because, I mean, I worked with Patti LaBelle. Patti LaBelle to me is the greatest singer I know in R&B and gospel. I mean, the woman's amazing. Chaka Khan. And I worked with all these wonderful, incredible singers. Even the background singers for Patti LaBelle were these incredible singers. And even at sound check, when Patti would be hitting these spiritual notes, these background singers would be crying, and they were all amazing singers in their own right, but she was something special.

We were talking earlier about Bob Dylan and George Harrison, and people like that are at a certain level, and when they talk, we listen, and Jimi was at that too. He's no color. I've been to biker events that don't like Latinos or Blacks—or anybody, really, but bikers—and they embrace Jimi and Jimi's music like he was as White as they were. Because he is a colorless icon. And

---

[14] Founded by Chick Corea in 1971, the band Return to Forever was an American jazz fusion band featuring Stanley Clarke, Airto Moreira, and Al Di Meola. John McLaughlin (b. 1942) is a British guitarist that blended numerous musical styles into his particular brand of jazz fusion. His notable recordings include playing with Miles Davis on *Bitches Brew* (1970) and Carlos Santana on *Love Devotion Surrender* (1973). Al Di Meola (b. 1954) is an American guitarist who rose to prominence as the lead guitarist in the band Return to Forever. His style is best characterized as jazz fusion.

[15] Also known as tumbao, montuno is a highly syncopated rhythm associated with the blind Cuban bandleader Arsenio Rodriguez.

[16] Chic was a band formed in 1972 by Niles Rodgers and Bernard Edwards, best known for disco hits like "Le Freak" (1978) and "Good Times" (1979).

30. Black and white wide-angle shot of the field and stage with farms in the background. Photograph by Henry Diltz.

that—I am so proud of that, that particular issue. Because we talked a lot about that.

Papa Hendrix was a really nice guy. Al Hendrix was such a sweetheart; he was a postman and he had a nice quiet life in Seattle. He married Jimi's mom, adopted Jimi, brought Jimi into his home, and did the same with Jimi's stepsister, Janie Hendrix. That's the kind of guy Papa Al was. So when you look at Jimi's upbringing, he was brought up in a really wholesome environment, although he came from a broken home, so to speak. Al was very important to him, and the type of person that Al was, a giving and loving person, bringing in all these kids. How much does a postman make? It didn't matter; the guy always had a beautiful smile on his face. And that brought him a lot of joy and that brought Jimi a lot of joy.

My point is, Jimi went to White schools, and you know maybe there were three Black families in the whole community. And I went to private schools, and I was the only Latino in the class for most of my educational years. And we talked about how it was to incorporate our people.

We played in Harlem, and they put us in this tent. It was in the summer, and it was ninety-five degrees outside, and it must have been one hundred and twenty in the tent.[17] And Jimi said, "I have to play for my people. I don't know how to reach out, I don't know how to reach out, man, you know they don't understand my music, and I'm trying to reach out. You know, I'm tired of playing 'Midnight Ride,' I'm tired of playing Wilson Pickett, and all this.[18] I can do all that. That's not what I want to do." And we went to Harlem, and it didn't work out because the sound wasn't great. We did the show, and we would always sit back and talk. Like I said, we're both lefties and we're both kind of outsiders who just felt that music was the only value, the only line that we had together. I could be talking about myself, who cares. Music's the most important thing that we are here about.

Moderator: I was wondering if you could talk a little bit about that inside/outside feeling that you both had, and did you feel that same pressure to communicate with the Latin community and moving between worlds, moving back and forth between worlds? I'm wondering if you had a similar experience to Jimi Hendrix.

Gerardo Velez: Ah, I don't think so, I don't think so, because my family had heritage in Puerto Rico and Spain. You know the African American experience is a totally different experience. I felt like I had roots and that I had a heritage. Most of my friends did not feel that. And that, to me, was a very sad situation. But the power of youthful energy changed that. I remember I went to a meeting for *Billboard* magazine with [Carlos] Alomar,[19] who was David Bowie's bandleader for a long time, thirteen years, and who was also the head of [LARAS] in New York.[20]

We went to this meeting and they [the *Billboard* representatives] said, "Listen, we're going to try to get Latin music to cross over and do bilingual

---

[17] The Harlem Street Fair took place on September 5, 1969, at the intersection of 138th Street and Lenox Avenue. Sponsored by the United Block Association, the street fair featured one of the final performances of Gypsy Sun and Rainbows.

[18] "Midnight Ride" is a blues standard that would have been de rigueur on the Chitlin' Circuit when Jimi Hendrix was a musician with Wilson Pickett in the early 1960s.

[19] Carlos Alomar (b. 1951) is a Puerto Rican guitarist and songwriter, known for his longtime collaboration with David Bowie, one product of which was the song "Fame" (1975), cowritten by Alomar, Bowie, and John Lennon. In addition, Alomar cofounded the National Rock Movement of Puerto Rico and is an advisor to the Latin Academy of Arts and Sciences.

[20] The Latin Academy of Arts and Sciences (LARAS) is known as the "Latin Grammys."

songs on radio." I looked at Carlos [Alomar] and I said, [*sarcastically*] "Yeah, that's going to happen." And look, it did happen.

Moderator: We have definitely had a good time with you today. From being a performer at Woodstock to being a jazz musician, I think your next step is to write your memoirs. We have time for one question from the audience.

Audience: Thanks for the talk; it was great. I have a two-part question. When you walked into the club with Jimi and Santana was playing, Jimi wasn't turned on to want to play with Carlos? He didn't say, wow, this guy can play? That's the first question. The second question is, you didn't mention the name of the guy who was Van Morrison's producer and manager and someone else's.

Gerardo Velez: That was my brother-in-law, Keith Johnson, and he was the musical director for Paul Butterfield, for Van Morrison, and then for Etta James until her passing. I love Etta James dearly, and she helped raise my nephew, Taj, and she would call me Uncle Titi because Titi is an aunt in Spanish. [*imitates Etta James speaking to him and calling him Uncle Titi*] And I always remember Etta for that particular reason. Anyway, that's Keith Johnson.

To answer your other question about Jimi: it was like this. I'll give you an example of what kind of guy he was. His ego was like, "I'm great, I'm watching Carlos Santana." He was stunned like I was, but I wasn't stunned for the same reason he was stunned. He loved the Latin with the rock because that's one of the things he and I were going after. I got up and jammed and he stood in the back because he didn't bum-rush the stage or anything like that. That's me. He didn't do that kind of stuff; he wasn't that kind of guy.

For instance, when we jammed, Jeff Beck and Jimi were playing, and Jeff is like, blues, and Jeff can rip, but he didn't have the fluidity that Jimi had, so Jeff would play something—[*pretends to play the guitar and imitates Beck's sound*]—something like that, right, really in the blues spirit, and Jimi would go.... [*does the same with Jimi Hendrix's sound and mimics a musical dialog between Beck and Hendrix*] He was like, "Bro relax, just play something. Don't mess with me." [*mimics intense playing*]

Moderator: Well, thank you so much. Please join me in a round of applause for Gerardo Velez.

PROFILES OF FEATURED WOODSTOCK LUMINARIES

RESEARCHED AND WRITTEN BY RONA ELLIOT

HENRY DILTZ

Henry Stanford Diltz was born on September 6, 1938, in Kansas City, Missouri, and occupies a unique role in the world of rock and roll. A pioneering rock photographer and accomplished musician, Henry's calm and kind demeanor and his personal generosity have made him a legend in his own time among musicians and fans alike. He is a respected and beloved elder in the world of music photography and 1960s cultural history.

Henry's background would not have obviously led him directly into photography, and his global reputation for capturing many of the most iconic images of twentieth-century music superstars would also seem highly unlikely, but it happened.

As Henry tells it, his entire family bounced around the world, following his father's work in the US diplomatic corps. Henry lived in a number of countries, including Thailand, Japan, and Germany; he attended schools in Munich, Germany, the West Point Military Academy in New York, and the University of Hawaii. As a child, Henry alternately dreamed of being a zookeeper, or a forest ranger living in the wilderness, or even a psychologist.

But the universe played tricks on his aspirations. While living in Hawaii, Henry became an accomplished banjo player and joined the Modern Folk Quartet, an acoustic band known for its vocal harmonies in the tradition of the Kingston Trio. Grounded in the folk music revival of the early 1960s, the Modern Folk Quartet recorded two albums in 1965, working in the studio with two of the most influential producers at that time, Jack Nitzsche and Phil Spector. Over the decades, the band has separated and then regrouped, and has continued to record together at different times. The Modern Folk Quartet remains a working band that still enjoys a large fan base in Japan, where they occasionally tour.[1]

As the Modern Folk Quartet played their a tour in Michigan (concert dates: February 4, 1966, Michigan State University, East Lansing; February 5, 1966, Hill Auditorium of the University of Michigan, Ann Arbor), they stopped at a thrift store to look around. At that point, destiny intervened, and a used camera entered Henry's life. A few of the other guys bought cameras too.

Among Henry's many friends in those days were people who took lots of photos. Henry also began to shoot whatever caught his eye, whether it was a fire hydrant or flowers, street signs or gas stations, and of course people. Among his circle, a tradition developed where friends would get together once a month and hold a slideshow at someone's house, using a slide projector to show enlarged images on an old-fashioned standing screen. The slideshow became an institution, and another crazy, stoned night in Los Angeles became a must-attend event.

Around that same time, the Laurel Canyon neighborhood in the Hollywood Hills was heating up as ground zero for the folk-rock explosion in Southern California. Henry would jam with his friends and then hang out and take their pictures. A remarkable career was born as he captured these fledgling artists who would grow into rock superstars. Henry's images have documented the emergence of influential performers including Crosby, Stills & Nash, Joni Mitchell, The Doors, James Taylor, the Mamas and the Papas, Neil Young, Linda Ronstadt, the Eagles, and Paul McCartney. Henry's now-iconic images have graced the covers of more than two hundred and fifty albums, and include thousands of publicity photos as well.

Henry's work has appeared in the *Los Angeles Times*, the *New York Times, Life, People, Rolling Stone, High Times, Billboard Magazine*, and in too many books to count. He is often called on for his expertise and to provide his recollections of the 1960s for documentaries, films, articles,

---

[1] The Modern Folk Quartet disbanded in 1966, but then reformed again in the mid-1970s.

and television shows. His own books include *California Dreaming*, a 2007 Genesis Publications UK Limited Edition that tells the story of the Southern California music scene as it unfolded between 1968 and 1972, through Henry's photographs. As a co-owner of the Morrison Hotel Gallery, with locations in New York, Los Angeles, and Maui, Henry has created a singular showcase for music photography and elevated the appreciation and respect for its photographers.

Henry was a photographer at the June 1967 Monterey Pop Festival and the official photographer for the Miami Pop Festival held in December 1968, but it is his work as the official staff photographer for Woodstock in August 1969 that was his defining moment. He arrived at the construction site at Yasgur's farm three weeks before the concert, and began recording much of the construction, chaos, and magic that went into what became those three days of peace, love, and music.

Henry has been honored as the Herb Alpert Scholar-in-Residence at Berklee College of Music for the years 2019 and 2020. Also in 2020, he was granted a Lifetime Achievement Award by the International Photography Hall of Fame.

Henry is always happy to share his images—along with wisdom, stories, advice, and techniques—with students and admirers of all ages from all over the world. He remains enthusiastic when sharing his eyewitness recollections with people who just wish they had been there too. Fortunately, through his pictures, Henry Diltz captured one moment after another for the rest of us to enjoy and imagine through his work.

RONA ELLIOT

Rona Elliot was born on February 22, 1947, in Brooklyn, New York, which confirms her status as a true baby boomer. The then-recent devastating events of World War II were a frequent and endless topic of conversation in her home. Rona quickly discovered that for her own well-being, listening to music—and rock and roll in particular—was an escape from the pain and suffering her parents both carried and shared. Rona also understood that music somehow magically connected her to love when she was in its grip, simply the finest experience possible. That much was obvious.

As a preteen, Rona knew that while being around music was her destiny, she discovered that she couldn't sing or play, but even so she was driven by a curiosity about how some artists created such transformational music. She realized she wanted to figure out ways to talk with artists and perhaps get to the bottom of this mystery, thereby opening the doors for herself and others to gain access to that spiritual place.

Few women were on the air in radio or television in the early to mid-1960s, and they were often relegated to the style and recipe sections in newspapers. Rona trusted that the path for her to somehow marry her passion for music and communication would reveal itself sooner or later. It did. With a combination of good fortune and focused determination, Rona's life unfolded as she had dreamed might be possible.

Rona is an eyewitness to music and pop-culture history. Her three greatest music credentials are attending Bob Dylan's performance when he "went electric" at the Newport Folk Festival in 1965, watching the Beatles perform at Dodger Stadium in 1966, and working at Woodstock in 1969. Her career in television, radio, print, and digital media has seen her interview musicians and world movers and shakers, from the Dalai Lama to Dolly Parton. Her in-depth interviews and profiles remain a standard for communicating not only about musicians, artists, and cultural icons, but also about where their inspirations come from.

Rona's career began at the powerhouse radio station KHJ in Los Angeles, and continued with jobs at major festivals like Newport Pop in Southern California (June 1968), Miami Pop (December 1968), and Woodstock (August 1969). In 1970, Rona moved to the Bay Area and worked at San Francisco's two legendary underground stations, KSAN and KMPX. In radio, she held every job on and off air, from hard news reporter to interviewer, at stations around the country.

At the NBC Radio Network in New York City, Rona worked in management and on air, producing and hosting daily, weekly, and monthly shows. With bandleader Paul Shaffer, she cohosted the *Live From the Hard Rock Cafe,* a radio broadcast series that began in 1985 with the opening of the Hard Rock Cafe in New York City. The series featured interviews and live performances from artists ranging from James Brown to Martha Reeves, who sang "Dancin' in the Street" on a flatbed truck outside the restaurant on Fifty-Seventh Street, before being shut down by police.

During a live international broadcast with Duran Duran from Abbey Road in London, Rona broke the Band Aid story and the song "Do They Know it's Christmas," leading to her work with Bob Geldof. Along with Hard Rock founder Isaac Tigrett, Rona was instrumental in placing the Cafe backstage at Live Aid in Philadelphia and in London, where artists gathered and Rona created her own broadcasting booth.

Her move to television began as the on-air journalist for VH1, which was quickly followed by her ideal job as the music correspondent for the *Today Show* on NBC. In this position, she traveled the world, interviewing the greatest artists and watching them perform. With Tina Turner, George Harrison, Paul McCartney, the Rolling Stones, U2, David Bowie, Yoko Ono, Billy Joel, Sting, the Bee Gees, Peter Gabriel, Ray Charles, the Who, Eric Clapton, Aretha Franklin, Cyndi Lauper, the Traveling Wilburys, Van Morrison, Joe Cocker and countless others, Rona was there conducting in-depth interviews and providing concert coverage. She stood in Berlin's No Man's Land with rock stars during Pink Floyd's The Wall—Live in Berlin concert after the wall fell, and covered benefit events like Farm Aid, the Nelson Mandela tributes, and the Prince's Trust Concerts, Amnesty International, and the Secret Policeman's Ball shows in the UK, and the list goes on.

Never Stop, Rona's e-book celebrating the Rolling Stones' fiftieth anniversary, was published in 2012. It contains hours of her television interviews with band members. She contributed interviews to the limited-edition volumes *California Dreaming*, by photographer Henry Diltz, and *The Woodstock Experience*, a celebration of the festival's fortieth anniversary, both for Genesis Publications in the UK. And she currently serves as the associate editor for the forthcoming Genesis book *Janis Joplin: Days and Summers*, for which Rona also conducted dozens of interviews with artists who were active in the San Francisco musical revolution of the 1960s.

Rona has written for *USA Today* and worked with the Grammy Foundation on their Musicares program and oral histories. She has written liner notes for albums and shot an album cover for Art Garfunkel. Rona created newspaper ads in the 1970s that highlighted the famine in Cambodia and raised millions of dollars for famine relief.

In honor of the fourteenth Dalai Lama's eightieth birthday in 2015, Rona conducted interviews for a documentary with people that the Dalai Lama called his inspirations. She consulted on a variety of shows in 2019, including the Emmy-nominated PBS *American Masters* documentary *Raúl Juliá: The World's a Stage*, and the PBS *American Experience* documentary, *Woodstock: Three Days that Rocked the World*.

Rona's life and work has been informed by a connection to counterculture, service, and spirituality. From her days living in a community with Zen Buddhist philosopher Alan Watts to being roommates with yippie turned yuppie Jerry Rubin, to her interviews with Holocaust survivors for

Steven Spielberg's Shoah Foundation, she has brought a sense of curiosity and commonality to her subjects and her search.

Her passion for music continues to be a primary focus as Rona shares her stories with a new generation of music journalists, professionals, and fans. She has taught a course on the history of Woodstock at the Gallatin School at New York University, and has served as a visiting artist at Berklee College of Music. Rona also serves as a trustee on the board of the Rock & Roll Hall of Fame and Museum in Cleveland.

For the record, Rona did manage to live her musical dream once, as a member of a parents' band at her kids' school. The group was the opening act for a charity concert headlined by the Beach Boys' Brian Wilson. Rona sang backup and played percussion, and was thrilled. However, there are many other things Rona has done that she has not and never will share with her children. The 1960s were like that sometimes, but for many like Rona, it was also a time to stand up for peace, love, and of course great rock and roll.

BILL HANLEY

Born in Medford, Massachusetts, on March 4, 1937, Bill Hanley was the son of a police officer, a lieutenant in the vice squad who was nicknamed "Chief Straight Arrow." Following in the footsteps of his father and becoming a police officer was not Bill's destiny. As a small child, Bill was intensely focused on building things, first radios, and then electric motors and radio crystal sets. This was all before the second grade. Bill lived for electronics: by the time he was a young teen, Bill was determined to figure out how to deliver better sound to audiences at games and concerts.

Bill's other passions were music and dancing. His experience performing at the Bal-A-Roue Rollaway skating rink in his hometown of Medford made him aware of disparities in the sound systems in use at the time. The sound was great when a live organist accompanied Bill and his friends as they were skating, but in Bill's opinion the sound was terrible when recorded songs were pumped in. The noise was so intolerable that Bill decided he would have to be the person to figure out how to fix it.

Bill's unique approach to and understanding of sound techniques and how sound works has become the stuff of legend. He was the go-to person for the famous Newport Folk and Jazz Festivals in Rhode Island, as well as the Cafe Au Go Go nightclub and the Fillmore East in New York, home to some of the greatest rock shows ever.

Bill was the audio engineer at the Newport Folk Festival in 1965, where Bob Dylan turned the world of folk music upside down. When Dylan abandoned his acoustic guitar for an electric one, the incident became mythic in music history. Contrary to the many versions about what actually happened, Bill says the whole production team knew what Dylan planned for that performance. Bill's only concern was about the amplification and whether the speakers could handle harder rock and roll. He needed to make sure the equipment was readjusted so that the intensity and vibrations from the sound wouldn't blow out the speakers. Bill adds that there was even a rehearsal before Dylan's set to test the equipment.

The only person who missed that Dylan rehearsal was Pete Seeger: when Dylan started with his electric guitar, Seeger was astonished as Dylan's band changed their tune, literally. In this story, the sound seemed shocking to Seeger because of its quantity, not its quality. The rest is history, even though the stories ebb and flow and the debate still rages about what happened on July 25, 1965. What is not in question is that Bill Hanley was on hand, helping Bob Dylan usher his music in a different direction.

But no previous achievement during Bill's notable career compares to his design and implementation of the sound system for the legendary Woodstock Festival in 1969, an endeavor that earned him the title of "Father of Festival Sound." Prior to Woodstock, there had never been a sound system that could handle a job of that scale and complexity. Woodstock producer Michael Lang said that he talked to others who felt they could do the job, but he admired Bill's confidence, saying it made him feel "comfortable." Lang remembers: "We came to a situation where I wanted great sound. Bill [Hanley] said to me, 'Great sound for an event like yours doesn't exist, but I can build it,' and he sold me."

Despite mud, rain, and a half million souls scattered over multiple acres, the sound system Bill created from scratch was so extraordinary and effective that people could hear superb rock and roll for three days from one end of Yasgur's farm to the other. Bill's commitment was to make sure that the people farthest from the stage could hear as well as the lucky ones in the front row, and they did.

Bill's other huge insight and subsequent contribution occurred long before Woodstock, when he moved the mixing table into the audience in a central location facing the stage and in the action. Previously, the mixing table and the engineer were squirreled away from the live performances. After Hanley moved out into the audience, it became standard operating procedure for future sound engineers.

Bill sheepishly admits that he maybe missed one opportunity. In 1966, he was the sound engineer for the Beatles at their Shea Stadium concert, where he says you couldn't hear yourself think with all the screaming. A few musicians in the stands reported that the songs sounded good and that the Beatles were impressed. They invited Bill to come back to England with them and work together. He declined, and told them that he was too busy building his business. No matter: Bill Hanley has secured his place in history as the sound genius who created systems to deliver incredible sound to audiences. His calculations and intuitive understanding of sound has become the standard for delivering excellence in what audiences hear to this day.

In addition to bringing music to audiences, Bill also provided the sound for President Lyndon B. Johnson's inauguration in 1965, as well as the Nixon-Agnew whistle-stop campaign tour of 1968. After Woodstock, Hanley Sound became the foremost sound provider for the largest and most important civil-rights and antiwar rallies and demonstrations in the following years.

The fear and fallout from Woodstock and the political climate resulted in laws that had a lasting and negative effect on Hanley Sound's ability to do business. Court injunctions forced large concerts everywhere to be cancelled, and opportunities to work events ground to a halt. But all was not lost: Bill continued to remain active in the field and consulted on events, and he found a way to repurpose his equipment to contribute to social justice efforts at the same time.

One member of Bill's Woodstock team, David Marks, was active in the anti-apartheid movement of his home country, South Africa.[2] At that time, Black and White artists were forbidden from playing on the same bill. But David found a loophole in the regulations: if shows were free and not intended to make money, artists of any race could appear together.

Bill was no longer able to use this large stockpile of sound equipment because of the canceled concerts in the United States, so he sent it to South Africa. This equipment was quickly named the "Woodstock Bins," and David used it to stage shows all over South Africa, where Black and White artists performed for Black and White fans. The sound was on equipment from Hanley Sound, which in its recent life had delivered three days of music at the peaceful Woodstock Festival.[3]

---

[2] David Marks (b. 1944).

[3] David Marks began using Bill Hanley's equipment in South Africa in 1971.

In 2006, the National Association of Music Merchants honored Bill Hanley with the Parnelli Innovator Award for his contributions to innovations in the live-event industry. At every concert and event, whether the audience realizes it or not, they are hearing Bill Hanley's imagination all around them, in the audio delivered by the sound system.

In his eighth decade, Hanley has seen and heard his dreams come true. But he continues to listen closely for something else that he might be able to figure out and improve, that is just waiting for his transformative touch.

ELLIOTT LANDY

Born in New York City in 1942, Elliott Landy began his career as a photojournalist for a variety of underground newspapers in the city. The 1960s offered many opportunities to shoot antiwar and social-activism events, which heralded the profound political and cultural shifts taking place at that time in America. Elliott was there with his camera to document them.

Music, of course, was a critical element in this changing landscape, and it offered Landy an entrée to a world of artists who were enormously influential politically and socially, and who were happy to have their photos taken by him. Elliott's ability to connect with these people through his lens has produced some of the most familiar and celebrated photos from that time. His portraits of Bob Dylan, The Band, Jim Morrison, Van Morrison, Janis Joplin and Big Brother and the Holding Company, and Jimi Hendrix are recognized around the world. His photos of the 1969 Woodstock Festival clearly evince the spirit of the time in a single glance.

Elliott's work has been published in *Rolling Stone*, the *Saturday Evening Post*, and *Life Magazine*. His images have also been selected as album covers, and his work is included in many book collections about that period. Elliott's collection of photographs has been shown all over the world, and his books include *The Band Photographs: 1968–1969*, *Woodstock Vision: The Spirit of a Generation* and *Elliott Landy's Woodstock*.

In addition to photography and writing, Elliott's commitment is to share a spiritual and meditation practice with others that supports healing and expanding the wonder of love.

MICHAEL LANG

On December 11, 1944, Michael Lang was born in Brooklyn, New York, making him one of the millions of baby boomers born in the shadow of war and devastation that defined the first half of the twentieth century. Like others in his generation, Michael was deeply inspired by the emergence of post-Elvis rock and roll, with its power to connect and move people. The new language of rock, based in the values of peace, love, and compassion, would help illuminate the deepening divide between America's past and the up-and-coming counterculture of the late 1960s.

Coming of age during the civil rights movement, the war in Vietnam, and the conservative politics of the 1960s, Michael dropped out of his studies at New York University and moved to Coconut Grove, Florida, to open what would be the first head shop in the Southeast. Michael was an early proponent of the legalization of marijuana. His store, the Head Shop South, became an outpost for the counterculture in the South.

While in Florida, Michael produced the first Miami Pop festival on May 18, 1968, along with his friend Richard O'Barry. Among the artists who performed at that show were such celebrated musicians as Jimi Hendrix, Frank Zappa, John Lee Hooker, Arthur Brown, and Blue Cheer. Michael had found his path.

After Miami Pop, Michael moved back north to Woodstock, New York. With a successful festival behind him, he dreamed of producing an even bigger concert somewhere in the country, where people could hang out, smoke a joint with friends, and try to live the dream of peace, love, and music.

Small outdoor festivals in rock, folk, blues, and jazz had achieved popularity in the previous years, but Michael wanted to create something new that reflected and included the sensibilities of the 1960s. He was deeply influenced by the D. A. Pennebaker movie about the Monterey Pop Festival, where the performances of Janis Joplin and Otis Redding catapulted both performers to stardom overnight. Michael asked himself after watching the film, "What could be better than doing that?"

In Michael's festival fantasy, he envisioned three days of peace and music in a beautiful setting, on grounds with paths leading to unexpected environments and activities, and to experiences throughout the site for those who might want to wander away from the stage area. But of course, on that enormous stage that would be built in his dream, only the greatest rock and roll acts would be booked and would perform. Along with his good friend Artie Kornfeld, Michael teamed up with New Yorkers Joel Rosenman and John Roberts, and Woodstock Ventures was born.

In the early spring of 1969, the preparations for the Woodstock Festival began in earnest. They first found a site in what turned out to be the unwelcoming town of Wallkill, in upstate New York. Pressured by the local citizens, Michael and crew abandoned Wallkill with few regrets and began a search for the truly right place. Undaunted, Michael as pied piper managed to find what would be the perfect spot for the concert in Bethel, New York—Max Yasgur's dairy farm, which quickly became legendary as the site for the Woodstock Festival.

Despite the incomprehensible challenges of building a temporary city for half a million people, opposition from hostile locals and wary neighbors, storms sent by Mother Nature, and a legendary traffic jam, the Woodstock Music & Art Fair: 3 Days of Peace and Music, more simply known as Woodstock, was a spectacular cultural moment. It is now recognized historically as one of the most influential music events ever held.

Since then, the word "Woodstock" has become universally associated with the possibility of peace, love, and music. Woodstock still remains a beacon of hope for a better world, spotlighting what those times came to stand for, even though many of the ideas from that period still remain a work in progress. Michael's vision came to pass and then some, and he was just twenty-four years old.

There was life after Woodstock '69 for Michael Lang, though admittedly it was a hard act to follow. Michael went on to produce the Woodstock '94 and '99 festivals. He has run a record company, Just Sunshine Records, produced albums, and managed superstars, including Billy Joel and Joe Cocker.

Michael's 2010 book with Holly George Warren, *The Road to Woodstock*, became a *New York Times* bestseller. Michael has been featured in movies and documentaries, and been written up in books and scholarly papers. His curly hair is recognized worldwide, and walking down the street in almost any major city, someone will invariably come up to him and say some variation of "You're the guy," shake his hand, and thank him.

Michael's current projects include the development of a Broadway musical based on Woodstock '69 with Woodstock Ventures, and production of a film based on the novel *The Master and Margarita* by Mikhail Bulgakov. Michael works with organizations like HeadCount, which supports voter registration, and is active in the fight against climate change. He also serves on the board of the Woodstock Film Festival, Farmhearts, and the Felix Organization for Adoptees. He and his family have lived in the town of Woodstock, New York, for over forty years.

In September 2019, Michael Lang was honored with the Muhammad Ali Humanitarian Award for Lifetime Achievement for his commitment to creating a more peaceful world. Michael has said that if anything he has done has contributed to making peace more of a reality on this planet and has served others, he has done his part. That said, he quickly adds—in true Woodstock fashion—it takes a village.

Michael Lang passed away on January 8, 2022 from complications due to non-Hodgkin's lymphona. He was 77.

CHIP MONCK

Chip Monck was born in Wellesley, Massachusetts, on March 5, 1939. The given name on his birth certificate appears as Edward Herbert Beresford Monck. The boys who taunted him and nicknamed him "Chip Monck" did not anticipate how enthusiastically he would embrace the moniker. Being Chip Monck has created distinct benefits throughout the course of his life and career and certainly foiled what the teasers originally intended.

Chip's early foray into the world of lighting design was influenced by his mother. She regularly spirited him out of school on the pretense of having a doctor's appointment. Instead, the two would take a train to New York City and go to see Broadway shows, which his mother enthusiastically appreciated and wanted to share. The young Chip was enchanted by the magical world being created on stage as well.

Chip discovered that he liked to build and tinker with equipment, and apprenticed with a summer theatre group at Wellesley College, learning the basics of theatrical lighting. By 1959, he began lighting the stage at the legendary Village Gate nightclub in New York, where jazz and folk artists performed. From there he lit performances for the influential Newport Folk and Jazz Festivals and the stage at the Apollo Theatre in Harlem.

As the world of production and staging shifted towards new technology in the 1960s, Chip was on the ground floor creating and implementing transformational techniques. In June 1967, he was in charge of lighting the three-day Monterey Pop festival, which would catapult Janis Joplin, Jimi Hendrix, and Otis Redding into immediate stardom. That show was followed by the Miami Pop Festival in December 1968, which showcased artists performing on two stages simultaneously.

In addition to his professional accolades, Chip cemented his legacy in the pantheon of rock and roll at Woodstock. He performed the role of master of ceremonies with respect, calm, and the dulcet tones of his unique voice, telling the gathered mass that eating the brown acid was perhaps not such a good idea, and urging those close to the stage to shift further away to avoid injury. Chip spoke, the masses moved, and the rest is well-documented history.

After Woodstock, Chip worked at the Altamont Free Festival where the Rolling Stones performed and where violence upended the dream of reprising Woodstock. A long-lived relationship with the Rolling Stones saw him light their extraordinary global performances for years. During the Fillmore East and West renovations, Chip's creative approach to lighting set a new standard in the world of performance venues.

Chip has worked his craft with most of the greatest performers on stages worldwide. On Broadway, he was the lighting director for Bette Midler's show *The Divine Miss M*, and the lighting director for *The Rocky Horror Show*, for which he received a Tony nomination. Chip also lit the opening and closing ceremonies for the 1984 Summer Olympics in Los Angeles, and consulted on staging for the 2000 Summer Olympics in Sydney. In 1989, he worked on a huge production at Dodgers Stadium in Los Angeles, where Pope John Paul II said Mass.

Among his most meaningful engagements was the production work he did in Zaire, Africa, on the famous Rumble in the Jungle boxing match between Muhammed Ali and George Foreman, and its accompanying three-day festival. The fight was delayed, but the concert, known as Zaire 74, went on as scheduled, with the added purpose of promoting racial and cultural solidarity. Trumpeter Hugh Masekela was one of the producers, and the event featured seventeen groups from Zaire along with fourteen groups from other countries, including Miriam Makeba, James Brown, Celia Cruz, B.B. King, Bill Withers, and the Spinners.

Chip Monck is the 2004 recipient of the Parnelli Lifetime Achievement Award, the stage and lighting industry's highest honor. Chip is also respected for his myriad contributions to the field; he is universally recognized for elevating stage and lighting production into the artistic spectacle we have now come to expect and enjoy in all entertainment production. He has lived in Australia since 1988, and continues to consult and to contemplate the future of his art.

GERARDO VELEZ

Gerardo "Jerry" Velez was born in the Bronx on August 15, 1947, into a family that had moved to New York City from Puerto Rico in the 1930s. The family members who remained in the islands were all professionals:

doctors, lawyers, and businesspeople. Jerry's parents had success in the Bronx owning three bodegas (markets), and it was expected that he would eventually become a professional too, most likely in the world of business.

At the age of six, Jerry and his older sister Martha, then ten, developed a dance act. Within three years, Jerry was playing bongos, and he and Martha were regulars on the dance competition circuit in New York and Puerto Rico. Jerry soon discovered that when he played percussion and danced he was an ecstatic human, and everything in his body and soul seemed in sync. He was too young to recognize that a muse had arrived at his doorstep.

A scuffle in the fifth grade threw water on life as he knew it after he landed a punch on another boy. His parents removed him from public school and quickly installed him in a more structured Catholic school. He stayed in Catholic schools through high school. It was around the seventh grade that Jerry considered becoming a veterinarian. At home, he had a fish and birds, but no dog was permitted, as the family lived in an apartment. At age twelve he enthusiastically took a job in a pet store in the Bronx, and then another job as a stable boy at the horse-riding academy in Pelham Bay Park, in the Bronx. A dream came true years later when, during summer visits to Puerto Rico, Velez was allowed to exercise horses at the famous El Comandante Racetrack in Canóvanas.

After high school, Jerry went to a Catholic college, where he decided that the priesthood would be his calling. He entered a seminary program, but quickly realized that with his energy, perhaps the priesthood was not his cup of tea after all.[4]

Jerry met Jimi Hendrix in the winter of 1968 when Jerry was playing with Jeff Beck, Rick Derringer, and the McCoys at Steve Paul's legendary nightclub, the Scene, in New York. Sitting back down after the set, Jerry was tapped on the shoulder by someone behind him. It was Jimi Hendrix, who then asked him to come up on stage and play with him when it was his turn that night.

The friendship grew between Jerry and Jimi Hendrix based on their mutual love of music and the magic they made when jamming or playing together. In the group they created, Band of Gypsys, Jimi and Jerry took a deep dive into the examination of all styles of music, from funk and R&B,

---

[4] In a communication with the editors, Velez stated: "My desire has always been to help those less fortunate than I was, and my duty to my fellow man. My impetus with regard to the seminary was to be a part of the community, a part of the process."

to classical, Latin, and world music. The future direction music might take was always a topic of discussion between them, particularly the fusion of different sounds which they were both excited about exploring. In a historic musical footnote, in 1969, Jerry brought Jimi Hendrix to Miles Davis's home in Harlem and introduced the two otherworldly players. To be a fly on the wall in that moment of musical majesty!

During the run-up to the Woodstock Music Festival in 1969, Jerry and Jimi shared a rented house in Phoenicia, not far from the festival grounds. They rehearsed together for their upcoming Band of Gypsys set at Woodstock, and Jerry had an eyewitness opportunity to watch Hendrix practice his version of "The Star-Spangled Banner" over and over and over in their music room. Hendrix's legendary performance at Woodstock continues to capture the world's attention as new generations of fans absorb its breathtaking originality. Jerry celebrated his twenty-second birthday playing alongside Jimi Hendrix at Woodstock, in what was his first professional performance. It was a birthday never to be forgotten, where he made music alongside the man many consider to have been the greatest guitarist ever

After Hendrix's passing, it took time before Jerry was ready to delve into fusion, the music he was so passionate about. Velez was an original member of Spyro Gyra, a six-piece band that made its name and reputation as the best-selling jazz fusion band of all time. With them, Velez was recognized by the National Academy of Recording Arts and Sciences with seven Grammy nominations.

Velez has performed with David Bowie, Elton John, Stevie Wonder, Chaka Khan, Stevie Nicks, and countless other greats. He plays, performs, and lectures with his enormous energy, a personal trademark, always eager and grateful to share his extraordinary professional and life-altering experiences in the whirlwind of music as he has lived it.

INDEX

Abbey Road (studio) 126, 168
Abruzzi, William xiv, 89–90
Adler, Lou 13, 45
Ali, Muhammad 150, 175
Allman Brothers 95, 134
Alomar, Carlos 163
Altamont Free Festival xiii, 63-64, 66, 177
    see also Violence at Festivals
Alternative Media Conference 124
American Experience 70, 169
Apollo Theatre (New York) 176
Apple Records 50
    see also Beatles
Art Crew 56
Atlantic Records 26n24, 124n17
Auger, Brian 149

Band, The xiv, 3, 16–17, 30, 134, 173
    see also Dylan, Bob
Band of Gypsys 83, 157–58, 178–79
Baez, Joan 17, 29, 30, 39, 128
Beach Boys 127, 170
Beatles xiv, 4–5, 13, 79, 82, 92, 108–9, 113, 115, 140–42, 168, 172
    "With a Little Help From My Friends" xv
    not appearing at Woodstock 50
Beck, Jeff 160, 164, 178
Bee Gees 169
Berklee College of Music vii, xvi–xviii, 1–2, 5, 57, 59, 77, 107, 147, 167, 170
Bernuth, Ticia 19

Bethel (New York) xxi, 11, 15, 45, 88, 92–93, 102-3, 149, 175
Bieler, Richard 117
Big Brother and the Holding Company 5, 173
    see also Joplin, Janis
Bindy Bazaar xxi, xxiii–xxiv
Black Lives Matter (social movement) 73
Black Sabbath 127
Bonnaroo 114, 138
Bonham, John 136
    see also Led Zeppelin
Bono 126–27
    see also U2
Booker T & the MGs 13
Bowie, David 147, 163, 169, 179
Boy George 127
Brady, Mathew 40
Brown, Arthur 174
Brown, James 168, 177
Browne, Jackson 128, 140–41
Bruce, Lenny 71
Buffalo (New York) 153, 156, 160
Burke, Patrick vii, 37
Burning Man 114, 138
Butterfield, Paul 10, 30, 46, 148–49, 164
    see also Paul Butterfield Blues Band

Cactus (band) 124
Café Espresso 17, 86n24
    see also Tinker Street Cafe; Woodstock (New York)

California, Randy 157
Calta, Louis 102
Capaldi, Jim 149
Catskills 2, 11, 104, 110, 144
Charles, Ray 169
Cheer, Blue 174
Chicago Democratic National Convention (1968) 4, 7–8, 36n31, 105
Chicago Seven 7, 118–19
   see also Hoffman, Abbie
Civil Rights Movement 4, 18, 73–74, 155, 172, 174
Clague, Mark 85n23
Clapton, Eric 139, 148–49, 157, 169
Clarke, Stanley 161n14
Clayton, Adam 126
   see also U2
Cleaver, Eldrige 11, 110, 113
Coachella 76, 99, 114, 138
Cocker, Joe xv, 3, 30, 40, 48, 152, 169, 175
   "With a Little Help From My Friends" xv
   see also Lang, Michael
Coconut Grove (Florida) 16, 174
Cohen, Harold 47
Cohen, Steve 22
Collier, Barnard L. 102, 105
Collins, Phil 127
Corea, Chick 161n14
Cox, Billy 158–59
Crosby, David 12n16
Crosby, Stills & Nash 44, 109, 134, 166
Crosby, Stills, Nash & Young xiv, 30, 44n36, 83, 109n4
Cruz, Celia 177
Cyrus, Miley 57

Dalai Lama 168–69
Daltrey, Roger 120, 121n14
   see also Who, the
Dass, Ram 124
Davies, Roger 125
Davis, Miles 83, 154–55, 161n14, 179
   Bitches Brew 83, 161n14

Dentsu 57
Denver Pop xiii, 63–64, 68, 92, 158
   see also Violence at Festivals
Derringer, Rick 159, 178
Diamond Horseshoe 88
   see also Bethel (New York)
Diltz, Henry xvi, 12, 53, 75–76, 78–80, 109–10, 121, 129–30, 165–67
   Abbie Hoffman assaulting Pete Townsend 118–19
   Eagles album cover shoot 131–33
   Herb Alpert Visiting Professor Program (Berklee College of Music) 76–77, 167
   Miami Pop Festival 12
Di Meola, Al 161
DiMucci, Dion 159
Doors, The 109, 159n9, 166
Dr. John 124
drugs xv, 11, 51, 89, 90, 92, 104–5, 117, 135–36, 156
   cannabis/marijuana 37, 44, 102, 135–136, 174
   peyote 132
   psychedelic drugs/LSD 11n12, 16, 27, 32, 46, 82, 104, 135, 156
Duran Duran 126, 147, 168
Dylan, Bob xiv, 3, 16, 17, 71, 79, 86, 108–9, 113, 128, 138–40, 161, 168, 171, 173
   see also Band, The

Eagles 12, 131–32, 166
Edge, The 126
   see also U2
Edwards, Bernard 161n16
Elliot, Rona xvi, 9, 11–12, 52–53, 75, 113–15, 124–27, 130–31, 167–70
   art of interviewing 139
   hearing Hendrix's "Star-Spangled Banner" at Woodstock 45
   interview with Mel Lawrence 36, 67
   interview with Stan Goldstein 61, 65–66

philosophy of "peace and love" 143–45
on Michael Lang's leadership at Woodstock 63, 100
women working in media 108–9, 113, 124–27, 130–31, 169
El Monaco Motel (New York) 11, 18–19
Entwistle, John 136
see also Who, the
Environmental Movement 18, 73–74
Evans, Dale 51

Fey, Barry 64, 68, 92
see also Denver Pop
Fillmore West (San Francisco) 31n28, 177
see also Bill Graham
Fillmore East (New York City) 26, 31n28, 47, 96–98, 158, 170, 177
see also Bill Graham
Fogerty, John 57
Ford, Allen 70
Foreman, George 177
Franklin, Aretha 169
Frey, Glenn 133
see also Eagles
Fyre Festival 138

Gabriel, Peter 169
Ganoung, Don 69–70, 81
Garfunkel, Art 135, 169
Garson, Dan viii, 151–52
Gaye, Marvin 82, 115
Geffen, David 54
Geldof, Bob 126–27, 168
"Generation H: Hendrix by Hendrix" 85n22
Goldstein, Stan 6, 10, 15, 19, 61, 65, 69, 71, 81
Goodrich, Peter 70
Graham, Bill xv, 31, 70, 95–100, 150
see also Fillmore West, Fillmore East
Grateful Dead 10, 13, 16, 30–31, 38, 45, 47, 64, 102, 121

Gravy, Wavy (Hugh Romney) 6n3, 51, 71–73
Green, Carol 88
Grogan, Emmett 68
Gypsy Sun and Rainbows 83–84, 147, 156–58, 163n17
see also Hendrix, Jimi

Hammond, John, Jr. 157
Hanley, Bill xvi, 12, 15, 22, 47, 92, 99, 170–73
Hanley Sound 47, 172
Hard Rock Cafe 126, 168
Hardin, Tim 30, 35, 49
Harlem Street Fair 163n17
see also Gypsy Sun and Rainbows
Harrison, George 115, 140n33, 141, 161, 169
Havens, Richie 10, 17, 25–26, 30, 35, 48–51
"Freedom" 50–51
Hells Angels 64, 66
see also Violence at Festivals
Hendrix, Al 162
Hendrix, Jimi xiii, xviii, 3, 10, 13, 30, 40, 45, 55, 82–83, 85, 87, 94, 114–15, 136, 147–50, 152–64, 173–74, 176, 178–79
exploitation of sound design 155
"The Star-Spangled Banner" Performance 40, 45, 85, 86, 91, 179
see also Jimi Hendrix Experience; Gypsy Sun and Rainbows
Henley, Don 133
see also Eagles
Heron, Mike 54n50
see also Incredible String Band
Hoffman, Abbie 7, 36–37, 118–19
Hog Farm xviii, xxi, 6, 13, 24, 32, 35, 51, 65, 70–72, 90–91, 151
see also Gravy, Wavy (Hugh Romney)
Hooker, John Lee 174
Hudson River Valley xiv
Hunter, Meredith 64

Incredible String Band 54
Isley Brothers 157

Jablonka, Tom viii, xxi, xxiii
Jagger, Mick 136
   see also Rolling Stones
James, Etta 164
Jay-Z 57, 144n36
Jefferson Airplane 13, 30, 64, 95, 102
J. Geils Band 124n17
Jimi Hendrix Experience 10, 13, 157–59
   see also Jimi Hendrix; Gypsy Sun and Rainbows
Jobs, Steve 142
Joel, Billy 169, 175
John, Elton 147, 179
John, Mike 105
Johnson, Keith 148–49, 164
Johnson, Lyndon B. 7, 172
Joplin, Janis xiii, 5, 30, 48–49, 92n31, 102, 136, 169, 173–74, 176
   see also Big Brother and the Holding Company

Kantner, Paul 96
   see also Jefferson Airplane
Keith, Linda 157
Kesey, Ken 71
   see also Merry Pranksters
Khan, Chaka 147, 161, 179
King, B.B. 71, 177
King, Martin Luther, Jr. 4
Kingston Trio 165
KMPX 124, 168
Kornfeld, Artie xiv, 8, 23, 27, 46, 70, 89–91, 102, 105–6, 174
Kramer, Eddie 10, 158

LaBelle, Patti 161
Landy, Elliott xvi, 16–17, 28–29, 41–42, 43–44, 173
Lang, Michael xiv, 29, 38, 46, 53, 72, 79, 90–94, 173–76

   Abbie Hoffman versus Pete Townshend 36–37
   choosing Bill Hanley to do sound 15–16
   growth of concert industry xv, 94
   leaving Wallkill 17–18
   managing Joe Cocker xvn1
   Miami Pop Festival (May, 1968) 10
   negotiating with Bill Graham 95–98
   on Richie Havens's performance at Woodstock 25, 50
   planning for Woodstock 5, 29–31, 48, 53, 63
   political echoes between 1969 and the 50th anniversary 72–73
   promoting Chip Monck to announcer at Woodstock 33
   security for Woodstock 6, 8–9, 23, 72
   Woodstock 50 56, 76, 146
   see also Woodstock Ventures
Langhart, Chris xxiii, 29, 30n26
Lauper, Cyndi 169
Laurel Canyon (California) 12, 136, 166
Lawrence, Denise xxiv
Lawrence, Mel 10–11, 19, 29, 36, 39, 56, 67, 69–70
Leary, Timothy 11, 110, 113, 124n17
Led Zeppelin 50, 127
Lee, Larry 84, 156, 158
LeMee, Brad 152
Lennon, John 50, 157, 163n19
   Plastic Ono Band 50
Liis, Ron and Phyllis 56
   see also Art Crew
Lipsius, Fred 5
Little Richard 157

Mackler, Lee 70
Madison Square Garden 4, 94, 113
Maharishi Mahesh Yogi 142n35
Makeba, Miriam 177
Makota, Leo 19
Mamas and the Papas 12, 45n38, 166

INDEX

"San Francisco (Be Sure to Wear Flowers in Your Hair)" 48n45
Mann, Sally 96
   see also Jefferson Airplane
Marks, David 172
Marley, Bob 149
Masekela, Hugh 177
McCartney, Paul 82, 115, 157, 166, 169
McLaughlin, John 160–61
Me Too (social movement) 73, 130, 131n23
Mead, Margaret 56
Merry Pranksters 71
Miami Pop Festival (May) 3, 9–10, 15–16, 26, 82, 174
Miami Pop Festival (December) 9-10, 11n13, 12, 56, 167–68, 176
Michael, George 127
Miles, Buddy 158, 160
Mitchell, Joni 54, 141, 166
   "Woodstock" (song) xiii, xv, 84
Mitchell, Mitch 83, 149, 157–58
   see also Jimi Hendrix Experience
Mizsak, Richard 117
Modern Folk Quartet 165–66
   see also Diltz, Henry
Monck, Edward Herbert Beresford "Chip" xvi, 14–15, 19–20, 22–23, 33, 45, 62–63, 137, 176–177
   "brown acid" 32, 113n7
   lighting designer 3, 12–13, 20, 22, 47, 89n27, 111–12, 135, 137–38, 176–177
   Monterey Pop Festival 13, 135
   on-stage announcer 33-34, 111–12, 123–24
Monterey Pop Festival xiii-xiv, 3, 12–13, 26, 45, 48, 135, 157, 167, 174, 176
Moody Blues 50
Moon, Keith 136
   see also Who, the
Moreira, Airto 161n14
Morris, John 96, 106

Morrison Hotel Gallery 167
Morrison, Jim 136, 173
   see also Doors, The
Moss, Stanley 130
Mountain 30, 46, 81
Movement City xiii, xxi, 37n32
Mullen, Larry, Jr. 126
   see also U2

Nahko Bear 55n52
Napster 95
Nash, Graham 54
   see also Crosby, Stills & Nash; Crosby, Stills, Nash & Young
Newport Folk Festival (Rhode Island) 3, 46, 108n1, 168, 170–71, 176
Newport Jazz Festival (Rhode Island) 3, 170, 176
Newport Pop Festival (California) 9, 168
Nicks, Stevie 179
Nitzsche, Jack 166
Nixon, Richard 4, 8, 50, 74
   whistle-stop campaign 172
Nyro, Laura 137

Obama, Barack 101
O'Barry, Richard 10, 174
Ono, Yoko 169
Osbourne, Lee 26
Osbourne, Ozzy 127
Outside Lands 138
Owsley, Stanley 16, 46
   see also Grateful Dead

Pan-African Cultural Festival 11, 110
Pappalardi, Felix 81
Parton, Dolly 168
Passaro, Alan 64
Paul Butterfield Blues Band 10, 30
Paul, Steve 159, 178
Pennebaker, D. A. 13, 174
Pepper, John Henry 99n37

Petty, Tom 128
Pickett, Wilson 157, 163
Pink Floyd 169
Pomeroy, Wes 6, 69, 71, 81, 102
Presley, Elvis 140, 174
Pressman, Gabe 91
Preston, Billy 50
    see also Apple Records
Puente, Tito 150

Quill 30, 31

Rankin, Kenny 159
Ratner, Louis 102
Redding, Noel 157–59
Redding, Otis 31, 115, 174, 176
Red Hot Chili Peppers 3, 121
Reeves, Martha 168
Reeves, Richard 105
Richards, Keith 136, 157
    see also Rolling Stones
Roberts, John xiv, 8–9, 38, 70, 102–3, 105–6, 120, 174
Rock & Roll Hall of Fame xix, 3, 131, 170
Rodgers, Nile 161
Rogers, Roy 51
Rolling Stones 3, 5, 64, 82, 113, 135, 137n29, 157, 169, 177
Romney, Hugh 6, 71
    see also Wavy Gravy
Ronstadt, Linda 166
Rosenman, Joel xiv, 8–9, 70, 105, 174
Ross, Jackie 106
Rothschild, Amalie Randolph 44
Rubin, Jerry 7, 169

Santana, Carlos xiii, xv, 30–31, 48, 57, 97, 150, 161n14, 164
    see also Shrieve, Michael
Swami Satchidananda 30, 75, 77, 129, 142
Scene (nightclub) 159, 178
Scorsese, Martin xvi, 42–43

Scully, Rock 68
Sebastian, John 27–28, 30, 80, 91
Seeger, Pete 171
Shaffer, Paul 126, 168
Sha Na Na xiii, 30, 47
Shankar, Ravi xiii, 13, 30, 42, 48, 140–42
Shepard, Richard F. 103
Shrieve, Michael 31n29
Sidebars
    Art Crew 56
    Band Aid and Live Aid 127
    Chicago Democratic National Convention 7
    Dan Garson 151–52
    Environmental Movement 74
    Interview with Mel Lawrence 36, 67
    Interview with Stan Goldstein 61, 65–66
    Jimi Hendrix and "The Star-Spangled Banner" 85
    Jimi Hendrix Performing Ensembles 157–58
    List of Performances at Woodstock 30
    Medical Issues at Woodstock 117
    Miami Pop Festivals 10
    Monterey Pop Festival 13
    Violence at Festivals 64
    Wavy Gravy and the Hog Farm 71
    "White Lake Happening" 90
    Woodstock Cultural History 17
    Woodstock in the News 102–6
    Woodstock Site Plans xxi–xxiv
    Woodstock 50th Anniversary Concert 57
Simon, Paul 141
Sinatra, Frank 140
Slick, Grace 96
    see also Jefferson Airplane
Sly and the Family Stone 30, 40–41, 48
social movements 144
    see also Black Lives Matter; Civil Rights; Environment; Me Too

Sommer, Bert 30, 46, 49
Spector, Phil 166
Spielberg, Steven 170
Spinners 177
Springsteen, Bruce 3, 95
Spyro Gyra 83–84, 147, 153, 156, 160, 179
Starr, Ringo xviii, 77–78
"Star-Spangled Banner" 40, 45, 85–86, 91, 179
   see also Hendrix, Jimi
Stickells, Gerry 82
Stills, Stephen 160
   see also Crosby, Stills & Nash; Crosby, Stills, Nash & Young
Sting 127, 169
Students for a Democratic Society (SDS) xxi, 7
Sultan, Juma 84, 158
Summer of Love xviii, 5, 13

Taylor, Derek 13
Taylor, James 50, 141, 166
   see also Apple Records
Tiber, Elliot 11n14, 18–19
   See also El Monaco Motel
Tigrett, Isaac 126, 168
Tinker Street Cafe 17, 86, 150
   see also Café Espresso; Woodstock (New York)
Today Show 3, 109, 119, 131, 169
Townshend, Pete 37–38, 118–20, 157
   see also Who, the
Traveling Wilburys 169
Tribeca Film Festival 60, 70
Trump, Donald 73, 144
Turner, Tina 82, 125–26, 169

U2 82, 126, 169
   see also Bono
Ure, Midge 127

Van Morrison 3, 5, 164, 169, 173

Velez, Geraldo "Jerry" xvi, 82–86, 94–95, 148, 177–79
Velez, Martha 148–49, 178
Vietnam War 4, 7, 16, 42, 51, 73–74, 85, 150, 152, 174
Village Gate (New York) 3, 176
Violence at Festivals 64

Wallkill (New York) xiv, 9, 17–18, 22, 47–48, 51, 103, 175
   Zoning Board of Appeals 9n9, 12n15
   Concerned Citizens Committee 18
Ward, Bill and Jean 56
   see also Art Crew
Wartoke (PR company) 11, 47, 151
Waters, Roger 138
Watkins Glen (New York) xiv, 3, 57, 92–93, 134, 142
Watts, Alan 169
Watts, Charlie 100
   see also Rolling Stones
WGBH 72
Weintraub, Fred 27
Wellesley College 176
White Lake (New York) 18, 90, 149
Who, the 5, 13, 30, 36–38, 118, 138, 169
Williamson, Robin 54n50
   see also Incredible String Band
Wilson, Brian 127, 170
Winter, Edgar 159
Winter, Johnny 30, 45–46, 159
Withers, Bill 177
Wonder, Stevie 128, 179
Woodstock Music and Art Fair
   diversity of performers 48
   documentary film 3, 13, 27, 42–43, 45–47, 51, 60, 81, 111, 114
   Filippini Farm xxi–xxiii, 13, 151
   Gempler Farm xxi
   initial plans and inspiration 5–6, 8–9, 12, 18–21, 113–14
   see also Yasgur, Max

medical issues xiv, 32, 90, 117
selling and taking tickets 17, 23, 65, 92, 97n36
site plans xxi–xxiv
turntable stage 20, 38, 111
women at Woodstock 41, 88, 144
Woodstock (New York) xiv, 17, 86, 149
Woodstock Ventures 107, 176
founders xiv, 8–9
Woodstock (1994) xv, xix, 52, 61–62, 93, 175
Woodstock (1999) xv, xix, 52, 61-62, 93, 175
Woodstock (2019) vii, xix, 3, 34, 53, 55–57, 60–61, 68, 72, 74–75, 92–93, 133–35, 143–44
World War II 75, 141, 167

Yasgur, Max xiv, xxi, 15, 19, 21, 29, 42–43, 67, 70, 88n25, 102, 103, 114, 167, 171, 175
Yogananda, Paramahansa 129
Young Lords 150
Young, Neil 138, 141, 166
see also Crosby, Stills, Nash & Young
Yurdin, Larry 124

Zappa, Frank 174